The METRE of
BEOWULF

By A. J. BLISS

Professor of English Language
in the University of Istanbul

BASIL BLACKWELL
OXFORD . MCMLXII

© BASIL BLACKWELL AND MOTT LTD.

FIRST PUBLISHED 1958
REPRINTED   1962

PRINTED IN GREAT BRITAIN BY
ROBERT CUNNINGHAM AND SONS LTD.
ALVA

In Memoriam
E. H. BLISS

PREFACE

THIS study of the metre of *Beowulf* had its origin some ten years ago in an attempt to check the validity of the statistical conclusions of Eduard Sievers, which had remained almost unchallenged for three quarters of a century. For this purpose it was necessary to re-examine the whole text of *Beowulf* with an open mind, and to derive a system of scansion step by step from the beginning. The result of this re-examination was a triumphant vindication of Sievers: every one of his major conclusions proved to be amply justified by the evidence. At the same time, however, it began to appear that, although Sievers' results were incontrovertible as far as they went, his own methods could be taken much further than he had taken them himself; and the further application of these methods led to a number of interesting discoveries which, once discovered, seemed so obvious that it was difficult to understand how they had been overlooked for so long.

A perusal of the extensive 'literature' of Old English metre (nearly all in German) revealed that they had not, in fact, been overlooked: nearly all of them had been anticipated, however vaguely and partially, either before or shortly after the appearance of Sievers' monumental work. Unfortunately Sievers' prestige was so great, and his conclusions were so rapidly accepted as the last word on Old English metre, that the work of his predecessors and contemporaries was soon consigned to oblivion; thus his achievement, remarkable as it was, actually came to act as an obstacle to further progress in the understanding of Old English metre. This obstacle has remained effective until the present day: all recent studies of Old English metre have tended to by-pass Sievers and to adopt quite a different approach from his.

Although the conclusions here presented were in the first place reached in ignorance of the fact that they had been anticipated, there is in fact little in this study that is absolutely new. The most that can be claimed is that a number of important facts about the metre of *Beowulf* which had been neglected by several generations of scholars have now been resurrected, investigated, placed on a secure statistical basis and assembled into a coherent system of scansion. It is precisely the coherence of the conclusions here presented, and the consequent necessity for frequent cross-reference, which has precluded piecemeal publication in a series of articles: hence the appearance of this work in book form before it has been submitted to the critical examination of a wider circle of scholars than could be reached by private correspondence.

Unfortunately the present costs of publication are such that this study has necessarily been presented in a somewhat condensed form: the result is a terseness of expression which tends sometimes to obscurity and sometimes to dogmatism. These failings are particularly noticeable in the phonological appendices, which would have had to be expanded to many times their present length if all the problems raised were to be discussed in full. However, the condensation of the text is to some extent counterbalanced by the inclusion of full tables of the statistical data on which the discussion in the text is based, so that those who disagree with the conclusions reached can examine for themselves the evidence on which they are based. A complete index to the scansion both of *Beowulf* and of the hypermetric verses in other Old English texts has also been included, for two reasons: firstly, no system of scansion can be considered successful unless it can be shown to account for all but a small fraction of the material considered; secondly, no such index has been attempted before, so that it often requires considerable labour to discover which scansion of a particular line is accepted by the various writers on Old English metre.

My thanks are due to the many friends and pupils who helped me with the drudgery of transferring the six thousand odd verses in *Beowulf* to index cards; to Mr A. Campbell and Professor C. E. Bazell, as a result of whose criticism the first draft of this book was substantially revised; to Mr Jonathan Wordsworth, always ready to check references for me; to Mme Tatyana Moran, who read the galley-proofs; to Professor Kemp Malone, who read the page proofs and made several helpful suggestions, one of which is incorporated in the Addendum on page 166; to my wife, always willing to help me with the most wearisome parts of my work; and, above all, to those whose anonymous generosity has made possible the publication of this book.

A. J. B.

KANDILLI, ISTANBUL

PREFACE TO THE SECOND EDITION

IN this Second Edition I have added a new Appendix on the combination of verses into lines, an important question which was scarcely touched on in the First Edition. A few small errors in the body of the work have been corrected, but otherwise the text remains unchanged.

A. J. B.

October, 1961

CONTENTS

CHAPTER

1 INTRODUCTORY   1
2 'LIGHT', 'NORMAL' AND 'HEAVY' VERSES   6
3 STRESS AND QUANTITY   24
4 RESOLUTION   27
5 THE CÆSURA   36
6 ANACRUSIS   40
7 SIEVERS' TYPE A   44
8 SIEVERS' TYPES B AND C   51
9 SIEVERS' TYPES D AND E   55
10 LIGHT VERSES   61
11 HEAVY VERSES   69
12 REMAINDERS   76
13 CLASSIFICATION   80
14 HYPERMETRIC VERSES   88
15 THE OLDEST ENGLISH VERSE   98
16 LATE OLD ENGLISH VERSE   100
17 TOWARDS AN INTERPRETATION   106

APPENDIX

A SECONDARY AND TERTIARY STRESS   113
B VOCALIC ENDINGS IN OLD ENGLISH   118
C THE SCANSION OF *Beowulf*: STATISTICAL
    INFORMATION   122
D HYPERMETRIC VERSES: STATISTICAL INFORMATION   129
E THE COMBINATION OF VERSES INTO LINES   135
  INDEX TO THE SCANSION OF *Beowulf*   139
  INDEX TO THE SCANSION OF THE HYPERMETRIC
    VERSES IN OLD ENGLISH   162
  INDEX OF VERSES SPECIALLY DISCUSSED   169
  ADDENDUM   170

CHAPTER ONE

INTRODUCTORY

1. The study of any metre involves two distinct processes: firstly, the description and classification of the metrical forms which actually occur; secondly, the discussion and interpretation of the resulting classification, with a consideration of the æsthetic effect produced. The first convincing classification of the metrical forms found in Old English poetry was achieved by Eduard Sievers in 1885,[1] and with few modifications it remains the standard classification, even though Sievers himself partially repudiated it in later life.[2] None of the alternative classifications proposed at various times has found many followers, though it will be shown below that the work of Möller[3] and Kaluza[4] is in some respects very sound. Most of the studies of Old English metre which have appeared in recent years have been devoted rather to discussion and interpretation, Sievers' classification being rather grudgingly accepted as a basis; the work of Heusler[5] and Pope[6] in particular has achieved very general recognition.

2. Heusler and Pope, whose systems differ only in detail, attempt to show that each of Sievers' five types of verse[7] can

---

[1] E. Sievers, 'Zur Rhythmik des germanischen Alliterationsverses', *PBB* x (1885) 209-314; *Altgermanische Metrik* (1893). A knowledge of Sievers' system has been assumed throughout this study; the notation followed is that of 1893, which differs in some respects from that of 1885.

[2] E. Sievers, 'Zu Cynewulf', *Festgabe Karl Luick* (1925) 60-81. Sievers' later conclusions, based as they are on the purely subjective criteria of *Schallanalyse*, have been almost completely ignored in subsequent work on Old English metre; but it will be shown below that some of Sievers' results can be justified on objective grounds.

[3] W. Möller, *Zur althochdeutschen Alliterationspoesie* (1888).

[4] M. Kaluza, *Der altenglische Vers: eine metrische Untersuchung* (1894); *A Short History of English Versification* (1911).

[5] A. Heusler, *Deutsche Versgeschichte mit Einschluss des altenglischen und altnordischen Stabreimverses* (1925).

[6] J. C. Pope, *The Rhythm of Beowulf* (1942).

[7] The term 'verse' is here used instead of the more cumbrous 'half-line' or 'hemistich'. The first verse in the line is called the 'a-verse', the second the 'b-verse'; similarly an *a* or *b* after a line-reference indicates the first or the second verse respectively.

be fitted into two musical measures; the five types can then be considered different ways of filling the two standard measures. Of the two systems, that of Pope represents a distinct advance on Heusler's, and Pope's scansion of Types B and C is certainly far preferable, though it is not lacking in inconsistency. However, any 'measure system' of this kind is open to a number of very serious objections. Firstly, some of the readings necessitated by such a system are implausible in the extreme; in the verse

wis welþungen   1927a[1]

for instance, the single syllable *wis* must somehow be made to occupy as much time as the three syllables of *welþungen*, either by drawling out *wis* to an impossible length, or by inserting between the two words a pause which breaks up the sense of the verse. Though it would seem that the use of such a pause or 'rest' where none is required by the sense should be self-condemnatory, it is not eschewed by either Heusler or Pope.

3. Furthermore, if Sievers' five types of verse are no more than different ways of filling the two standard measures, there is no obvious reason why such verses as

*hreas blac   2488a
wrætlicne wundurmaððum   2173a

should not be as permissible as any other. Yet in fact verses of this kind are exceedingly rare: the first is almost certainly corrupt (it is emended by all editors), the second is perhaps hypermetrical (§ 106). It is of course possible to argue that, even within the limits of the 'measure system', the verse must be neither too light nor too heavy; if the first measure contains only one syllable then the second must contain three, and *vice versa*. But this argument introduces quite a new consideration, and in fact puts us back exactly where we started—with Sievers' five types, which at least have the merit of establishing a comparatively stable length and weight for the verse.

4. It must be admitted that an adequate interpretation of the Old English metrical forms is still to seek. Since a study of the metrical forms which actually occur has hitherto proved an in-

---

[1] Unless otherwise indicated all references are to *Beowulf*. The text followed is that of Klaeber's third edition; any departure, however slight, from Klaeber's text is indicated by an asterisk prefixed to the verse quoted.

sufficient basis for interpretation, it is possible that a study of
the metrical forms which do not occur may be more rewarding;
for this purpose Sievers' classification, though generally sound
as far as it goes, is insufficient, since within each of Sievers' five
types a number of possible subtypes, which are not excluded by
his description, are in fact never found. A simple example may
be pointed out in Sievers' Type A*, in which the first foot never
in *Beowulf* consists of a single word[1]; an apparent exception

(wigen)des egesan   3154b

proves to be without manuscript support, since the true reading,
revealed by ultra-violet light, is *werudes egesan*.[2] The purpose
of this study is to provide a more accurate and complete classification of the Old English metrical types, as a basis for a fresh
interpretation.

5. The logical processes involved in classification have never
been adequately described, and even so acute a scholar as Henry
Sweet can be guilty of some misconception on this point. 'These
critics,' he writes,[3] 'seem to forget that Sievers' classification of
the Old-English metrical forms into types is not a theory, but
a statement of facts, and that the complexity and irregularity
to which they object is a fact, not a theory.' Sweet fails to
observe that any process of classification involves the assumption that certain differences between verses are not metrically
significant; and unless the underlying assumptions are valid the
resulting classification will not be valid. The statement that the
verse *Beowulf maðelode* occurs twelve times in the poem of
Beowulf is a statement of fact; but the statement that the verse
Beowulf maðelode and the verse *Hroðgar maðelode* belong to the
same type involves the assumption that the difference between
Beowulf and *Hroðgar* is not metrically significant. In this particular instance few would doubt the validity of the assumption;
but other cases may not be so clear, and it is important to
remember that the usefulness of any classification depends entirely on the validity of the underlying assumptions.

---

[1] This peculiarity of Type A* has of course been noticed before, but no
adequate explanation has yet been given; Sweet's attempted explanation
(*Anglo-Saxon Reader*, Introduction § 365) is quite insufficient.
[2] A. H. Smith, 'The Photography of Manuscripts', *London Mediæval Studies*
i (1938) 179-207.
[3] H. Sweet, *op. cit.* Preface to Seventh Edition (1894).

6. The assumptions of insignificance underlying the classifications of Sievers, Möller, Kaluza, Trautmann and others seem to be based almost entirely on subjective grounds; since it is obvious that no such subjective decision can hope to command general assent, it is desirable to establish objective criteria of what is and what is not a metrically significant difference between two types of verse. Wherever possible, I have used the following statistical criteria:

(1) the proportion of *a*-verses to *b*-verses;

(2) the proportion of *a*-verses with double alliteration.[1]

In practice it will be found that a metrically significant difference between two types of verse generally causes a marked variation in both of these criteria; in other words, the criteria are not really independent of each other. It will be shown below that types of verse in which double alliteration is quasi-compulsory occur more frequently in *a*-verses than in *b*-verses; it will also be shown that the occurrence of anacrusis is intimately linked to the question of double alliteration (see Chapter Six).

7. These criteria are not arbitrary or mechanical, but have a real relationship to the natural rhythm of the verse, and to the author's feeling for it. It is well known, for instance, that the structure of a *b*-verse is in general lighter and less complex than that of an *a*-verse; it follows, therefore, that if the poet finds a certain type more suited to a *b*-verse than to an *a*-verse, and another type more suited to an *a*-verse than to a *b*-verse, there must be a genuine rhythmical difference between the two types. In the same way, the fact that a certain type requires strengthening by double alliteration while another type does not suggests a similar rhythmical difference. Thus we are able to supplement the deficiencies of our own untutored ears by intercepting, at second hand, the author's own feeling for his verse.

8. At this stage it may be well to insert a note on emendation *metri causa*. The question is a singularly difficult one, since the necessity for emendation may seem at first sight to discredit the rule on which the emendation is based. The extravagancies of Trautmann and his followers rightly resulted in a reaction against

---

[1] The phrase 'double alliteration' is here used to indicate that there are two alliterating words in the *a*-verse, not that there is alliteration on two distinct letters.

this kind of emendation; yet it remains true that Old English manuscripts abound in minor corruptions, and it is not to be expected that none of them should affect the metre. Used with discretion, emendation *metri causa* can still serve a useful purpose, and I have not hesitated to indulge in it provided that one or more of the following conditions is fulfilled:

(1) that the verse emended offends against more than one metrical 'rule' at the same time;

(2) that the sense or grammar of the verse emended is also objectionable, or at least doubtful[1];

(3) that a number of exceptional or irregular verses have some common factor, so that a single type of emendation will correct them all.[2]

If none of these conditions is fulfilled emendation is not permissible: instead, if the number of irregular verses is small, they must be recognized as exceptions to the rule; if the number is large, a new rule must be formulated to include the exceptions.

---

[1] In practice it will very often be found that an emendation required *metri causa* has already been suggested by one or other of the many editors of *Beowulf* on quite other grounds.

[2] The outstanding example is Sievers' discovery that a very large number of irregular verses can be corrected by substituting uncontracted for contracted forms.

CHAPTER TWO

'LIGHT', 'NORMAL' AND 'HEAVY' VERSES

9. In any discussion of an accentual metre the first point to be determined must be, which of the words in the verse-clause bear metrically significant stresses? The observations of Kuhn[1] provide a useful basis from which to begin to answer this question. Kuhn observed that, if we accept Sievers' scheme of scansion, the various components of a verse-clause in OE may be divided into three groups, which he called 'stressed elements' (*Satzteile*), 'particles' (*Satzpartikeln*) and 'proclitics' (*Satzteilpartikeln*). Stressed elements bear a metrical stress irrespective of the position they occupy in the verse-clause: they include nouns, infinitives, participles, adjectives and certain adverbs. Particles normally[2] stand either before or after the first stressed element (that is, in the first thesis of the verse-clause), and in this position they are unstressed; if they are displaced from this position they acquire a positional stress, and are treated in all respects like stressed elements: they include finite verbs, certain adverbs, certain pronouns, and conjunctions. Proclitics normally stand immediately before the stressed element with which they are most closely connected, and are then unstressed; but, like particles, if they are displaced they acquire a positional stress, and are treated like stressed elements: they include prepositions, certain pronouns, and articles. The verse-clause, therefore, consists of a series of stressed elements; each stressed element may be preceded by one or more proclitics; and the first stressed element may be preceded or followed by one or more particles. As an example of the construction of a verse-clause we may take *Beowulf* 109b-110: *ac he hine* || *feor* | *forwræc,* | *Metod* | *for þy mane* | *mancynne* | *fram.* Here the stressed elements are four in

---

[1] H. Kuhn, 'Wortstellung und -betonung im Altgermanischen', *PBB* lvii (1933) 1-109. I have simplified Kuhn's cumbrous terminology, and my description of the structure of the verse-clause differs in some respects from his.
[2] The use of the word 'normal' does not necessarily imply that this is statistically the most frequent position.

number, *feor, Metod, mane* and *mancynne*; the stressed element
mane is preceded by the proclitics *for* and *þy*; the first stressed
element *feor* is preceded by the particles *ac, he* and *hine*; the
proclitic *fram* and the particle *forwræc* have been displaced
from their normal positions and are therefore treated as stressed
elements.

10. The normal verse contains two stressed elements, each
of which may be accompanied by its quota of proclitics. The
following examples are taken at random:

> þrym | gefrunon   2b
> monegum | mægþum   5a
> weox | under wolcnum   8a
> on fæder | (bea)rme   21b
> leof | landfruma   31a

In many cases the two stressed elements are preceded by one or
more particles:

> Oft || Scyld | Scefing   4a
> syððan || ærest | wearð   6b
> he þæs || frofre | gebad   7b
> þæt wæs || god | cyning   11b
> Swa sceal || (geong | g)uma   20a

But in addition to these normal verses, there are many verses
which consist only of a single stressed element, usually preceded
by one or more particles:

> hu || ða æþelingas   3a
> oð þæt him || æghwylc   9a
> him þæs || Liffrea   16b
> þæt hine || on ylde   22a
> ne hyrde ic || cymlicor   38a

Sometimes there are no particles, but the single stressed element
is preceded by one or more proclitics:

> in geardagum   1b
> ofer hronrade   10a
> to gescæphwile   26b
> of feorwegum   37a
> **buton** folcscare   73a

B

Sometimes there are neither particles nor proclitics:

> þeodcyninga   2a
> ymbsittendra   9b
> wilgesiþas   23a
> hringedstefna 32b
> hildewæpnum   39a

All verses which consist of only one stressed element are here termed 'light' verses. On the other hand, there are also many verses which contain three stressed elements instead of the normal two:

> blæd | wide | sprang   18b
> fæder | ellor | hwearf   55b
> swutol | sang | scopes   90a
> lif | eac | gesceop   97b
> gearo | sona | wæs   121b

All verses of this kind are here termed 'heavy' verses.

11. Since the conventional systems of scanning Old English verse—Sievers' and others—recognize only two-stress verses,[1] these light and heavy verses have to be forced into a two-stress mould. The light verses are made to conform by wresting an additional stress either from among the particles (Sievers' Type A3) or from the body of the stressed element itself, whenever it consists of a compound word, or even of a word containing a long derivative ending; Sievers, for instance, makes no distinction between *ac* ‖ *se maga* | *geonga* with two stressed elements and *hu* ‖ *ða æþelingas* with only one, classing them both as Type C2. It is, of course, possible that the distinction between these two types of verse is not metrically significant, but their equivalence must not be assumed without discussion. The heavy verses are made to conform to the two-stress pattern by arbitrarily[2] subordinating the stress on one of the three elements

---

[1] The difference between the *Zweihebung* and *Vierhebung* theories is not relevant here, since both recognize two main stresses in each verse. Sievers' later work on Old English metre recognizes one-stress verses (*Festgabe Karl Luick* p. 63, § 8), and Pope envisages verses in which one of the two stresses is replaced by a rest.

[2] Supporters of Sievers would claim that the procedure is not arbitrary: but the choice of the element to be subordinated is purely subjective, and the difficulty is glossed over. It will be shown in Chapter Eleven that one of the elements must in fact be subordinated: but an objective criterion will be provided for choosing which element to subordinate

and calling it a 'half' or 'secondary' stress; unfortunately the
exponents of the conventional systems are often unable to decide which of the three stresses is to be subordinated.[1] In the
third of the five examples of heavy verses quoted above the
alliteration shows that the verse belongs to Type D2, not to
Type A2k; the other four examples, however, may belong equally
well to Type D4 or to Type E1. The relationship between the
light and heavy verses and the normal verses will be discussed
in Chapters Ten and Eleven; in the meantime, 'verse' implies a
normal verse unless the contrary is stated.

12. It is not in general difficult to distinguish between a light
verse and a normal verse, or between a normal verse and a
heavy verse; but when the verse contains a finite verb which
is not preceded by a stressed element and which shares in the
alliteration, it may appear that the finite verb must bear a stress;
and in fact Sievers always attributes stress to verbs in this
position, provided they share in the alliteration. On the other
hand, the possibility of 'accidental' alliteration must not be
dismissed too lightly. The whole question has been recently
discussed by Slay,[2] who concludes on rather slender grounds that
Sievers' attitude is justified. Clearly the problem can only be
solved by the examination of a large number of verses containing a finite verb which is not preceded by a stressed element,
whether the verb alliterates or not. There are in *Beowulf* 580[3]
verses of this kind, almost exactly one verse in eleven; of these,
165 contain auxiliary or similarly unstressed verbs. The auxiliaries in question are *weorþan, habban, willan, sculan, magan,
motan* and *durran*; with these are included the quasi-auxiliaries
wutun, onginnan, hatan, lætan and *myntan*, the verbs *cuman* and
gewitan when construed with a dependent infinitive, and the
verb *cweþan*, which never alliterates. Of these fifteen verbs,
weorþan, habban, myntan, cuman and *gewitan* are also used as
independent verbs. The 165 verses containing unstressed verbs
of this kind are reserved for later consideration in §§ 27-29.

13. The remaining 415 verses containing independent finite

---

[1] Cf. A. Campbell, *The Battle of Brunanburh* (1938) pp. 29-30.
[2] D. Slay, 'Some Aspects of the Technique of Composition of Old English
Verse', *Transactions of the Philological Society* (1952) 1-14.
[3] This total does not include the rare verses which consist of a single finite
verb (e.g. *andswarode* 258b, 340b) nor the very numerous verses containing
some form of the verb 'to be'.

verbs may be divided into nine groups according to the position of the verb in the verse clause:

(1) The verb is preceded by a stressed element;

(2) The verb is in apposition to a verb in group (1) which immediately precedes it;

(3) The verb is the only particle before the first stressed element;

(4) The verb is the last particle before the first stressed element;

(5) The verb is the last particle but one before the first stressed element;

(6) The verb is the last particle but two before the first stressed element;

(7) The verb forms a whole clause in itself;

(8) The verb is the last particle in a clause which contains no stressed elements;

(9) The verb is the last particle but one in a clause which contains no stressed elements.

14. In group (1) the finite verb has been displaced from its normal position among the particles at the beginning of the clause, and must therefore be treated as a stressed element; in the 65 examples of this group in *Beowulf*[1] the finite verb invariably alliterates, as is to be expected. The following are representative examples:

hringiren scir

song in searwum   323a

Hine sorhwylmas

lemede to lange   905a

Hie dygel lond

warigeað wulfhleoþu   1358a

Syððan heofones gim

glad ofer grundas   2073a

Beorh eallgearo

wunode on wonge   2242a

[1] 105b, 276a, 323a, 505a, 560a, 702a, 709a, 772a, 782a, 814a, 905a, 922a, 1008a, 1128a, 1231a, 1257a, 1312a, 1337a, 1358a, 1452a, 1493a, 1510a, 1554a, 1581a, 1622a, 1667a, 1701a, 1724a, 1739a, 1741a, 1751a, 1767a, 1770a, 1837a, 1854a, 2003a, 2062a, 2065a, 2073a, 2096a, 2110a, 2132a, 2183a, 2242a, 2260a, 2270a, 2277a, 2279a, 2319a, 2344b, 2488a, 2491a, 2629a, 2632a, 2663b, 2703a, 2717a, 2831a, 2882a, 2883a, 2899b, 3055b, 3067a, 3121a, 3152a.

In group (2) the finite verb would seem to begin a new clause, since strictly there cannot be more than one finite verb to a clause; in this case the verb would be in the normal position for a particle, and should not alliterate. But in fact, out of the 33 examples of this group in *Beowulf*,[1] the verb alliterates in no less than 31. It seems probable that when two consecutive finite verbs stand in apposition to each other the second does not open a new clause; from the point of view of stress the two verbs are treated as equivalent, so that the stress of the second depends on the stress of the first. The following are representative examples of this group:

> Guman onetton,
> *sigon* ætsomne   307a
> þær git eagorstream   earmum þehton,
> *mæton* merestræta,   mundum brugdon, 514a
> *glidon* ofer garsecg   515a
> Ides gnornode,
> *geomrode* giddum   1118a
> nu se wyrm ligeð,
> *swefeð* sare wund   2746a

It should be noticed that in every instance in this group the first finite verb ends a line and the second begins the next line. The two instances in which the finite verb does not alliterate are the following[2]:

> he þe æt sunde oferflat,
> *hæfde* mare mægen   518a
> ond eowic gretan het,
> *bæd* þæt ge geworhton   æfter wines dædum ... 3096a

It seems reasonable to assume that, apart from these two exceptions, the finite verbs in verses of groups (1) and (2) bear a

---

[1] 6a, 8a, 131a, 307a, 421a, 423a, 514a, 515a, 532a, 660a, 726a, 896a, 926a, 1118a, 1132a, 1150a, 1159a, 1274a, 1453a, 1604a, 1610a, 1909a, 1954a, 2018a, 2051a, 2085a, 2439a, 2476a, 2919a, 2930a, 2975a; 518a, 3096a.

[2] It is possible to suggest an explanation for these two exceptions to the rule. In the first instance the verb *hæfde* is most often used as an auxiliary, and is then lightly stressed; although it is fully meaningful here, the light stress has perhaps been transferred from the auxiliary use. In the second instance the verb *bæd* is in apposition to the quasi-auxiliary *het*, and is in fact itself used as a quasi-auxiliary.

positional stress, and that the verses concerned are therefore normal verses.

15. Out of the 83 examples of group (3) in *Beowulf*,[1] the finite verb alliterates in 64. Since in this group the verb stands in the normal position for a particle, it might be supposed that the verb does not bear a stress, and that the alliteration is only 'accidental'; but there are serious objections to this view. In the first place, alliteration is far too frequent to be accidental. Ross has shown[2] that the probability of chance alliteration is about one in twelve; here the proportion is about three in four. Furthermore, it is highly improbable that an Anglo-Saxon poet, with his ear trained to alliteration, would fail to notice its occurrence; and in fact the incidence of accidental alliteration in the *b*-verse, where its presence would apparently be objectionable, is negligible.[3] 'Accidental' alliteration is only to be assumed where the word concerned is so insignificant that its participation in the alliteration might reasonably escape the notice of the poet. However, even if 'accidental' alliteration is improbable, there remains the possibility of 'ornamental' or 'non-functional' alliteration; that is to say, a word whose stress is not significant in the metrical pattern may be made to alliterate by the poet as a work of supererogation. It will be shown below that there is some evidence in *Beowulf* for this kind of 'non-functional' alliteration (§ 21).

16. Yet even this explanation will not suffice to account for the alliteration of the finite verb in verses of group (3), since in twelve instances the verse cannot be scanned at all unless the finite verb is stressed. Of these twelve, eleven are *b*-verses, where the assumption that the verb is not stressed robs the verse of all alliteration:

> *slat* unwearnum   741b
> *ræhte* ongean   747b

---

[1] 49a, 94a, 204a, 302a, 311a, 325a, 358a, 402a, 411a, 424a, 448a, 449a, 450a, 496a, 501a, 598a, 614a, 625a, 659a, 714a, 741b, 742a, 747b, 818a, 821b, 839a, 1119a, 1120a, 1137b, 1161a, 1169a, 1216a, 1390a, 1512a, 1616a, 1632a, 1699b, 1713a, 1749a, 1755b, 1785b, 1917a, 1982a, 2119a, 2179a, 2252a, 2329a, 2455a, 2578b, 2582a, 2681a, 2690a, 2705a, 2717b, 2852a, 2863b, 2902a, 2909a, 2991a, 3031a, 3084a, 3123a, 3152b, 3173a; 264a, 376b, 452a, 459a, 539a, 609b, 612b, 640b, 646b, 672b, 764b, 918b, 1201b, 1233a, 1814b, 2604b, 2737b, 2986a, 3166a.
[2] A. S. C. Ross, 'Philological Probability Problems', *Journal of the Royal Statistical Society* B xii (1950) 19-59. See pp. 32-33.
[3] For one instance, see § 18.

> *wiste* þe geornor   821b
> *fundode* wrecca   1137b
> *swigedon* ealle   1699b
> *fehð* oþer to   1755b
> *geong* sona to   1785b
> *bat* unswiðor   2578b
> *seah* on enta geweorc   2717b
> *seah* on unleofe   2863b
> *sæde* geneahhe   3152b

The remaining verse is the following:

> *forgrand* gramum   424a

This verse can be scanned as Type C3 if the finite verb is stressed; otherwise it cannot be scanned at all. In these twelve verses, at least, the finite verb must be stressed even though it is not displaced from its normal position as a particle.

17. On the other hand, there are only two verses in group (3) which are metrically objectionable if the finite verb is stressed:

> *gesawon* seledream   2252a
> *seah* on enta geweorc   2717b

On the first of these two verses see § 48; the meaning is difficult, and there is a strong case for emendation. On the second verse, see § 87. This last verse, it will be noticed, also appears among the twelve verses which cannot be scanned at all if the verb is not stressed; clearly there is something badly wrong here. The remaining 81 verses in this group, however, offer no difficulty, and the evidence suggests that a finite verb which is the only particle in the clause may sometimes bear stress (and alliteration) and sometimes not. It is possible that the presence or absence of stress is dictated by circumstances that escape our untrained ears but were immediately obvious to the ear of the Anglo-Saxon.

18. Out of the 75 examples of group (4) in *Beowulf*,[1] the finite

---

[1] 28a, 47a, 96a, 136b, 333a, 372a, 377a, 415a, 429a, 463a, 480a, 489b, 520a, 535a, 538b, 560b, 630b, 731a, 740a, 748b, 751a, 778a, 1095a, 1142a, 1218b, 1265b, 1270a, 1327b, 1331b, 1347a, 1363a, 1384a, 1396b, 1465a, 1548b, 1563a, 1578a, 1661a, 1722b, 1819b, 1826a, 2036a, 2039a, 2158a, 2177a, 2195a, 2204a, 2208b, 2253a, 2395b, 2511b, 2544b, 2634a, 2656b, 2665a, 2738a, 2738b, 2855b, 2933a, 2934a, 2968b, 2980b, 2985a, 2990b, 3001a, 3002a, 3029b, 3038a, 3081a, 3096a, 3137a, 3159a, 3178a; 1600a, 1727b.

verb alliterates in all but two. It is true that in many cases the
verb must alliterate and bear a stress if the verse is to scan at all:

hi hyne þa *ætbæron*   to brimes faroðe   28a
Ic hine *cuðe*   cnihtwesende   372a
Ic him *þenode*   560b
deoran sweorde
ofer þæm *hongiað*   hrinde bearwas   1363a
Þenden *reafode*   rinc oðerne   2985a

Yet there are a number of instances in which the verse will scan
perfectly well even if the verb does not bear a stress:

Ne *sorga*, snotor guma   1384a
He *gefeng* þa fetelhilt   1563a
ne *sohte* searoniðas   2738a

The two examples in which the finite verb does not alliterate
are the following:

Ða *com* non dæges   1600a
he *ah* ealra geweald   1727b

In the second example the verb does in fact appear to alliterate,
but since the verse is a *b*-verse it must be assumed that the
alliteration is accidental; possibly *agan*, like *cweþan*, is a verb
which is never stressed, but it occurs too rarely in *Beowulf* for
any certainty on this point. The evidence seems to indicate
that when a finite verb is the last of a number of particles before
the first stressed element it is normally assimilated to the stressed
elements and treated as such.

19. Out of the 105 examples of group (5) in *Beowulf*,[1] the
finite verb alliterates in only 57, a little more than half the total.
In a number of the cases in which the verb alliterates the assumption that the verb is not stressed robs the verse of all
alliteration:

[1] 34a, 109a, 142b, 217a, 327a, 356a, 399a, 489a, 525a, 617a, 620a, 652a,
723a, 758a, 788b, 960b, 1013a, 1027a, 1219a, 1251a, 1408a, 1441b, 1501a,
1506a, 1518a, 1525b, 1531a, 1537a, 1539a, 1543a, 1545a, 1557a, 1665a, 1735a,
1758a, 1870a, 1872b, 1977a, 1987a, 2288a, 2339b, 2345a, 2367a, 2516a, 2529a,
2538a, 2593a, 2628a, 2640a, 2661a, 2697a, 2725b, 2756a, 2854a, 2936a, 2956b,
3156a; 38a, 78b, 118a, 181b, 270a, 336b, 359b, 455b, 471a, 487b, 675a, 681a,
728a, 746a, 1011a, 1020a, 1188a, 1210a, 1232a, 1242a, 1279a, 1316a, 1322a,
1397a, 1425a, 1474a, 1573a, 1601b, 1612a, 1730a, 1748a, 1782a, 1809b, 1842b,
1888a, 2014b, 2062b, 2361a, 2417a, 2431a, 2460a, 2461b, 2542a, 2606a, 2653a,
2994a, 3033a, 3141a.

> *heold* hyne syðþan   142b
> Ðonne *wene* ic to þe   525a
> *Gemunde* þa se goda   758a
> *Heold* hine fæste   788b
> *Uþe* ic swiþor   960b
> *Gyrede* hine Beowulf   1441b
> *ðolode* ær fela   1525b
> *Gefeng* þa be eaxle   1537a
> *hruron* him tearas   1872b
> *wisse* he gearwe   2339b, 2725b
> *beah* eft þonan   2956b

There are eight more instances which consist of a finite verb
followed by the particle *þa*:

> *aledon* þa   34a
> *Ymbeode* þa   620a
> *Gegrette* þa   652a, 2516a
> *Ofereode* þa   1408a
> *Gecyste* þa   1870a
> *Oferhogode* ða   2345a
> *Geworhton* ða   3156a

If the finite verb is stressed the particle following it may be
viewed in two ways: it may be considered to occupy the thesis
after the first stress, the second of the two allowable positions;
or it may be considered as displaced from its normal position
before the first stressed element, in which case it will bear a
positional stress. The verses in the second group quoted above
cannot be scanned unless the particle *þa* is stressed.

20. If the particle which follows the finite verb is not stressed
the verse concerned may offend against Kuhn's 'Law of Particles' (*Satzpartikelgesetz*), according to which 'if there are several
particles, they must not be distributed between both the possible positions [i.e. before and after the first stressed element];
nor may they be placed before the second stressed element if
the first is preceded by a proclitic or an unstressed prefix.'[1]

---

[1] 'Das Satzpartikelgesetz verbietet es, die Satzpartikeln, wenn mehrere da
sind, auf beide möglichen Stellen zu verteilen, sowie die vor das zweite betonte
Wort zu stellen, wenn vor dem ersten durch Satzpartikeln oder unbetonte
Vorsilben ein Auftakt gebildet wird' (Kuhn, *op. cit.* p. 9, § 3). Kuhn himself
specifically excepts from the operation of his law instances in which the first

The offending verses, then, are those in which the alliterating verb is preceded by a particle or by an unstressed prefix:

ne *gefeah* he þære fæhðe   109a
Gewat þa ofer wægholm   217a
Aras þa se rica   399a
Ðonne *wene* ic to þe   525a
onbræd þa bealohydig   723a
Gemunde þa se goda   758a
ne *gefrægn* ic freondlicor   1027a
Ongeat þa se goda   1518a
Gefeng þa be eaxle   1537a
oferwearþ þa werigmod   1543a
Ofsæt þa þone selegyst   1545a
Geseah ða on searwum   1557a
Ofsloh ða æt þære sæcce   1665a
Bebeorh þe ðone bealonið   1758a
Gesæt þa wið sylfne   1977a
Hu *lomp* eow on lade   1987a
Oferswam ða sioleða bigong   2367a
Gebide ge on beorge   2529a
Aras ða bi ronde   2538a
Ne *gemealt* him se modsefa   2628a
onmunde usic mærða   2640a
Ne *hedde* he þæs heafolan   2697a
Geseah ða sigehreðig   2756a
Besæt ða sinherge   2936a

If the finite verb is stressed in these verses, then the particles following them must also be stressed; but in many cases a stress on the particle, even a secondary stress, will produce an impossible metrical pattern. There is, for instance, no analogy for such patterns as *Gebíde gé on béorge* or *onmúnde úsic mǽrða*.[1] The only possible conclusion seems to be that in these verses the finite verb is not stressed, and that the alliteration of the verb is non-functional. Of the three verses which have only

stress of a verse-clause falls on a particle: such breaches of the law, he says, are only apparent (*ibid.*, and cf. Slay, *op. cit.* p. 12). Yet it is difficult to understand why a stressed particle, which in any other position is treated exactly like any other stressed element, should be differently treated here; and it will þe shown below that it is possible to devise a system of scansion which involves no breaches, apparent or otherwise, of Kuhn's law.

[1] The assumption that the *-e* of *onmunde* is elided does not help matters.

single alliteration, two can be disposed of by adopting the palmary emendations *Gemunde þa se* mod[g]*a* and *Gefeng þa be* [*f*]*eaxe*
(both due to Rieger); the third, *Ðonne wene ic to þe*, is less easy
to improve, and must be considered anomalous.[1]

21. The verses in this group which are neutral—in which a
stressed finite verb is neither essential nor objectionable—are
few in number:

> *bugon* þa to bence   327a, 1013a
> *Hwearf* þa hrædlice   356a
> *Site* nu to symle   489a
> *bæd* hine bliðne   617a
> *cen* þec mid cræfte   1219a
> *Sigon* þa to slæpe   1251a
> *Grap* þa togeanes   1501a
> *Bær* þa seo brimwyl[f]   1506a
> *wearþ* ða wundenmæl   1531a
> *brægd* þa beadwe heard   1539a
> *Wunað* he on wiste   1735a
> *stonc* ða æfter stane   2288a
> *Hyrte* hine hordweard   2593a
> *Wod* þa þurh þone wælrec   2661a
> *wehte* hyne wætre   2854a

Here there is no certain way of determining whether the verb
is stressed or not; but the heavy predominance of verses in
which alliteration of the verb is either lacking or non-functional
suggests that here also the verb is unstressed. It should further
be noticed that, apart from the eight instances in which *þa* must
be stressed, none of the verses in which the verb must be stressed
contains the particle *þa*[2]; but among the remaining verses in
this group the particle *þa* is extremely frequent. The evidence
seems to indicate that when a finite verb is the last particle but
one before the first stressed element it is only stressed when the
metre of the verse absolutely requires it; in all other cases
alliteration must be considered non-functional.[3]

[1] The omission of *ic* would solve the metrical problem, but would introduce
syntactic difficulties.

[2] The two exceptions in the list in § 19 have been removed by emendation.

[3] In the cases when the verb is stressed it must be decided whether the
particle is stressed or not (§ 19); no certainty is possible, but it seems most
probable that all particles are stressed except personal pronouns in the nominative case, which may be enclitic upon the preceding verb.

22. There are only nine instances in *Beowulf* of group (6), in six of which the finite verb alliterates. With alliteration:

>*Secge* ic þe to soðe   590a
>*Hylde* hine þa heaþodeor   688a
>ne *geweox* he him to willan   1711a
>*Reste* hine þa rumheort   1799a
>*Heald* þu nu, hruse   2247a
>*geaf* him ða mid Geatum   2623a

Without alliteration:

>*gesaga* him eac wordum   388a
>*Eodon* him þa togeanes   1626a
>*gedeð* him swa gewealdene   1732a

All of these verses are *a*-verses, and in none of them is the assumption that the verb is stressed necessary to the metre. Moreover, if the alliteration is mainly non-functional in group (5), then *a fortiori* it is likely to be so in group (6). If the verb is stressed, the verse *ne geweox he him to willan* offers difficulties: if the particles after the verb are unstressed the verse offends against Kuhn's Law of Particles; if they are stressed the result is an impossible metrical pattern. Three of the verses in which the verb alliterates contain the objectionable *þa*. All this evidence suggests that when the verb is the last particle but two before the stressed element the alliteration is non-functional.

23. Of the thirteen instances of group (7) in *Beowulf*, the finite verb alliterates in all but two:

>*heold* þenden lifde   57b
>*Sægde* se þe cuþe   90b
>*seomade* ond syrede   161a
>*fremme* se þe wille   1003b
>*bruc* þenden þu mote   1177b
>*frægn* gif him wære   1319b
>*sec* gif þu dyrre   1379b
>*wyrce* se þe mote   1387b
>*ga* þær he wille   1394b
>*breac* þonne moste   1487b
>*hyde* se ðe wylle   2766b

With one exception all these verses are *b*-verses, and the assumption that the verb is not stressed robs them of all alliteration;

the exception (*seomade ond syrede*) should perhaps not be included in this group, since it is not certain that the two verbs cannot be considered to belong to the same clause. The two verses in which the finite verb does not alliterate are the following[1]:

> *mynte* þæt he gedælde   731a
> *Nah*, hwa sweord wege   2252b

The evidence suggests that a finite verb is normally stressed when it forms a whole clause in itself.

24. In the 21 examples of group (8) in *Beowulf*,[2] the finite verb alliterates in every one; in each case the verse cannot be scanned at all unless the verb is stressed. The following are representative examples:

> Ic þæt *gehyre*,   þæt þis is hold weorod   290a
> frean Scyldinga.
>
> Hwæþere me *gesælde*,   þæt ic mid sweorde ofsloh 574a
> niceras nigene.
>
> hwæþre him *gesælde*,   ðæt þæt swurd þurhwod   890a
> wrætlicne wyrm.
>
> Me man *sægde*,   þæt þu ðe for sunu wolde   1175a
> hereri[n]c habban.
>
> ac he hyne *gewyrpte*,   þeah ðe him wund hrine.   2976a

In this group there is clearly no doubt at all that the finite verb is stressed.

25. Out of the ten examples of group (9) in *Beowulf*, the finite verb alliterates in seven. Two of the verses cannot be scanned at all unless both the verb and the particle which follow it are stressed:

> *Gæþ* eft se þe mot   603b
> *Hafa* nu ond geheald   658a

---

[1] It is possible to find an explanation for these two exceptions. In the first instance the verb *mynte* is most often used as a quasi-auxiliary, and is then lightly stressed; although it is fully meaningful here, the light stress has perhaps been transferred from the quasi-auxiliary use. In the second verse the verb is *nah*, and it has already been suggested in § 18 that *ah* may be always unstressed.

[2] 144a, 272b, 290a, 292b, 435a, 503a, 536a, 574a, 632a, 691a, 798a, 809a, 890a, 937a, 1175a, 1392a, 1671a, 1846a, 2668b, 2976a, 3103b.

The remaining five verses in which the verb alliterates have double alliteration, so there is no difficulty in assuming that the alliteration of the verb is non-functional:

> *Wen'* ic þæt ge for wlenco   338a
> *Wen'* ic þæt he wille   442a
> *Manað* swa ond myndgað   2057a
> *Hyrde* ic þæt he ðone healsbeah   2172a
> *heold* mec ond hæfde   2430a

In the following verses the verb does not alliterate:

> *hyrde* ic þæt [. . .]   62a
> *wene* ic þæt he mid gode   1184a
> *Hyrde* ic þæt þam frætwum   2163a

The analogy of group (5), which this group closely resembles, suggests that the finite verb is only stressed when the metre of the verse absolutely requires it.

26. The examination of these nine groups of verses reveals that (with trifling exceptions) the finite verb is always stressed in groups (1), (2), (4) and (8); that it is often, but not always, stressed in groups (3) and (7); that in groups (5) and (9) it is stressed only when the metre absolutely requires it; and that it is never stressed in group (6). Even in the groups in which the finite verb is not normally stressed it may, and often does, bear non-functional alliteration. From the point of view of practical scansion, this conclusion may be much more simply expressed: alliteration is always to be accepted as evidence that the finite verb is stressed, except when it is followed by one or more particles in the same clause; in this case it is only stressed if the metre absolutely requires it. It is not difficult to understand why this state of affairs should exist. Leaving aside groups (1) and (2), which are already explained by Kuhn's discoveries, we may notice that the finite verb seems to occupy a kind of half-way house between the particles and the stressed elements. When it is followed by one or more particles it is associated with them and not normally stressed; when it stands between one or more particles and the first stressed element it is assimilated to the stressed elements and is treated as such; when it forms or concludes a clause which contains no stressed element it supplies the place of the missing stressed element. Only when it stands alone before the **first** stressed element of a clause is there any doubt, because the context does not clearly associate it either with particles or with the first stressed element.

27. It only remains to consider the auxiliaries and quasi-auxiliaries which have hitherto been left out of consideration. In general it may be stated that these verbs do not normally alliterate, no matter what group they belong to; but there are a few instances, mostly in group (4), where the verse cannot be scanned at all unless the auxiliary is stressed, and in these cases, of course, the auxiliary alliterates; there are also a few instances of what is probably genuine accidental alliteration. The verb 'to be' alliterates only four times:

> ond ge him *syndon* 393a
> *Wes*, þenden þu lifige 1224b
> þæt hie oft *wæron* 1247a
> cwædon þæt he *wære* 3180a

Weorþan never alliterates. *Habban* alliterates only twice, and in each case the alliteration is almost certainly accidental:

> *hæfdon* hy forhealden 2381a
> *hæfde* Higelaces 2952a

Willan alliterates twice; in the first instance the verse cannot be scanned unless the auxiliary is stressed, in the second the alliteration is doubtless accidental:

> Wen' ic þæt he *wille* 442a
> *wolde* wigfruma 664a

Sculan never alliterates. Out of 24 instances of *magan*, there are no less than eight instances of alliteration, of which one is doubtless accidental:

> *Meaht* ðu, min wine 2047a

In the other seven examples the verse cannot be scanned at all unless the verb is stressed:

> (þ)ær he *meahte* swa 762b
> ðær hie *meahton* swa 797b
> ic hine ne *mihte* 967a
> þæt he ne *mehte* 1082a
> þeah þe ne *meahte* 1130a
> swa he ne *mihte* 1508a
> hyt ne *mihte* swa 2091b

Motan alliterates three times, and in each case the verb must be stressed:

> þæt hie ne *moste*   706a
> Noðer hy hine ne *moston*   2124a
> þæs ðe ic *moste*   2797a

Durran alliterates twice, and in each case the verb must be stressed:

> nænig þæt *dorste*   1933a
> ða ne *dorston* ær   2848a

28. Among the quasi-auxiliaries, *wutun* alliterates only once:

> *Uton* nu efstan   3101a

Here there can be little doubt that the alliteration is accidental. *Onginnan* also alliterates once, and again the alliteration is probably accidental:

> *onginneð* geomormod   2044a

Hatan alliterates four times, and in each case the alliteration seems to be accidental:

> *Het* ða Hildeburh   1114a
> *Heht* þa se hearda   1807a
> *Hatað* heaðomære   2802a
> *Heht* ða þæt heaðoweorc   2892a

Lætan alliterates twice:

> *læteð* hworfan   1728b
> *lete* hyne licgean   3082a

The first instance has long been recognized as anomalous; in the second the alliteration is probably accidental; the verse is of the same type as *bæd hine bliðne* and *Hyrte hine hordweard*, discussed in § 21. *Myntan* occurs only twice, and alliterates each time:

> *mynte* se manscaða   712a
> *Mynte* se mæra   762a

In each case the alliteration seems to be accidental.

29. *Cuman* never alliterates, but *gewitan* alliterates twice:

> *Gewat* him þa to waroðe   234a
> *Gewiton* him ða wigend   1125a

In each case the alliteration is probably accidental. *Cweþan* never alliterates. Out of 165 instances of these auxiliary and quasi-auxiliary verbs, the verb alliterates in only 29, or about 18 per cent (the verb 'to be' is not included in the count); in 15 cases the alliteration seems to be accidental, a proportion of exactly one in eleven—very nearly the proportion calculated by Ross. Out of 415 instances of fully meaningful verbs, however, the verb alliterates in no less than 335, or about 81 per cent. The independent treatment of these two groups of verbs is thus fully justified. As far as the auxiliary and quasi-auxiliary verbs are concerned, alliteration is only to be taken as evidence that the verb is stressed when the stress is absolutely required by the metre.

CHAPTER THREE

STRESS AND QUANTITY

30. The attributes of stress and quantity are entirely independent of each other by nature, though in practice there is often a link between them.[1] Quantity is a physiological attribute, and, although it may be partly conventionalized, it depends ultimately on the actual time required to pronounce the sounds of a given syllable. Stress, on the other hand, is a psychological attribute, and depends on the importance attached by the speaker to the meaning of a given syllable.[2] Stress may vary considerably from speaker to speaker, and from context to context, but quantity can only vary within very narrow limits. Sievers recognized two degrees of stress in Old English, full stress and 'half' or 'secondary' stress. According to him, a full stress is found in every word which is neither a particle nor a proclitic (see § 9); a secondary stress is found not only on the second element of all compounds, but also on a number of derivative endings, usually in long syllables, but occasionally in short syllables. This view of secondary stress is defended on both metrical and phonological grounds: here we are concerned primarily with metrical considerations, but the phonological aspect is discussed in Appendix A.

31. In such a verse as

æþeling manig   1112b

Sievers attributes secondary stress to the derivative syllable *-ing*, on the grounds that a short syllable like *ma-* may only act as a metrical lift when it is preceded by a long *stressed* syllable. On the other hand, in such a verse as

---

[1] In Latin, for instance, the position of the stress depends on the quantity of the penultimate vowel.

[2] Cf. Daniel Jones, *The Phoneme: its Nature and Use* (1950) pp. 134-5, § 425: 'Stresses are essentially subjective activities of the speaker. A strongly stressed syllable, for instance, is one which he consciously utters with greater effort than other neighbouring syllables in the word or sentence.'

Oft Scyld Scefing 4a

a secondary stress on -*ing* would be metrically objectionable,
and it is therefore ignored. The secondary stress on the second
element in a compound, however, is never thus ignored, apart
from proper names whose composition is less consciously recognized. Sievers himself, therefore, implicitly recognizes a metrical
difference between the secondary stress on derivative endings
and secondary stress in compounds, in so far as the first may be
ignored when necessary and the second may not. On metrical
grounds, indeed, there is no need to assume any degree of stress
on -*ing* in *æpeling manig*: it would be just as easy to state that
a short syllable may only act as a metrical lift when it is preceded by a *long* syllable, irrespective of the degree of stress on it.
Since, however, the phonological evidence for some degree of
stress on derivative and formative syllables is by no means
negligible, it will be convenient to refer to the secondary stress
which cannot be ignored as 'secondary' stress, and to the secondary stress which can be ignored as 'tertiary' stress, without
prejudice to the possibility that 'tertiary' stress may in fact
prove to be equivalent to lack of stress.

32. It is obviously desirable to find clear definitions of secondary and tertiary stress. Secondary stress is not difficult to define,
once it is recognized that stress is a psychological attribute re-
quiring conscious effort on the part of the speaker: it is found
in compounds whose meaning can be deduced from the meaning
of its elements, both of which also occur as independent words.[1]
Tertiary stress is found in all other types of compound, which
may be classified as follows:

(1) Compounds in which the meaning of the whole word is so
far removed from the apparent meaning of the elements that
the mode of composition is obscure: e.g. *garsecg* 'ocean'.

(2) Compounds in which one of the elements has become obsolete: e.g. *siðfæt* 'expedition', in which *fæt* 'journey' is obsolete.

(3) Compounds whose composition has become obscured
through phonetic change: e.g. *hlaford* 'lord'.

(4) Proper names standing for a single person or place, in

[1] Cf. Fuhr, *Die Metrik des westgermanischen Alliterationsverses* (1892) 17ff.
The proviso that the elements of the compound must exist as independent
words is required to exclude such compounds as *uncup*, whose meaning can be
deduced from the meanings of its elements.

which the individual elements have no independent significance:
e.g. *Beowulf*.[1]

(5) Compounds containing suffixes like *-lic*, *-leas*, *-scipe*, *-weard*.

(6) Compounds containing prefixes like *un-*, *oð-*, *or-*, *in-*; the prefix normally bears full stress and the primary element loses its stress.

(7) Pronominal compounds like *æghwæs*, *nathwylc*.

Tertiary stress is also found on all long or disyllabic derivative or formative endings.

33. That the distinction between secondary and tertiary stress is of real metrical significance will be clear from the table below. Under each of the types of verse considered the first row, marked (1), gives the number of *a*-verses and the number of *b*-verses in *Beowulf*, with percentage equivalents in brackets; the second row, marked (2), gives the number of *a*-verses with double alliteration and the number of *a*-verses with single alliteration, with percentage equivalents in brackets.

		With secondary stress		*With tertiary stress*	
Type A2k	(1)	23 : 25	(48 : 52)	3 : 12	(20 : 80)
	(2)	16 : 7	(70 : 30)	2 : 1	(67 : 30)
Type A2l	(1)	54 : 8	(87 : 13)	30 : 21	(59 : 41)
	(2)	54 : 0	(100 : 0)	17 : 13	(57 : 43)
Type A2b	(1)	65 : 0	(100 : 0)	47 : 27	(64 : 36)
	(2)	65 : 0	(100 : 0)	35 : 12	(74 : 26)
Type D1	(1)	20 : 2	(91 : 9)	38 :119	(24 : 76)
	(2)	20 : 0	(100 : 0)	19 : 19	(50 : 50)
Type D2	(1)	37 : 0	(100 : 0)	20 :111	(15 : 85)
	(2)	37 : 0	(100 : 0)	9 : 11	(45 : 55)

The very striking differences in the percentages leave no doubt that there is a real distinction between secondary and tertiary stress.

[1] Compounds like *Suð-Dene* must be considered doubtful, since it is not agreed whether the prefix is intended to distinguish a particular group of Danes or is merely conventional and ornamental.

CHAPTER FOUR

RESOLUTION

34. In Old English verse, a full stress usually falls on a single long syllable; it may, however, fall on a short syllable followed by another unstressed syllable, usually short, and this phenomenon is known as 'resolution'; it may also fall on a single short syllable when the preceding syllable is long. It follows that the sequence of syllables ∪× is metrically ambiguous, since it is equivalent sometimes to _ and sometimes to _×. It has never yet been established whether the equivalence depends entirely on the context (that is, whether the sequence is preceded by a long syllable or not), or whether some other factor is relevant. The question can only be decided by a comparison of types of verse in which one or other of the possible equivalences would be metrically objectionable. In the sequence of syllables ⌣̲ ∪ × ⌣̲ × absence of resolution would be metrically objectionable, since the sequence ⌣̲ ̲ × ⌣̲ × (to which, in the absence of resolution, it would be equivalent) is studiously avoided by the *Beowulf* poet when the first three syllables belong to the same word (see § 4). In the sequence of syllables ⌣̲ ̲ ∪ ×, on the other hand, resolution would be metrically objectionable, since the sequence ⌣̲ ̲ ̲ (to which, by resolution, it would be equivalent) is short of one syllable. The following paragraphs contain an analysis of all the verses in *Beowulf* belonging to these two types, according to the nature and origin of the final syllable of the compound word.

35. The sequence of syllables ⌣̲ ∪ × ⌣̲ × :

(*a*) neuter *a*-stem, nominative plural
        bengeato burston   1121a

(*b*) neuter *a*-stem, accusative plural
        brimclifu blican   222a
        sincfato sealde   622a
        banfatu bærnan   1116a
        Bencþelu beredon   1239a

(c) neuter *wa*-stem, nominative singular
    sweordbealu sliðen   1147a
    hreþerbealo hearde   1343a
    feorhbealu fægum   2077a
    feorhbealo frecne   2250a, 2537a

(d) neuter *wa*-stem, accusative singular
    morðbeala mare   136a
    feorhbealo feorran   156a
    morþorbealo maga   1079a, 2742a
    aldorbealu eorlum   1676a
    leodbealo longsum   1722a
    cwealmbealu cyðan   1940a
    wigbealu weccean   2046a

(e) neuter *wa*-stem, nominative plural
    guðsearo gumena   328a

(f) neuter *wa*-stem, accusative plural
    guðsearo geatolic   215a
    fyrdsearo fuslic   2618a

(g) feminine *ō*-stem, nominative singular
    nydwracu niþgrim   193a

(h) feminine *ō*-stem, accusative singular
    modceare micle   1778a
    modceare mændon   3149a

(i) masculine *i*-stem, nominative singular
    freowine folca   430a
    drihtsele dreorfah   485a
    gilpcwide Geates   640a
    Dryhtsele dynede   767a
    goldwine gumena   1171a, 1476a, 1602a
    beahsele beorhta   1177a
    wiggryre wifes   1284a
    færgripe flodes   1516a
    wighete Wedra   2120a
    freawine folca   2357a, 2429a
    goldwine Geata   2419a, 2584a

(j) masculine *i*-stem, accusative singular
    folcstede frætwan   76a
    goldsele gumena   715a
    mundgripe maran   753a
    gestsele gyredon   994a

>   folcstede fara   1463a
>   wighryre wraðra   1619a
>   ecghete eoweð   1738a
>   burhstede beateð   2265a
>   dryhtsele dyrnne   2320a
>   winsele westne   2456a
>   wicstede weligne   2607a

(k) masculine *i*-stem, dative singular
>   mundgripe mægenes   1534a

(l) masculine *i*-stem, nominative plural
>   laðbite lices   1122a

(m) masculine *u*-stem, nominative singular
>   gomenwudu greted   1065a
>   þrecwudu þrymlic   1246a
>   healwudu dynede   1317b
>   sundwudu þunede   1906b

(n) masculine *u*-stem, accusative singular
>   sundwudu sohte   208a
>   sæwudu sældon   226a
>   mægenwudu mundum   236a
>   holtwudu sece   1369b
>   gomenwudu grette   2108a

(o) masculine *u*-stem, accusative plural
>   bordwudu beorhtan   1243a

36. The sequence of syllables $\acute{\smile}\acute{\smile}\smile\times$:

(a) neuter *a*-stem, accusative plural
>   steap stanhliðo   1409a

(b) feminine *ō*-stem, genitive singular
>   gearo gyrnwræce   2118a

(c) masculine *i*-stem, genitive plural
>   wis wordcwida   1845a

(d) masculine *n*-stem, nominative singular
>   leof landfruma   31a
>   deorc deaþscua   160a
>   scearp scyldwiga   288a
>   fah feondscaða   554a
>   eald æscwiga   2042a
>   dior dædfruma   2090a
>   gomel guðwiga   2112a
>   eald uhtsceaða   2271a

nacod niðdraca   2273a
lað lyftfloga   2315a
earm anhaga   2368a
gearo guðfreca   2414a

(e) masculine adjective, nominative plural
  frome fyrdhwate   1641a, 2476a
  scaþan scirhame   1895a

(f) masculine *a*-stem, accusative plural
  oflet lifdagas   1622a

(g) masculine *n*-stem, accusative singular
  bat banlocan   742a

(h) feminine *n*-stem, accusative singular
  eft eardlufan   692a
  hiold heahlufan   1954a

(i) past participle
  heard hondlocen   322a, 551a
  guma gilphlæden   868a
  wea widscofen   936a
  gyfen goldhroden   1948a
  geong goldhroden   2025a
  wyrm wohbogen   2827a

(j) miscellaneous consonantal endings
  leof leodcyning   54a
  geweold wigsigor   1554a
  secg synbysig   2226a
  Gesyhð sorhcearig   2455a
  hwate helmberend   2517a, 2642a
  god guðcyning   2563a
  (song) sorhcearig   3152a

37. A comparison of these two lists reveals that, with one
exception, there is no duplication between them; that is, an
ending which appears in one does not appear in the other. The
exception is the ending of the neuter *a*-stem, accusative plural,
which appears four times in the first list and once in the second;
but the single instance in the second list is probably due to an
error on Klaeber's part. There are two forms of the word *hlið*,
one with a short vowel and one with a long vowel; it is highly
probable that *stanhliðo* has the long vowel, since it is the only
instance in *Beowulf* of the absence of back mutation in this
word; compare *misthleoþum* 710, *fenhleoðu* 820, *wulfhleoþu* 1358,

næshleoðum 1427. It is also remarkable that all the endings in
the first list are vocalic, although about half the endings in the
second list are consonantal. Most remarkable of all is the fact
that all but four of the endings in the first list are those which
are regularly lost after a long stem syllable, while (apart from
the exception dismissed above) all the endings in the second
list are those which are regularly retained after a long stem
syllable; we may say that, in metre as in grammar, *scipu* is
equivalent to *hus* in the nominative and accusative plural, but
scipa is equivalent to *husa* in the genitive plural.[1] The phonological implications of this remarkable distinction are discussed in
Appendix B; for the moment it is sufficient to notice that there
is metrical evidence of a distinction in Old English between two
types of vocalic ending, which we may, without prejudice to
the subsequent discovery of their real nature, conveniently call
'short' vocalic endings and 'long' vocalic endings.[2]

38. It is now clear that the presence or absence of resolution
in the sequence of syllables ◡ × depends not only on the context
but also on the quantity of the second syllable: in the types
of verse reviewed above, the sequence ◡ ◡ is resolved but the
sequence ◡ _ (where _ stands for a 'long' vocalic or consonantal
ending) is not. Unfortunately matters are not always as simple as
this. Among the instances of the sequence of syllables ◜◡×◜×,
for instance, which differs from the sequence considered in § 35
only in the substitution of tertiary for secondary stress, there
are a number of consonantal endings. The following is a complete list of the verses concerned:

> egsode eorl[as]   6a
> þreatedon þearle   560a
> freolicu folccwen   641a
> tryddode tirfæst   922a
> geomrode giddum   1118a

---

[1] The distinction between two types of ending, and its relevance to the question of resolution, was hinted at by Kaluza; see Max Kaluza, 'Zur Betonungs-
und Verslehre des Altenglischen', *Festschrift für O. Schrade* (1896) 120-31, and
A Short History of English Versification (1911) § 52 and § 65 Note. Unfortunately, Kaluza failed to describe his discovery accurately or to prove it
statistically.

[2] That there was really any distinction of quantity in unstressed final vowels
is highly improbable; but there can be no objection to writing *wordcwidā*, etc.
for metrical purposes; many of the conventional Old English quantities are in
fact prehistoric.

drihtscype dreogan   1470a
freondscipe fæstne   2069a
grapode gearofolm   2085a
weorðode weorcum   2096a
siðode sorhfull   2119a
healsode hreohmod   2132a
eorlscipe efnde   2133a, 3007a
eorlscype efne   2535a
eorlscipe efnan   2622a
sweðrian syððan   2702a

weardode hwile   105b
myndgiend wære   1105b
fundode wrecca   1137b
swigedon ealle   1699b

Most of these verses have short vocalic endings[1]; but there are
four consonantal endings, one of which has two consonants after
the vowel. It seems to follow that consonantal endings are
ambivalent, and do not necessarily preclude the possibility of
resolution.

39. Furthermore, an examination of the verses representing the
sequence of syllables $\acute{\_}\grave{\_}\cup\times$, which differs from the sequence considered in § 36 only in the substitution of tertiary for secondary
stress, reveals the following instances of apparently short vocalic
endings:

heah Healfdene   57a
weard maþelode   286a

Sele hlifade   81b
Heorot eardode   166b
secg wisade   208b, 402b
stig wisode   320b
hider wisade   370b
feo þingode   470b
hlyn swynsode   611b
Gode þancode   625b, 1397b
feond treddode   725b

---

[1] This is clearly true of the nominal forms; with the verbal forms no certainty is possible until the phonological basis of the distinction has been
established, since our present criterion (retention or loss after a long stem) is
not available. Forms like *demde* are not relevant, since in this case it is the
medial vowel which is lost.

Reced hlynsode   770b
trode sceawode   843b
hild sweðrode   901b
lean teohhode   951b
Dene weorþode   1090b
Ides gnornode   1117b
sinc ealgode   1204b
wean ahsode   1206b
Reced weardode   1237b
feo leanige   1380b
ham eahtode   1407b
ufan cunnode   1500b
heard grapode   1566b
drepe þrowade   1589b
Lagu drusade   1630b
*oft wisode   1663b
hylt sceawode   1687b
weorc þrowade   1721b
forð wisade   1795b
reced hliuade   1799b
mæst hlifade   1898b
feor wlatode   1916b
min costode   2084b
Glof hangode   2085b
swaðe weardade   2098b
fela leanode   2102b
last weardode   2164b
frea sceawode   2285b
wræce leornode   2336b
sele fælsode   2352b
sinc brytnade   2383b
nearo ðrowode   2594b
gled fæðmie   2652b
gearo sceawige   2748b
gold sceawode   2793b
grim andswaru   2860b
Lyt swigode   2897b
wæl reafode   3027b

The number is considerable (51 out of a total of 133 instances,

or rather more than a third) and there can be no doubt that
short vocalic endings are also ambivalent, and do not necessarily
impose resolution. There is no evidence, however, that long
vocalic endings are ever ambivalent; it appears that a long
vocalic ending necessarily precludes the possibility of resolution.

40. So far the discussion has been concerned only with resolution after a long syllable: it remains to determine whether the
possibility of resolution is affected by the nature of the second
syllable when no long syllable precedes. In one sense the problem is simpler, since the sequence ◡ × can never be equivalent
to the sequence _ × unless a long syllable precedes it; it is only
necessary to determine whether the sequence ◡ _ is avoided
altogether in contexts which require resolution. The amount of
material available is very great, since resolution is frequent in
all types of verse, but it will be sufficient to quote a representative group of examples; the group selected is one of the varieties
of Type B.

> We þurh holdne hige   267a
> hæfde mare mægen   518a
> Ða wæs haten hreþe   991a
> se þe secgan wile   1049a
> hire selfre sunu   1115a
> siþðan grimne gripe   1148a
> æfter deofla hryre   1680a
> on swa geongum feore   1843a
> þæt hie Geata clifu   1911a
> wið his sylfes sunu   2013a
> æfter billes bite   2060a
> syððan Geata cyning   2356a
>
> Þær wæs madma fela   36b
> ofer landa fela   311b
> sohte holdne wine   376b
> *þæt wæs geomuru ides   1075b
> þær he worna fela   2003b
> þær wæs swylcra fela   2231b
> Ic geneðde fela   2511b
> se ðe worna fela   2542b
> þæt we rondas beren   2653b
> þæt he ana scyle   2657b

Out of 22 endings, four are consonantal (one with two consonants), three are long vocalic endings (*hreþe, feore, scyle*); the remaining 15 are short vocalic endings. This proportion is representative, and it follows that long vocalic endings do not necessarily preclude the possibility of resolution when no long syllable precedes. It seems very likely that we can observe in *Beowulf* the decay of a poetic tradition. The primitive equivalences were doubtless clear and simple: a short syllable followed by a short vocalic ending was equivalent to a single long syllable, but a short syllable followed by a consonantal or a long vocalic ending could only be equivalent to a long syllable followed by a similar ending. These equivalences were most fully preserved in *Beowulf* in the second element of full compounds, less fully in disyllabic formative and derivative endings, less fully still in isolated disyllables. Even in isolated disyllables the degree of preservation is high; but no conclusions can be drawn about the vitality of poetic tradition until some conclusion has been reached about the antiquity of the tradition.[1] However, the degree to which the equivalences are preserved might provide a new criterion of the relative chronology of Old English verse.

[1] See Appendix B, § 6.

CHAPTER FIVE

THE CÆSURA

41. Sievers divided each of his five types of verse into two feet, and indicated the division in his notation by a vertical bar:

Type A $\acute{-}\times|\acute{-}\times$
Type B $\times\acute{-}|\times\acute{-}$
Type C $\times\acute{-}|\acute{-}\times$
Type D $\acute{-}|\acute{-}\grave{-}\times$
Type E $\acute{-}\grave{-}\times|\acute{-}$

The point of division was quite arbitrarily chosen, remained the same for every instance of a given type, and often came in the middle of a word, or between a proclitic and the following word. This feature of Sievers' system has been much criticized, especially by advocates of 'measure systems' of scansion, whose objections have been well summarized by Pope[1]: 'Rhythm is apprehended, not by the eye, but the ear. The bar has therefore no power—it cannot be heard. Unless it is used to indicate that the syllable following it is more heavily accented than its neighbours, it has no meaning whatever.' If Pope is right, there is no point in writing a bar at all, since the position of the stress can be more conveniently indicated by the usual accent-mark. If the bar is written, it may fall in a different place from Sievers' bar (notably in Type B) but it will still often fall in the middle of a word, or between a proclitic and the following word. Moreover, it is not true that a bar which does not mark a following accent cannot be heard: it may mark what in musical terms is called 'phrasing'; it may mark the division of a clause into units of sense or breath-groups.

42. As we have seen in § 9, a verse clause consists of a series of stressed elements; each stressed element may be preceded by one or more proclitics, and the whole series may be preceded by one or more particles. Each stressed element with its attendant

---

[1] J. C. Pope, *op. cit.* 10.

proclitics forms a unit of sense or breath-group, what Heusler calls a *Kolon*[1]: 'Über der Silbe kommt im Gerüste des Satz-rhythmus nicht das *Wort* (das ist keine Gehörgrösse), sondern das *Kolon*. . . . Ein treffender Name wäre "Atemgruppen"; denn die Kola werden zusammengehalten und begrenzt durch die Atemführung. Die Kolongrenzen liegen da, wo bei lang-samen Vortrag eine Atempause denkbar wäre.' If therefore the bar is used to mark the *Atempause* or cæsura, while the position of the stress is indicated by the usual accent-mark, *some* addi-tional information has been given, though it remains to be seen whether this information is metrically significant. This use of the bar has already been adopted by Möller, Lawrence and Vogt[2]; Lawrence points out that the cæsura within a verse is often marked by a point in the manuscripts.[3] Yet the metrical significance of the cæsura has been merely asserted, never proved.

43. It is not in fact difficult to prove the metrical significance of the cæsura, at least in certain types of verse. In the standard Type A verse, $\acute{-} \times (\times) \acute{-} \times$, the cæsura may fall in three different places; (i) $\acute{-} \times | \acute{-} \times$; (ii) $\acute{-} | \times \acute{-} \times$; (iii) $\acute{-} \times | \times \acute{-} \times$. In the table below, the first row, marked (1), gives the number of *a*-verses and the number of *b*-verses in *Beowulf*, with percentage equi-valents in brackets; the second row, marked (2), gives the num-ber of *a*-verses with double alliteration and the number of *a*-verses with single alliteration, with percentage equivalents in brackets.

Position (i)	*Positions* (ii) *and* (iii)
(1) 368 : 489 (43 : 57)	530 : 446 (54 : 46)
(2) 105 : 263 (29 : 71)	494 : 36 (93 : 7)

These figures show a very striking contrast between Position (i) on the one hand and Positions (ii) and (iii) on the other. The first variety of verse is more frequent in the *b*-verse, the second is more frequent in the *a*-verse; the numerical divergence is not great, but in view of the large number of instances it is clearly significant. In the first variety double alliteration is found in

---

[1] A. Heusler, *op. cit.* p. 55, § 65.
[2] W. Möller, *Zur althochdeutschen Alliterationspoesie* (1888); J. Lawrence, *Chapters on Alliterative Verse* (1893); W. H. Vogt, 'Altgermanische Druck-"Metrik": recht unbekummerte Meinungen eines Nicht-Metrikers', *PBB* lxiv (1940) 124-64.
[3] *op. cit.* Chapter I [MS Junius 11]. For traces of a similar pointing in *Beowulf*, see Klaeber, *op. cit.* c.

less than a third of the instances, but in the second variety it is quasi-compulsory. It is impossible to doubt that the position of the cæsura is of the first importance. Here, for instance, lies the explanation of the peculiarity of Type A* noticed in § 4: although the sequence ´_|×´× is permissible, the sequence ´_×|´× is not—the only difference being in the position of the cæsura.

44. The position of the cæsura is also important in Type D*. In the majority of instances the cæsura falls immediately before the second full stress; all the instances in which the cæsura falls immediately after the first stress are susceptible either of an alternative explanation, or of simple emendation. In Type D*1 the following verses are outstanding:

> brond | ne beadomecas   1454a
> lac | ond luftacen   1863a
> seah | on unleofe   2863b

In the first instance the reading *brodne* improves the sense and is metrically unobjectionable.[1] In the second instance the syncopation of *e* in the last syllable (*luftacẹn*) makes an unobjectionable example of Type A2b. In the third instance *unleofe* must be stressed on the second syllable, giving an example of Type A1; stress on compounds with *un-* is variable; compare *únmurnlice* 449 and *unmúrnlice* 1756, in both of which the position of the stress is attested by the alliteration. The following instances must be considered together:

> Sorh | is me to secganne   473a
> Wundor | is to secganne   1724b
> idese | to efnanne   1941a
> To lang | ys to reccenne   2093a
> sæcce | to seceanne   2562a

In each instance the substitution of the uninflected for the inflected form of the infinitive gives a regular example of Type A1.[2]

45. In Type D*2 the following verses are outstanding:

> word | wæron wynsume   612a
> fleon | on fenhopu   764a

---

[1] Trautmann, Holthausen and Sedgefield read *brogdne*, but *brodne* is palæographically preferable; compare the frequent accidental omission of *n* in *Beowulf* (Klaeber, *op. cit.* xcviii Note 2).

[2] For references see Klaeber, *op. cit.* 277 § 12; see also Pope, *op. cit.* 237.

     win | of wundẹrfatum   1162a
     Dead | is Æschere   1323b
     eard | ond eorlscipe   1727a
     deorc | ofer dryhtgumum   1790a
     him | on andsware   1840b
     wongas | ond wicstede   2462a
     lond | ond leodbyrig   2471a
     lif | ond leodscipe   2751a

In every instance the final syllable consists either of a short
vocalic ending or of a consonantal ending; as we have seen in
§ 40, both these endings are ambivalent, and there is no reason
why these verses should not belong to Type A2b, with resolution
of the secondary stress. It is noteworthy that two lines in which
this solution is not available have already been eliminated on
quite other grounds (§§ 28, 20):

        mynte se manscaða   712a
        Ne gemealt him se modsefa   2628a

In Type D*4 only one verse requires consideration:

        Heold | on heahgesceap   3084a

Here the MS reading *heoldon* is metrically unobjectionable; and
whatever the difficulty of the passage, it is not permissible to
indulge in emendation which produces a metrically unsatisfac-
tory verse.

D

CHAPTER SIX

ANACRUSIS

46. The types of verse which begin with a stressed syllable
(Types A and D; it is doubtful whether Type E should be included here) may occasionally be preceded by one, or exceptionally two unstressed syllables; this extrametrical prelude to the
verse is known as anacrusis or *Auftakt*. It has hitherto been
assumed that the occurrence of anacrusis is entirely casual; but
this view is not supported by the facts. In Type A1, when the
cæsura falls in position (i), there are only two instances of
anacrusis:

> [be] Finnes eaferum   1068a
> under heofenes hador   414a

If Sievers' suggestion that *ai* in *Caines* is a diphthong is accepted[1]
a third instance must be added:

> in Caines cynne   107a

When the cæsura falls in positions (ii) or (iii), on the other hand,
anacrusis is frequent:

> in mægþa gehwære   25a
> ongunnen on geogoþe   409a
> gehede under heofenum   505a
> genered wið niðe   827a
> ahæfen of horde   1108a
> forhabban in hreþre   1151a
> Onfoh þissum fulle   1169a
> geworden in wicun   1304a
> wið ord ond wið ecge   1549a
> forgyteð ond forgymeð   1751a
> forsiteð ond forsworceð   1767a
> *To lang ys to reccan   2093a
> gewac æt wige   2629a

[1] E. Sievers, *Zum angelsächsischen Vocalismus* (1900) 7.

    gesigan æt sæcce   2659a
    geswac æt sæcce   2681a
    geweold his gewitte   2703a
    gesæt on sesse   2717a
    ætgifan æt guðe   2878a
    acigde of corðre   3121a

    swa wæter bebugeð   93b
    swa guman gefrungon   666b
    swa sæ bebugeð   1223b
    ðurhfon ne mihte   1504b
    gesacan ne tealde   1773b
    forberan ne mehte   1877b
    nu hæleð ne mostan   2247b
    hy eft gemetton   2592b

    ge æt ham ge on herge   1248a

47. The three apparent instances of anacrusis when the cæsura is in position (i) are all doubtful in various ways. The first instance depends on an emendation, itself highly controversial, and may safely be neglected, since the emendation falls if the supposed metrical type cannot be substantiated elsewhere. The second instance gives a very doubtful meaning, and the palmary emendation *haðor* (Grein, Holthausen, Schücking) gives a verse of Type B; if the manuscript reading must be retained, it is possible to syncopate the *o* of the last syllable (*hador*). In the third instance the manuscript originally read *cames*, which gives a verse of Type C2; *Caines* is a later alteration, which must not be accepted in the face of the metrical objection.[1] It appears, then, that anacrusis is not permissible when the cæsura is in position (i). It is also remarkable that, with two exceptions, all the instances of anacrusis in the *a*-verse when the cæsura is in positions (ii) or (iii) have double alliteration; it is true that double alliteration is quasi-compulsory in these varieties of Type A (§ 43), but this does not seem sufficient to explain the complete regularity of double alliteration here. The following are the two exceptions to the rule:

[1] In line 1261 the manuscript reading *camp* (emended to *Cain*) clearly depends on an original *cam*; but in this case an original *Cain* is confirmed by the metre. This inconsistency is tiresome, but must be accepted as a fact.

in mægþa gehwære   25a
*To lang ys to reccan   2093a

In the first instance Sievers proposed to read *gehwæm* on his-
torical grounds,[1] and this reading is metrically unexceptionable
(Type B2); the second instance depends on an emendation, and
cannot be held to invalidate the rule. It seems best to assume
that anacrusis cannot be used in the *a*-verse without double
alliteration, and to regard verse 2093a as anomalous.

48. In Types A2a and A2ab the cæsura always falls in position (i), so that anacrusis is not to be expected. There are in
fact only two possible instances of anacrusis in these types, and
both are susceptible of alternative explanations:

se ðe lengest leofað   2008a
Him Beowulf þanan   1880b

These verses could be scanned as Type A2k with anacrusis, but
the apparent anomaly can be avoided by scanning them as
Type B, with resolution of the second stress. In Type A2b the
cæsura may fall in any of the three positions. There are a
number of examples of anacrusis, of which only one has the
cæsura in position (i):

gesawon seledream   2252a

Since the manuscript reading offers considerable difficulties of
interpretation, it is better to adopt Trautmann's emendation
secga seledream, which gives excellent sense and metre, and is
palæographically satisfactory. All the instances of anacrusis
when the cæsura is in positions (ii) or (iii) have double alliteration.

49. In Types D and D* anacrusis is frequent, but it is found
almost exclusively in the varieties with secondary (rather than
tertiary) stress (see § 33). Three apparent instances of anacrusis
in verses with tertiary stress are the following:

gesægd soðlice   141a
þa secg wisode   402b
gewrecen wraðlice   3062a

The second of these verses can easily be improved by dropping
the *þa*, which is not required by the sense[2]; but the two *a*-verses

---

[1] *PBB* x (1885) 485.   [2] Sievers, *ibid.*, 256; Pope, *op. cit.* 237.

must be accepted. It is interesting to note that all the types of verse in which anacrusis is found have certain qualities in common.

(1) In all the types of verse concerned the second breath-group is longer than the first. It is not a question of mere weight; in Type A2b with the cæsura in position (i) the second breath-group is noticeably heavier than the first, but anacrusis is not found; the number of metrical units in the second breath-group must be greater than the number in the first.[1] It seems that anacrusis may serve to counterbalance the greater length of the second breath-group (see § 126).

(2) In all the types of verse concerned double alliteration in the first half-line is compulsory or quasi-compulsory; double alliteration is a pre-requisite not only of the anacrusis itself, but of the type of verse in which anacrusis may occur.

50. In the light of these considerations anacrusis is not to be expected in Type E, in which the second breath-group cannot be longer than the first, and in which double alliteration is comparatively rare; in fact, the nine possible instances are all susceptible of alternative explanations:

> Da him Hroþgar gewat   662a
> ond him Hroþgar gewat   1236a
> Þæt wæs feohleas gefeoht   2441a
>
> wæs him Beowulfes sið   501b
> þæt ic ænigra me   932b
> Ne bið þe [n]ænigre gad   949b
> Ic on Higelace wat   1830b
>
> swylc Æschere wæs   1329b
> þeah ðe hio ænlicu sy   1941b

The first seven instances could be scanned as Type E1 with anacrusis, the last two as Type E2 with anacrusis; but it is better to take them all as Type B, particularly since disyllabic anacrusis is exceedingly rare, and trisyllabic anacrusis unparalleled. It is further noteworthy that all these verses have tertiary stress.

---

[1] For an alternative view, see the Addendum, page 170.

CHAPTER SEVEN

SIEVERS' TYPE A

51. At this stage it may be convenient to conduct a cursory survey of Sievers' five types in the light of the discoveries reported in the preceding chapters. Type A1 must be divided into three varieties, according to the position of the cæsura. The first variety has the sequence $\acute{}\times|\acute{}\times$ without any variations; the first breath-group, like the second, can have only one unstressed syllable after the stress.[1] Apparent exceptions to this rule are due to a variety of causes. In the first group the scribe has written a vowel which was syncopated in pronunciation:

> mistige moras   162a
> windige weallas   572a
> hæþene sawle   852a
> Eotena treowe   1072a
> mihtigan Drihtne   1398a
> sawele hyrde   1742a
> modige mannes   2698a

> Geotena leode   443b
> nænegum arað   598b
> ænige þinga   791b, 2374b, 2905b
> windige næssas   1358b
> Grendeles maga   2006b
> hindeman siðe   2049b, 2517b[2]
> Grendeles modor   2118b, 2139b
> Grendeles mægum   2353b

---

[1] This peculiarity is not, of course, a rule of metre, as is sometimes stated, but a detail of classification. An originally short medial vowel was syncopated in prehistoric Old English; an originally long vowel survived. But if the medial vowel survives in the second breath-group, the verse is classified as Type D*; if it survives in the first breath-group, the verse is classified as Type A2l—compare the verses quoted in § 38.

[2] The word *hindema* is found only in *Beowulf* and there only twice; but there is every reason to suppose that the medial vowel would have been syncopated after the long stem syllable.

blodigan gare   2440b
ænige hwile   2548b

In all these verses the medial vowel should be underdotted in the text and ignored in scansion. The second group of exceptions contains only three verses:

Uþe ic swiþor   960b
wisse he gearwe   2339b, 2725b

Here the final -*e* of the verb must be elided before the vowel or *h*- of the following pronoun; elision before *h*- has not hitherto been envisaged in Old English, but there seems to be no reason why it should not occur when the *h*- belongs to a lightly-stressed word such as a pronoun. Some further exceptions have already been eliminated on other grounds (§§ 20, 22)[1]:

onmunde usic mærða   2640a
Heald þu nu, hruse   2247a

52. The second variety has the sequence $\acute{\,}|(\times\times)\times\acute{\,}\times$, with a variable number of unstressed syllables before the second stress. One syllable is most frequent, two syllables are not uncommon, but there are only four instances of three syllables:

*Sorh is me to secga*n   473a
wesan, þenden ic wealde   1859a

bruc þenden þu mote   1177b
Wes þenden þu lifige   1224b

It is curious that three of these examples should contain the conjunction *þenden*, and it is tempting to reduce the number of unstressed syllables to two by omitting the pronoun (compare *heold þenden lifde* 57b); but the pronoun can hardly be omitted in verse 1859a, since it cannot be understood from the preceding clause. Since there seems to be no theoretical objection to three unstressed syllables, it is better to let these verses stand. The third variety has the sequence $\acute{\,}\times|(\times\times)\times\acute{\,}\times$, again with one, two or three unstressed syllables before the second stress. In

---

[1] The position of the cæsura in these verses is uncertain, and this in itself suggests that they have been rightly eliminated; the most natural position seems to be immediately before the second stress.

three instances a syncopated vowel has been written by the scribe:

> modige on meþle   1876a
> omige þurhetone   3049a
>
> ænige gefremman   2449b

In these verses the medial vowel should be underdotted in the text and ignored in scansion. Some other anomalous varieties have already been eliminated on other grounds (§§ 20, 22):

> Secge ic þe to soðe   590a
> ne geweox he him to willan   1711a
> Gebide ge on beorge   2529a
> geaf him ða mid Geatum   2623a

There are three examples of three unstressed syllables before the second stress, and these must be allowed to stand:

> þegnas syndon geþwære   1230a
> ræsde on ðone rofan   2690a
>
> sealde þam ðe he wolde   3055b

53. In examining any variety of Type A2 it is important to distinguish varieties with secondary stress from varieties with tertiary stress (see § 33). In Type A2k the variety with tertiary stress is much more frequent in the *b*-verse than in the *a*-verse; the variety with secondary stress is nearly equally divided between the two verses; in neither variety is double alliteration compulsory. In Type A2l the variety with tertiary stress is slightly more frequent in the *a*-verse, the variety with secondary stress is very much more frequent in the *a*-verse. There are, in fact, only eight *b*-verses representing this variety, and a number of these are suspicious:

> [heaþorinc eode]   403b
> mandream flêon   1264b
> deaþwic sêon   1275b
> foldweg mæton   1633b
> hringnet bæron   1889b
> Hordweard sohte   2293b
> morþorbed strêd   2436b
> meduseld buan   3065b

Verse 403b need not be considered, since it is editorial. Verse 1275b might belong to Type A2k, if the contracted form *séon* is expanded as *sĕhan* or *sĕohan* rather than *sēoan*.[1] Verse 1889b might also belong to Type A2k if *bæron* is emended to *beran* (infinitive dependent on *cwom*),[2] and there seems to be no reason why verse 1633b should not be treated in the same way (*metan* dependent on *ferdon*). However, since the remaining four verses belong unmistakably to Type A2l it is wiser to refrain from emendation. Double alliteration in the *a*-verse is compulsory in the variety with secondary stress. In the variety of Type A2l which has resolution of the long thesis (for a list of the verses concerned see §§ 35 and 38) conditions are similar though not identical: the proportion of *a*-verses to *b*-verses is rather higher, and double alliteration is compulsory even with tertiary stress.

54. Like Type A1, Type A2b must be divided into three, according to the position of the cæsura. The first variety has the sequence $\acute{\_} \times | \acute{\_} \_$, with only one syllable after the first stress; an apparent exception is due to the writing of a vowel which had been syncopated in pronunciation:

dogera dægrim   823a

In this verse the medial vowel should be underdotted in the text and ignored in scansion. Some other anomalous varieties have already been eliminated on other grounds (§ 22):

Hylde hine þa heaþodeor   688a
Reste hine þa rumheort   1799a

The variety with tertiary stress is rather more frequent in the *a*-verse than in the *b*-verse; double alliteration in the *a*-verse is not compulsory. Here must be included the verse

wæpen hafenade   1573b

with resolution of the long second thesis.[3] The variety with

---

[1] The only other instance of contracted *séon* in *Beowulf* (*metodsceaft sĕon* 1180a) could also belong to Type A2k.

[2] Sievers, *PBB* x (1885) 224.

[3] If it is assumed that the *e* of *wæpen* is only scribal, it is possible to scan this verse as Type D2; compare *Weard mapelode* 286a. But this last verse is anomalous, since a short syllable can only replace a long syllable when it is preceded by a single long syllable, and it is better not to multiply anomalies.

secondary stress is found only in the *a*-verse, and double alliteration is compulsory. Here must be included the verse

modges merefaran   502a

with resolution of the long second thesis. The second variety has the sequence $\angle|(\times)\times\angle\_$, with one or two unstressed syllables before the second stress. The variety with tertiary stress is much more frequent in the *a*-verse than in the *b*-verse, and double alliteration in the *a*-verse is compulsory. Here belong a number of verses with resolution of the long second thesis (§ 45):

eard ond eorlscipe   1727a
lif ond leodscipe   2751a

Dead is Æschere   1323b
him on andsware   1840b

and, with two unstressed syllables before the second stress,

word wæron wynsume   612a

The variety with secondary stress is found only in the *a*-verse, and double alliteration is compulsory. Here belong a number of verses with resolution of the long second thesis (§ 45):

fleon on fenhopu   764a
lond ond leodbyrig   2471a
win of wunderfatum   1162a

and, with two unstressed syllables before the second stress,

deorc ofer dryhtgumum   1790a

The third variety has the sequence $\angle\times|(\times)\times\angle\times$, with one or two unstressed syllables before the second stress. The variety with tertiary stress is much more frequent in the *a*-verse than in the *b*-verse, and double alliteration in the *a*-verse is compulsory. The variety with secondary stress is found only in the *a*-verse, and double alliteration is compulsory. Here belongs a verse with resolution of the long second thesis (§ 45):

wongas ond wicstede   2462a

55. In Type A2ab it is important to distinguish four varieties, according to the distribution of secondary and tertiary stress.

In the first variety, with tertiary stress in both theses, double alliteration in the *a*-verse is not compulsory, and there is one *b*-verse:

æghwær selest 1059b

Here belong 25 verses of the type *Beowulf mapelode*, with resolution of the long second thesis.[1] In the second variety, with secondary stress in the first thesis and tertiary in the second, double alliteration in the *a*-verse is compulsory, and there is one *b*-verse:

glædman Hroðgar 367b

Here belongs one verse with resolution of both theses (§ 65):

fyrdsearu fuslicu 232a

The third variety, with tertiary stress in the first thesis and secondary in the second, is found only in the *a*-verse, and double alliteration is compulsory. The fourth variety, with secondary stress in both theses, is also found only in the *a*-verse, and double alliteration is again compulsory.

56. Type A* always has the sequence $\acute{-}\_|\times\acute{-}\times$ or $\acute{-}\_|\times\acute{-}\_$ (§§ 4, 43), and is really equivalent to Type A2a or Type A2ab with the cæsura in position (iii). The sequence $\acute{-}\_|\times\acute{-}\times$ must be divided into two varieties, one with tertiary and the other with secondary stress. In the variety with tertiary stress double alliteration in the *a*-verse is not compulsory, and there is one *b*-verse:

ærest gesohton 2926b

Here belongs a verse with resolution of the long first thesis:

earfeþo on yþum 534a

There is only one instance of the variety with secondary stress:

gealorand to guþe 438a

The sequence $\acute{-}\_|\times\acute{-}\_$ must be divided into four varieties, according to the distribution of secondary and tertiary stress. In the first variety, with tertiary stress in both theses, double alliteration in the *a*-verse is compulsory, and there is one *b*-verse:

Guðlaf ond Oslaf 1148b

---

[1] In this paragraph resolution of the long first thesis is not specially noted.

The second variety, with secondary stress in the first thesis and tertiary in the second, is not represented in *Beowulf*, and there are only two examples each of the third and fourth varieties, with secondary stress in the second thesis and in both theses respectively:

> geatolic ond goldfah   308a
> *b*etlic ond banfag   780a
>
> gamolfeax ond guðrof   608a
> wreoþenhilt ond wyrmfah   1698a

CHAPTER EIGHT

SIEVERS' TYPES B AND C

57. Like Type A1, Type B must be divided into three varieties according to the position of the cæsura; this division cuts across Sievers' division into Type B1 with one unstressed syllable in the second thesis and Type B2 with two unstressed syllables in the second thesis. The first variety has the sequence $(\times\times\times\times)\times\underline{\prime}|(\times)\times\underline{\prime}$, with one to five unstressed syllables before the first stress and one or two before the second; the variety with five unstressed syllables before the first stress and two before the second is not found. This variety is four times as frequent in the *b*-verse as in the *a*-verse; double alliteration is found in nearly half the *a*-verses. Here must be included the verse

he þe æt sunde oferflat   517b

which requires elision of the final *-e* of *sunde* (see § 59). The second variety has the sequence $(\times\times\times\times)\times\underline{\prime}\times(\times)|\underline{\prime}$, with one to five unstressed syllables before the first stress and one or two after it. This variety is more than twice as frequent in the *b*-verse as in the *a*-verse, and double alliteration is comparatively rare. The most frequent number of syllables before the first stress is two, then three, one, four and five in that order.

58. The vast majority of verses of this type have only one unstressed syllable after the first stress, and some apparent instances of two syllables are only scribal. In the following verses the scribe has written a vowel which had been syncopated in pronunciation:

Næfre ic ænegum men   655a
wið Eotena bearn   1088a
þæt he Eotena bearn   1141a

wes þu us larena god   269b
He mid Eotenum wearð   902b
þæt wæs geomuru ides   1075b

swa he Fresena cyn   1093b
oððe eagena bearhtm   1766b
he geblodegod wearð   2692b

In all these verses the medial vowel should be underdotted in the text and ignored in scansion. Another group of verses might seem to belong here, but is better scanned as Type C3:

ymb aldor Dena   668a
Þa wæs wundor micel   771a

him wæs geomor sefa   49b, 2419b
hwæt me Grendel hafað   474b
þonne Grendel hine   678b
scolde Grendel þonan   819b
Þæt wæs tacen sweotol   833b
Ða wæs winter scacen   1136b
þeah þæt wæpen duge   1660b
ond þone maðþum byreð   2055b
him se oðer þonan   2061b

Here the endings of the last word in each verse are noteworthy: four are long vocalic endings (*Dena, sefa, duge*), seven are consonantal endings, and there is only one short vocalic ending. A comparison with the conditions described in § 40 shows that resolution is here improbable; it is therefore better to underdot the last vowel in the preceding word in each verse, and to scan as Type C3.

59. In a considerable number of verses belonging to this variety of Type B tertiary stress is found in the second thesis; but there are no instances of secondary stress. Here must be included the verse

*Þær gene*hh*ost brægd   794b

in which the manuscript simplification of the double consonant is purely scribal. Two verses of this variety which have resolution of the second stress have already been discussed in § 48. In two verses the long syllable in the second thesis has been resolved:

swylc Æschere wæs   1329b
þeah ðe hio ænlicu sy   1941b

In four cases the sequence (×)× ×⏑́× ×|⏑́ is found:

> wæs him Beowulfes sið   501b
> þæt ic ænigra rᵐᵃ   932b
> Ne bið þe [n]ænigre gad   949b
> Ic on Higelace wat   1830b

These four verses all have tertiary stress, and there are no instances of secondary stress; but even so the metrical pattern
seems anomalous, and it is tempting to classify these verses as
Type E with anacrusis; however, this possibility has already
been discussed and rejected in § 50. The third variety of Type B
has the sequence (× × × ×)× ⏑́ ×|× ⏑́, with one to five unstressed
syllables before the first stress, but only one before the second.
One apparent instance of two unstressed syllables before the
second stress can be corrected by elision:

> se wæs betera ðonne ic   469b

This variety is more than twice as frequent in the b-verse as in
the a-verse, and double alliteration is comparatively rare.   In
the following verse the scribe has written a vowel which had
been syncopated in pronunciation:

> no þær ænige swa þeah   972b

The medial vowel must be underdotted and ignored in scansion.
In a number of verses belonging to this variety there is a long
syllable after the first stress; in no case is there secondary stress.

60. Sievers divided his Type C into three sub-types, C1 with
the sequence × ⏑́|⏑́ ×, C2 with the sequence × ⏑̆×|⏑́ ×, and C3
with the sequence × ⏑́|⏑̆ ×; the distinction between C1 and C2
is anomalous, since the presence or absence of resolution is
not specially noted elsewhere. Here the type is divided into
two varieties, the first comprising Sievers' C1 and C2, the
second equivalent to his C3. The first variety has the sequence
(× × × ×)× ⏑́|⏑́ ×, with one to five syllables before the first
stress; the most frequent number of unstressed syllables is one,
then two, three, four and five in that order. This variety is
seven times as frequent in the b-verse as in the a-verse, and
double alliteration is found in three-quarters of the a-verses.
Here must be included two verses printed by Klaeber with
false quantities:

of hliðes nosan   1892b
æt brimes nosan   2803b

In each case Klaeber prints *nosan* with a short *o*; by making
the *i* of *hliðes* long, he produces a verse of Type B for the first
instance, but the second remains anomalous. There are two
forms of the word *hlið*, one with a short vowel and one with a
long vowel (§ 37); and *nose* should have a long vowel.[1] Three
verses have a long syllable in the second thesis:

Oft Scyld Scefing   4a
ne gesacu ohwær   1737b
Wæs se fruma egeslic   2309b

All three verses have tertiary stress. The second variety of
Type C has the sequence $(\times \times \times \times) \times \stackrel{\,\_}{} | \stackrel{\smile}{} \times$, with one to five
unstressed syllables before the first stress; the most frequent
number of unstressed syllables is two, then three, one, four and
five in that order. This variety is four times as frequent in the
b-verse as in the *a*-verse, and double alliteration is found in
only a quarter of the *a*-verses.

[1] F. Holthausen, *Altenglisches etymologisches Wörterbuch*, s.v.

CHAPTER NINE

SIEVERS' TYPES D AND E

61. In examining any variety of Type D it is important to distinguish verses with secondary stress from verses with tertiary stress (see § 33). In Type D1 the variety with tertiary stress is about three times as frequent in the *b*-verse as in the *a*-verse, and double alliteration is found in half the *a*-verses. One verse which might seem to belong here is better scanned as Type A:

milts ungyfeðe   2921b

If this verse belonged to Type D1, it would be the only instance of resolution of the long first thesis; it has already been shown that stress on compounds with *un-* is variable (§ 44). The variety with secondary stress is much more frequent in the *a*-verse than in the *b*-verse, and double alliteration in the *a*-verse is compulsory. There are only four examples of this variety in the *b*-verse:

feond mancynnes   164b
hroden ealowæge   495b
swyn ealgylden   1111b
segn eallgylden   2767b

The last two instances are suspicious, since two of the three apparent examples of Type D2 with secondary stress in the *b*-verse also contain compounds with *eal(l)-*; it is better to divide the compounds (*swyn eal gylden*, etc.) and treat them as heavy verses. The first two instances seem unexceptionable, however, and although they are the only certain instances of any variety of Type D with secondary stress in the *b*-verse, they must be allowed to stand.

62. In Type D2 the variety with tertiary stress is nearly six times as frequent in the *b*-verse as in the *a*-verse, and double alliteration is found in about half the *a*-verses. Here must be included three anomalous verses with resolution of the second stress:

> Weard maþelode   286a
> gold glitinian   2758a
> hord openian   3056b

In general a short syllable can only replace a long one when it is preceded by a single long syllable; but it is difficult to see how these three verses can be scanned if not as Type D2. The variety with secondary stress is found only in the *a*-verse, and double alliteration is compulsory. There are three apparent examples in the *b*-verse:

> þeod ealgearo   1230b
> Beorh eallgearo   2241b
> hwate scild*wigan*   3005b

In the first two instances the compounds must be divided, and they must be treated as heavy verses. In the third instance the difficulty is editorial: the manuscript reading *hwate Scildingas* is metrically unexceptionable, since it belongs to Type D1 with tertiary stress, a type which is frequent in the *b*-verse. Admittedly the manuscript reading is not easy to understand in its context; but whatever remedy is adopted, it must not introduce an unparalleled metrical pattern. Type D3 occurs only twice, in each case with tertiary stress, and in each case in the *b*-verse.

63. There are only five instances of the variety of Type D4 with tertiary stress:

> eal inneweard   998a
> bonan Ongenþeoęs   1968a
> eorl Ongenþio   2951a
>
> Heort innanweard   991b
> flet innanweard   1976b

The variety with secondary stress is found only in the *a*-verse, and double alliteration is compulsory. An apparent instance in the *b*-verse is easy to correct:

> eofor heafodsegn   2152b

The reading *eoforheafodsegn*, adopted by most editors, gives a light verse of an unexceptionable type (§ 74). This variety can be further subdivided according to the position of the division in the compound word forming the second breath-group; there are three possible positions, corresponding to the three possible positions of the cæsura in Type B. If the division of the compound is indicated by the symbol ⦂, the following are the three possible sequences: ´|´⦂×`, ´|´×⦂`, and ´|´×⦂×`. Of these, the second is by far the most frequent; there are only two instances of the third, both containing the word *sibbegedriht*:

> seon sibbegedriht 387a
> swefan sibbegedriht 729a

64. In Type D*1, the variety with tertiary stress is found only in the *a*-verse, and double alliteration is compulsory. There are a number of apparently anomalous verses (lacking double alliteration, or occurring in the *b*-verse), but all of these can easily be corrected:

> eþel Scyldinga 913a
> þeoden Scyldinga 1675a, 1871a
> broðor oðerne 2440a
>
> dohtor Hroðgares 2020b
> ðeod*ne* Heaðo-Beardna 2032b
> laðra owihte 2432b

The first five cases can be corrected by reading *eþel, þeoden, broðor, dohtor*. The same remedy is applicable to the manuscript reading in the sixth case—*ðeoden Heaðo-Beardna*; it is doubtful whether the objection to the accusative after *ofþyncan* is necessarily valid; but perhaps the best solution is to read *ðeoden' Heaðo-Beardna*, assuming elision before *H-*.[1] In the last case the reading *ohte* for *owihte* removes all difficulties. A number of verses have a long syllable in the first thesis:

> Sceotend Scyldinga 1154a
> æghwæs untæle 1865a
> æghwæs orleahtre 1886a
> æðeling anhydig 2667a
> wigend weorðfullost 3099a

---

[1] M. Rieger, *Zeitschrift für deutsche Philologie* iii (1871) 404. Elision before stressed *h*- is less probable than before unstressed *h*-; compare § 51.

All these verses have tertiary stress. One apparent instance in a *b*-verse requires emendation:

Beowulf Scyldinga   53b

Here the occurrence of the hero's name applied to a different character, a Dane, is suspicious; and the reading *Beow Scyldinga* has much to recommend it. Some apparent instances of the cæsura in positions (ii) and (iii) have been discussed in § 44. The variety with secondary stress is found only in the *a*-verse, and double alliteration is compulsory. There are two verses with a long syllable in the first thesis:

hatost heaþoswate   1668a
siðas[t] sigehwile   2710a

Both these verses have tertiary stress. Some apparent instances of the cæsura in positions (ii) and (iii) have been discussed in § 44.

65. In Type D*2, the variety with tertiary stress is found only in the *a*-verse, and double alliteration is compulsory. There are a number of apparently anomalous verses (lacking double alliteration, or occurring in the *b*-verse), but all of these can easily be corrected:

dennes niosian   3045a
wundor sceawian   840b, 3032b
wica neosian   1125b
oftost wisode   1663b
fionda nios(i)an   2671b

All of these verses might be scanned as Type A2b or Type A2ab, with resolution of the long second thesis; but there are a number of obvious corrections which make this unnecessary. The verses with *neosian* require the alternative form *neosan*, and belong to Type A1; the *o* of *wundor* should be underdotted and ignored in scansion; *oftost* should be emended to *oft*. A number of verses have a long syllable in the first thesis:

æðeling unwrecen   2443a

and, with resolution of the long syllable,

eahtodan eorlscipe   3173a

Both verses have tertiary stress. There is one apparent instance of secondary stress, with resolution of the long syllable:

fyrdsearu fuslicu   232a

This verse is best considered as an example of Type A2ab, with resolution in both the theses (§ 55). Some apparent instances of the cæsura in positions (ii) and (iii) have been discussed in § 45. The variety with secondary stress is found only in the *a*-verse, and double alliteration is compulsory. In one instance the scribe has written a vowel which had been syncopated in pronunciation:

hæþenes handsporu   986a

The medial vowel must be underdotted and ignored in scansion. There are a number of verses with a long syllable in the first thesis:

ærest East-Dena   616a
wundǫrlic wægbora   1440a
leoflic lindwiga   2603a
egeslic eorðdraca   2825a

and, with resolution of the long syllable,

sellice sædracan   1426a

All these verses have tertiary stress. Some apparent instances of the cæsura in positions (ii) and (iii) have been discussed in § 45. In Type D*4 the variety with tertiary stress is not found in *Beowulf*; the variety with secondary stress is found only in the *a*-verse, and double alliteration is compulsory. The sequence $\angle × | \angle × ⋮ × \angle$ is not found. An apparent instance of the cæsura in position (ii) has been discussed in § 45.

66. Type E1 must be divided into three varieties according to the position of the cæsura. The first variety has the sequence $\angle - | (×) × \angle$, with one or two unstressed syllables before the second stress. The variety with tertiary stress is found only in the *b*-verse; the variety with secondary stress is three times as frequent in the *b*-verse as in the *a*-verse, and double alliteration in the *a*-verse is compulsory. The variety with two unstressed syllables before the second stress is rare; there are only two

examples in *Beowulf*, one with tertiary stress and one with secondary:

> Beowulf is min nama   343b
> feorhsweng ne ofteah   2489b

The second variety has the sequence $\acute{\,}\_\times|\acute{\,}$. The variety with tertiary stress is twice as frequent in the *b*-verse as in the *a*-verse, and double alliteration is found in three quarters of the *a*-verses. Here must be included two verses in which a late spelling hides the true quantity:

> irena cyst   673a, 1697a

The spelling must be emended to *iren[n]a*.[1] The variety with secondary stress occurs in about the same proportions as the last variety. In four examples the syllable bearing secondary stress is resolved:

> umborwesendum ær   1187a
> gledegesa grim   2650a
> wigheafolan bær   2661b
> ligegesan wæg   2780b

The third variety has the sequence $\acute{\,}\_\times|\times\acute{\,}$, and occurs in about the same proportions as the second variety; it is rare, either with tertiary or with secondary stress. In two examples the syllable bearing secondary stress is resolved:

> fæderæþelum onfon   911a
> Hreðsigora ne gealp   2583b

The sub-type of Type E1 in which the second syllable is short is rare in *Beowulf*, and with one exception it is found only in the *b*-verse. The single exception is the following:

> wundorsmiþa geweorc   1681a

It is tempting to scan this verse as an example of the first variety of Type E1, with resolution of the syllable bearing secondary stress; but resolution is forbidden by the long vocalic ending of *wundorsmiþa* (§ 40); the verse must belong to the sub-type in which a short syllable bears the secondary stress; the cæsura is in position (iii).

---

[1] Sievers, *PBB* x (1885) 308; Pope, *op. cit.* 235. The same word must also be emended in 2259b.

CHAPTER TEN

LIGHT VERSES

67. All the verses considered so far have been normal verses: it remains to consider the light and heavy verses, to see how far they can be fitted into the scheme of types already established. Light verses are those which contain only one stressed element (§ 10), and therefore (apparently, at least) only one full stress; they may be classified according to the sequence of syllables beginning at the single full stress: $\_$, $\_\times$, $\_\_$, $\_\_\times$, etc. The first variety, classified by Sievers as Type B3, is that in which the single full stress ends the verse; the stress may be preceded by a number of unstressed syllables varying from two to five. It must be considered doubtful whether this type has any genuine existence; certainly the only instance with only two unstressed syllables before the stress must be considered anomalous:

Wæs min fæder   262a

There are only seven examples of this type, and in all but one the stress is resolved—a highly suspicious feature; it is possible that in the examples with resolution the sequence $\smile\times$ is exceptionally equivalent to $\_\times$. The single example without resolution is the following:

þenden he wið wulf   3027a

Here the emendation *wulf[e]* offers no difficulty; but it is perhaps wiser to reserve these verses of Type B3 for further consideration later (§ 73).

68. The second variety, classified by Sievers as Type A3, is that in which the full stress is followed by a single unstressed syllable; the stress may be preceded by a number of unstressed syllables varying from two to six. This variety, like the last, is found only in the *a*-verse, for obvious reasons. Sievers considered that his Type A3 differed from his Type A1 only in the position of the alliteration; Type A3 is, in fact, only Type A1 with postponed alliteration. There are several objections to this view. If Type A3 is structurally the same as Type A1, it is necessary to find a full stress to precede the stress which bears the alliteration; but, by definition, there are no other stressed elements, and the first part of the verse consists only of particles and proclitics. In such a verse as

ond ge him syndon   393a

the choice of a syllable to bear the first stress is embarrassing. *Ond* can hardly be stressed at the expense of *ge* and *him*; if *ge* is stressed, not only is the anacrusis irregular (since the cæsura, if there must be one, comes rather after than before *him*) but the verse offends against Kuhn's Law of Particles (§ 20); if *him* is stressed, the verse no longer belongs to Type A but to Type C, and Type C with postponed alliteration is unparalleled. In this verse (and there are a great many like it) it is not possible to stress any of the particles without producing some anomaly.

69. There is in fact clear evidence of a structural difference between Type A1 and Type A3: the number of syllables before the second stress in Type A1, or before the only stress in Type A3. In Type A1, the most frequent number of syllables before the second stress is two, then three, four and five in that order; there are no examples of six syllables; the average number of syllables is 2·6. In Type A3, the most frequent number of syllables before the only stress is four, then three, five, six and two in that order; the average number of syllables is 3·9. It is obvious that for some reason Type A3 requires a substantially greater number of syllables than Type A1, and it is probable that the reason is the need for extra weight to compensate for the absence of one of the usual two stresses; what the verse lacks in stress it makes up in length. We must, in fact, recognize the possibility of one-stress verses. Sievers himself in later life envisaged such one-stress verses[1]; Pope, too, makes one-stress verses a mainstay of his new theory,[2] though he postulates an initial rest, marked by a chord on the harp. Neither of these writers, however, is willing to recognize that all verses of Type A3 are one-stress verses, nor has either observed that the missing stress is replaced by additional unstressed syllables.

---

[1] E. Sievers, 'Zu Cynewulf', *Festgabe Karl Luick* (1925) 63.
[2] *op. cit. passim*, especially 88-95.

70. The third variety, also classified by Sievers as Type A3, is that in which the full stress is followed by a long syllable bearing either secondary or tertiary stress; it bears the same relationship to Type A2b as the last type does to Type A1, and offers no difficulty. The fourth and fifth varieties, however, are in quite a different category; they have two syllables after the full stress, and were not distinguished by Sievers from normal verses of Types B and C; yet they bear exactly the same relationship to Type D as Type A3 does to Type A1. The true relationship of these varieties cannot be decided subjectively; but fortunately it is very easy to decide statistically. In the table below the rows marked (1) give the number of *a*-verses and the number of *b*-verses in *Beowulf*, with percentage equivalents in brackets; the rows marked (2) give the number of *a*-verses with double alliteration and the number of *a*-verses with single alliteration, with percentage equivalents in brackets. Among the light verses, it is only those which have secondary stress which are strictly comparable with the normal verses, and only these are considered in the table.

		Normal verses	*Light verses*
Type B	(1)	255 : 613 (29 : 71)	53 : 30 (64 : 36)
	(2)	86 : 169 (34 : 66)	2 : 51 (4 : 96)
Type C1 and C2	(1)	37 : 246 (13 : 87)	125 : 41 (75 : 25)
	(2)	27 : 10 (73 : 27)	5 : 120 (4 : 96)
Type C3	(1)	47 : 213 (18 : 82)	159 : 63 (72 : 28)
	(2)	13 : 34 (28 : 72)	9 : 150 (6 : 94)
Totals	(1)	339 : 1072 (24 : 76)	337 : 134 (72 : 28)
	(2)	126 : 213 (37 : 63)	16 : 321 (5 : 95)

These figures leave no possible doubt that Sievers was quite mistaken in associating light verses of these varieties with normal verses of Types B and C; it would be hard to imagine a wider divergence of usage than is revealed by the above table. Whereas the normal verses are three times as frequent in the *b*-verse as in the *a*-verse, the light verses are three times as frequent in the *a*-verse as in the *b*-verse; and whereas double alliteration is not uncommon in the normal verses it is excessively rare in the light verses.

71. We are thrown back, then, upon the alternative hypothesis: that these light verses bear the same relationship to Type D as Type A3 does to Type A1. This hypothesis seems incapable of statistical proof, since the example of Type A3 shows that an entirely different distribution from that of Type D is to be expected; and the exact nature of the difference of distribution can only be a matter of surmise. Type A3, as is well known, is found only in the *a*-verse; these varieties of light verse are much more frequent in the *a*-verse than in the *b*-verse: this measure of agreement is in favour of the hypothesis, and no more can be expected. The only argument against the hypothesis is the presence in these light verses of a few instances of double alliteration, which is never found in the second breath-group of a verse of Type D. The proportion of verses with double alliteration, however, is less than the proportion which could be attributed to chance (see § 15), so that even here double alliteration is avoided to some extent; all that can be said is that double alliteration is less scrupulously avoided in these verses than in verses of Type D—perhaps because double alliteration in the second breath-group of Type D would mean triple alliteration in the verse as a whole.[1] It should be noted that the wide divergence of usage revealed by the table in § 70 is inconsistent with Kaluza's view that normal verses of Types B and C should also be associated with Type D; the argument works both ways. If the light verses under discussion are to be considered as related to Type D, some new nomenclature is required to distinguish them from normal verses of Types B and C: they may be denoted by the symbols d1 (Sievers' Types C1 and C2), d2 (Sievers' Type C3) and d4 (Sievers' Type B); if this nomenclature is adopted, it will be convenient to denote Sievers' Type A3 by the symbols a1 and a2, the latter specifying the variety with a long syllable after the stress.

72. Type d1 (Sievers' Types C1 and C2) may have from one to four unstressed syllables before the stress; it must be divided into two varieties, one with secondary and one with tertiary stress; neither variety offers any difficulty. Type d2 (Sievers' Type C3) may have from one to five unstressed syllables before

---

[1] It should be remembered that in those varieties of Type D in which the second breath-group contains secondary stress (the only varieties in which double alliteration within the breath-group is possible) double alliteration in the verse as a whole is compulsory.

the stress, and must also be divided into two varieties, one with
secondary and one with tertiary stress. Here belong a number
of verses which might seem to belong rather to Type d4 (Sievers'
Type B)—compare § 57:.

> næfre he on aldordagum   718a
> swylce he on ealderdagum   757a
> ðæs morþorhetes   1105a
> æfter maþðumgife   1301a
> þurh hleoðorcwyde   1979a
> oððe him Ongenðeowes   2475a
> æfter maððumwelan   2750a
> þæt he wið attorsceaðan   2839a
>
> to aldorceare   906b
> nalles facenstafas   1018b

As in § 57, an examination of the final syllables is interesting:
there are two long vocalic endings (-gife, -ceare), seven consonantal endings, and only one short vocalic ending. Resolution is
improbable, and it is better to underdot the second vowel in
the first element of each compound. Type d4 may have from
one to four unstressed syllables before the stress; the possible
variety with tertiary stress is not found. Like Type D4, this
variety can be subdivided according to the position of the
division in the compound word (compare § 63); of the three
possible positions the third is not found. There is one apparent
instance of the third position:

> Scolde his aldorgedal   805b

Here the o of aldor- must be underdotted and ignored in scansion. Here must be included the following verses:

> Hy on wiggetawum   368a
> þæt we him ða guðgetawa   2636a
>
> in eowrum guðgetawum   395b

Pope has shown that the a of getawa is short.[1]
   73. At this stage it may be desirable to reconsider the first

---

[1] J. C. Pope, *op. cit.* 235.

variety of light verse, already discussed in § 67, that in which the single full stress ends the verse. It has been shown that the second and third varieties are related to Type A, and the fourth and fifth to Type D; in each case the loss of the first stress of the basic type is compensated by an increased weight of unstressed syllables. If, then, the first variety of light verse has any real existence—if it has not been fabricated from a conglomeration of accidental errors—it must be related to some type of verse that ends with a stress; that is, either to Type B or to Type E. Sievers related it to Type B, and called it Type B3, but it seems rather to belong to Type E; Types A, D and E have in common the fact that they all begin with a stress.[1] Despite the considerable doubt which must be raised by the high proportion of resolution in this variety, it seems best to accept the relationship to Type E, and to denote it by the symbol e.

74. The sixth, seventh and eighth varieties of light verse are of quite a different character from the first five: they exactly resemble normal verses of Types A, D and E respectively, except that they each consist of a single word, invariably a compound, so that the second full stress of the normal verse is replaced by the secondary stress on the second element of the compound. There can be no question of relating these light verses to any other types of normal verse; if they are not special forms of Types A, D and E respectively they must be classified in a separate category of their own. The distribution of these verses is compared with that of the corresponding normal verses in the following table[2]: under each of the types of verse considered the first row, marked (1), gives the number of *a*-verses and the number of *b*-verses in *Beowulf*, with percentage equivalents in brackets; the second row, marked (2), gives the number of *a*-verses with double alliteration and the number of *a*-verses with single alliteration, with percentage equivalents in brackets.

---

[1] There can be no real objection to relating this first variety to Type B; but, if so, the second and third varieties might as well be related to Type C.

[2] The light verses of Type A are divided according to the position of the division of the compound, which corresponds to the cæsura in the normal verses. The light verses of Type D1 are compared with the variety of normal D1 which has tertiary stress; the remaining varieties of Type D and Type E are omitted because the number of light verses is too small to be statistically useful.

		Normal verses	Light verses
Type A (i)	(1)	368 : 489 (43 : 57)	78 : 43 (64 : 36)
	(2)	105 : 263 (29 : 71)	4 : 74 (5 : 95)
Type A (ii)	(1)	144 : 154 (48 : 52)	48 : 31 (61 : 39)
	(2)	133 : 11 (92 : 8)	3 : 45 (6 : 94)
Type D1	(1)	38 : 119 (24 : 76)	48 : 37 (56 : 44)
	(2)	19 : 19 (50 : 50)	6 : 42 (13 : 87)

This table shows several marked divergences between the distributions of the normal and the light verses. All the varieties of light verse are comparatively more frequent in the *a*-verse than the corresponding normal verses; and double alliteration is exceedingly rare, much rarer than in any type of normal verse. Of course it is not to be expected that double alliteration should be very common, since the number of alliterating compound words is strictly limited, so that verses of this kind could scarcely be used at all if double alliteration were insisted on. It is noteworthy that the proportion of instances of double alliteration does not differ very widely from the proportion to be expected by chance (about 8 per cent); in fact the proportion in these light verses taken as a whole is almost exactly 8 per cent. It is more than likely that the presence of double alliteration is in fact accidental. If it is assumed that double alliteration is not required in these light verses, then the difference in the proportion of *a*-verses and *b*-verses is not very disturbing; these light verses may be classified as special forms of the respective normal types. Yet they must be distinguished from the normal types (if only because of the absence of double alliteration), and it is convenient to use the symbols *A, D* and *E*.

75. Type *A* must be divided into two varieties, according to the position of the division of the compound, corresponding to the cæsura in normal verses of Type A. There are no instances of the division in the third position, though there are two apparent instances:

> dogorgerimes   2728a
> ealdorgewinna   2903b

In both of these verses the unstressed vowel of the first element of the compounds should be underdotted and ignored in scansion. Only one variety of Type *D*1 is found, that which is equivalent to the variety of the normal Type D1 with tertiary stress; since the second full stress is here replaced by secondary stress, it is naturally inconvenient to have another secondary stress immediately following it, even if it were possible to find triple compounds of the kind required. Here must be included **two** apparent instances of Type *D**:

ceasterbuendum   768a

ymbesittendra   2734a

In the first instance the unstressed vowel of *ceaster-* must be underdotted and ignored in scansion; in the second the restoration of the more regular form *ymbsittendra* removes all difficulty. Type *D*2 is exceedingly rare, and is represented only by the two regular verses

leassceaweras   253a

mægenfultuma   1455b

and the two anomalous verses

andswarode   258b, 340b

Type *D*3, on the other hand, is very much more frequent than the normal Type D3, which is exceedingly rare. In the verses

woruldcyninga   1684b, 3180b

the second vowel of *woruld-* should be underdotted. There are no instances of Type *D*4. On the single instance of Type *E* see § 63.

CHAPTER ELEVEN

HEAVY VERSES

76. Heavy verses are those which contain three stressed elements (§ 10), and therefore (apparently, at least) three full stresses; they can only be fitted into the normal scheme by subordinating one of the stresses to the other two. In many verses it is obvious which of the three stresses must be subordinated, since the alliteration shows which are the two main stresses; in other verses, however, this criterion fails, and the metrists disagree. The nature of the words which form the verse is no guide: no discrimination can be made between words which are stressed elements by nature and those which are stressed elements only by position, since a particle or even a proclitic, when displaced from its normal position in the first thesis of the verse clause, is treated in all respects as a stressed element. The following verses will serve as examples:

> seofon niht swuncon   517a
> geseon sunu Hrædles   1485a
> folc to sægon   1422b

The first two verses are distinguished by the alliteration as Type A2l and Type D1 with anacrusis respectively; but the third verse, which has only single alliteration, might belong to either Type A2l or to Type D1. Similarly such a verse as

> Werod eall aras   651b, 3030b

might belong to either Type D4 or to Type E. The true classification of such ambiguous verses will be discussed later in this chapter.

77. Heavy verses must, of course, correspond to one of the types of normal verse which may have secondary stress; that is, to Types A2, D, D* or E. Type A2k is not well represented among heavy verses, since there are no a-verses at all; the only verses which can be included here are ambiguous verses of the type

wyrd oft nereð   572b

At first glance these verses might be scanned as Type D2, but there is an insuperable objection to this scansion: the variety of Type D2 with secondary stress is found only in the *a*-verse and requires double alliteration; hence *a fortiori* a heavy verse of this type cannot appear in the *b*-verse. Type A2k, on the other hand, is more frequent in the *b*-verse than in the *a*-verse, and double alliteration is not compulsory; it follows that these heavy verses must belong to A2k rather than to D2. Here must be included two verses discussed in § 62:

*þeod eal gearo   1230b
*Beorh eall gearo   2241b

Here also belong two verses which require elision:

ðolode ær fela   1525b
snude eft cuman   1869b

These verses cannot belong to Type D*2, since the variety with secondary stress is found only in the *a*-verse; and there is no type which has the sequence $\acute{-} \times \acute{-} | \acute{\smile} \times$. If the final vowel of the first word in each verse is underdotted and ignored in scansion all difficulties are removed.

78. In Type A2l there are two verses whose scansion is assured by the alliteration:

seofon niht swuncon   517a
heard swyrd hilted   2987a

The remaining verses are ambiguous verses of the type

þreo hund wintra   2278b

It is just possible to scan these verses as Type D1, since there are two exceptional instances of this type in the *b*-verse (see § 61); but Type A2l is much more frequent in the *b*-verse than Type D1, and it is better to classify these ambiguous verses as Type A2l. Here must be included two verses discussed in § 61:

*swyn eal gylden   1111b
*segn eall gylden   2767b

Here also belong two verses which require elision or syncopation:

> Gode ic þanc secge   1997b
> Wundur hwar þonne   3062b

These verses cannot belong to Type D*1, since the variety with
secondary stress is found only in the a-verse (the first instance
also has the cæsura in an impossible position); and there is no
type which has the sequence ́× ́| ́×. The readings *Godę* and
Wundųr remove all difficulty. Here also belong a number of
verses with resolution of the secondary stress, the scansion of
the first being assured by the alliteration:

> beorht hofu bærnan   2313a

> heold hyne syðþan   142b
> Heold hine fæste   788b
> gladum suna Frodan   2025b

79. Since the variety of Type A2b with secondary stress is
found only in the a-verse and double alliteration is compulsory,
there is in general little doubt about the heavy verses which
belong here. So, with the cæsura in position (ii),

> hond ond heard sweord   2509a

and, with the cæsura in position (iii),

> helmas ond heard sweord   2638a
> beagas ond brad gold   3105a

> ðicgean ofer þa niht   736a

There is one verse with resolution of the secondary stress:

> bær on bearm scipes   896a

This verse cannot belong to Type D*2, since the cæsura is in an
impossible position; compare § 45. One apparent instance of
this type in a b-verse offers some difficulty:

> sceaðona ic nat hwylc   274b

Here the scribe seems to have expanded the pronoun *nathwylc*
into a clause; compare *nið[ð]a nathwylc* 2215a and *gumena
nathwylc* 2233b. The verse *sceaðona nathwylc* offers no difficulty,

F

since *nathwylc* has tertiary stress, and the variety of A2b with tertiary stress is not infrequent in the *b*-verse. There are few heavy verses belonging to Type A2ab. With secondary stress in the first thesis:

> wine min Beowulf   457b, 1704b
> wine min *Un*ferð   530b

Here must be included a verse with resolution of the secondary stress:

> Gyrede hine Beowulf   1441b

This verse requires elision before the *h-* of *hine*; the final *-e* of *gyrede* must be underdotted and ignored in scansion. With secondary stress in the second thesis:

> æscholt ufan græg   330a

80. There is only one heavy verse in Type D1:

> geseon sunu Hrædles   1485a

Type D2 is represented by three verses:

> swutol sang scopes   90a
> heard her cumen   376a
> beorht beacen Godes   570a

Ambiguous verses which at first glance might seem to belong to these two types have been discussed in §§ 77 and 78. Type D4 must be divided into three varieties according to the position of the cæsura between the second two words (compare § 63). In the first variety there is only one verse whose scansion is assured by the alliteration:

> Fyrst forð gewat   210a

But there are also a large number of ambiguous verses of the type

> lif eac gescop   97b

At first sight it might seem that these verses should indeed belong here, particularly since the third word is nearly always a finite verb; but there is an insuperable objection to this scansion. The variety of Type D4 with secondary stress is found only in the *a*-verse, and double alliteration is compulsory; *a fortiori*,

the same must be true of heavy verses. Type E, on the other
hand, is much more frequent in the *b*-verse than in the *a*-verse.
Since the verses under discussion are much more frequent in
the *b*-verse, and since the *a*-verses lack double alliteration, it
follows that they must belong to Type E rather than to Type D4.
The second variety is represented by a number of verses of
the type

> sweord swate fah   1286a

A large number of ambiguous verses of the type

> Flod blode weol   1422a

must be referred to Type E. The third variety is represented
by three verses:

> atol yða geswing   848a
> Metod manna gehwæs   2527a
> eald enta geweorc   2774a

A large number of ambiguous verses of the type

> word inne abead   390b

must be referred to Type E.

81. Type D*1 is represented by only one verse:

> bædde byre geonge   2018a

Type D*2 is represented by three verses, among which must be
included a verse which requires the syncopation of an unstressed
vowel:

> Ne sorga, snotor guma   1384a

This verse looks at first sight as though it belongs to Type A2b,
with resolution of the second full stress and the secondary
stress; but such a reading is forbidden by the presence of anacrusis, and by the difficulty of resolving *guma* with its long
vocalic ending. The reading *snotor* removes all difficulty. Type
D*4 is more amply represented, as the following selection of
varieties shows:

> yðde eotena cyn   421a
> þryðlic þegna heap   400a, 1627a
> licað leng swa wel   1854a
> oncyð eorla gehwæm   1420a

There are two apparently anomalous verses, one lacking double alliteration, the other in a *b*-verse:

> sti∂[r]a nægla gehwylc   985a
> Feþa eal gesæt   1424b

In the first instance the manuscript reading *steda nægla gehwylc* gives an unexceptionable verse of Type E; whatever difficulties the interpretation of the verse may offer, they must not be removed at the cost of producing an impossible metrical type. The second instance requires elision: the reading *Feþạ* removes all difficulties.

82. Type E is well represented by heavy verses, not only by the ambiguous verses already discussed in § 80 (though these are in the majority) but also by verses whose scansion is assured by the alliteration; it must be divided into three varieties according to the position of the cæsura between the second two words (compare § 63). The first variety is represented only by ambiguous verses of the type

> lif eac gescop   97b

However, the sub-variety with two unstressed syllables before the second stress is represented by one verse with double alliteration as well as three ambiguous verses:

> Hafa nu ond geheald   658a
>
> Gæþ eft se þe mot   603b
> hond sweng ne ofteah   1520b
> hlæw oft ymbehwearf   2296b

The last two of these verses could be reduced to the simpler pattern, the first by elision (*hond sweng nẹ ofteah*), the second by substituting the form *ymbhwearf*; but the first two instances are unobjectionable, so that there is no justification for tampering with the others. The second variety is represented by three verses with double alliteration, as well as a large number of ambiguous verses:

> twelf wintra tid   147a
> fif nihta fyrst   545a
> Ðys dogor þu   1395a

The third variety is represented only by ambiguous verses of the type

word inne abead   390b

There is one apparent instance of a sub-variety with two un-stressed syllables before the second stress:

heals ealne ymbefeng   2691b

This verse can be improved in two ways, either by assuming elision (*heals ealne̦ ymbefeng*) or by substituting the form *ymb-feng*; the latter alternative is preferable.

83. It will be noticed that there is no clash between light verses and heavy verses, since light verses correspond always to those varieties of normal verse which have no secondary stress, and heavy verses always to those which have secondary stress. If, therefore, it is necessary to find a special symbol for the heavy verses, the same device that has already been suggested for the light verses can be used: thus, *A*1 will stand for a light verse, *A*2 for a heavy verse. However, difficulties arise in Types D and E, since Sievers' scheme does not distinguish between the varieties of these types which have secondary stress and the varieties which have tertiary stress. In fact, there is no real need to distinguish heavy verses from normal verses, since their distribution does not differ substantially from that of normal verses.

CHAPTER TWELVE

REMAINDERS

84. Among the remainders must be included eight verses so corrupt that they cannot be classified: 62a, 2226b, 2227a, 2228b, 2229a, 2229b, 2230a, 2231a. Much more important than these, however, are some score of verses which cannot be fitted into any of the recognized types[1]; some of these may be due to mechanical errors, but it is always possible that others may belong to a type which has hitherto been overlooked. The first group to be considered consists of five verses with the sequence of syllables $\_\times|(\times)\times\_$:

> lissa gelong   2150a
> êam his nefan   881a
> dædum gefremed   954a
> ræhte ongean   747b
>
> niða ofercumen   845a

These verses have exactly the same sequence of syllables as verses of Type E with the cæsura in the first position, except that the second syllable is short instead of long. Sievers rejects the possibility of verses of this type, on the basis of his rule that 'a continuous sequence of unstressed syllables counts as a single thesis'[2]; but Sievers did not recognize the existence of the cæsura, which effectively divides the two theses one from the other. Once the existence of the cæsura is recognized there seems to be no reason why these verses should not be classified as a variety (indeed, the simplest and most fundamental variety) of Type E.

---

[1] The number of these difficult verses is much less in any edited text than in the manuscript, since all editions make use of emendation *metri causa* to a greater or less degree; Klaeber's text is extremely conservative, and the number of difficult verses is correspondingly large.

[2] 'Im allgemeinen hat jede ununterbrochene reihe sprachlich unbetonter silben als einheitliche senkung zu gelten'—E. Sievers, *Altgermanische Metrik* (1893) § 10.1.

85. The next group of remainders consists of a number of verses with the sequence $\acute{-}|\acute{-}\times$:

> secg betsta   947a, 1759a
> ðegn betstan   1871b

With these may be included the verse

> Hreðel cyning   2430b

if the second *e* of *Hreðel* is underdotted and ignored in scansion. With this group may be associated two verses with the sequence $\acute{-}|(\times)\times\acute{-}$:

> bord wið rond   2673a
> Raþe æfter þon   724b

These two groups of verses have exactly the same sequence of syllables as Types C and B respectively, except that the unstressed syllables forming the first thesis are lacking. Now, verses of Types A and D, which normally begin with a stressed syllable, may sometimes begin with an additional, extrametrical thesis—the phenomenon known as 'anacrusis'; it is not impossible that Types B and C may occasionally in a similar way lack the first thesis. If such a variety of Types B and C exists, it is to be expected that it should be very rare, since even the variety in which the first thesis consists of only one unstressed syllable is very rare.

86. The next group of remainders consists of six verses with the sequence $\acute{-}|(\times)\times\times\times\acute{-}$:

> Wa bið þæm ðe sceal   183b
> Wel bið þæm þe mot   186b
>
> Geat unigmetes wel   1792b
> wyrd ungemete neah   2420b
> þegn ungemete till   2721b
> deað ungemete neah   2728b

These verses form two clearly defined groups of similar structure, with the cæsura immediately after the first stress in each group. In the first group, the context would allow the stressing of *þæm*, but the result would be a heavy verse of Type D4 with the cæsura in an impossible position; all the particles must therefore be proclitic on the second stress. In the second group *ungemete*(s), though unusually long, is an adverb of degree, and must be proclitic on the adjective it qualifies. These verses are very difficult to classify: they can scarcely belong to Type B, like *bord wið rond* or *Raþe æfter þon*, since there are no instances of Type B with more than two syllables between the cæsura and the second stress; they can scarcely belong to Type E, since they lack the vital syllable after the first stress. Yet the fact that they are all *b*-verses and have such a clearly defined structure suggests that they do belong to a type of some kind, and are not merely corrupt (see § 110). Perhaps the evidence available to us is insufficient for the solution of this problem.

87. The last five remainders have nothing in common but their refusal to conform to any recognized type:

> hreas [heoro]blac   2488a
> ungedefelice   2435b
> seah on enta geweorc   2717b
> To lang ys to reccenne   2093a
> he is manna gehyld   3056a

The first, of course, is purely editorial. There seems to be no theoretical reason why such a verse should not occur, since the short syllable *heo-* is preceded by a long syllable and may therefore carry the stress without resolution; but there are in fact no instances of this licence. The alternative emendation *hreas [hilde]blac* is a regular verse of Type D4, and is much preferable. The second of these remainders might perhaps be hypermetrical, but cannot be explained in any other way; perhaps Sievers' suggestion *ungedefe* should be accepted. The third verse, *seah on enta geweorc*, is extremely difficult. There are two reasons why it cannot belong to Type D*4: firstly, this type is found only in the *a*-verse, and always has double alliteration; secondly the cæsura is in an impossible position (see § 45). It can hardly belong to Type E, since such a scansion would require resolution of the syllables *seah on*, and there is no parallel for resolution across the cæsura. The fourth verse has already been discussed in §§ 44 and 47. As it stands, it cannot belong to Type D*1, since it lacks double alliteration, and since the cæsura is in an impossible position. On the other hand, if *reccenne* is emended to *reccan*, it offends against the rule which requires double alliteration as a condition for anacrusis. The last verse seems at first to be a regular example of Type B; but the alliteration of the line is on *h-*. It differs from the verses of Type e (Sievers' Type B3) discussed in §§ 67 and 73 in so far as *manna* is a stressed element by nature, so that its stress cannot be ignored; all the instances of Type e contain one stressed element preceded by particles and proclitics.

CHAPTER THIRTEEN

CLASSIFICATION

88. The theory of classification has been briefly discussed in §5; now that the practical problem of classification has at last been reached the theoretical basis must be discussed at more length. Classification is the aggregation of units into classes possessing common features; since any two distinct units must possess features which are not in common, classification necessarily involves the neglect of differences which are assumed to be insignificant. The criteria employed in the classification of metrical forms must be, on the one hand, obvious rhythmical differences, on the other hand, substantial differences of distribution; neither of these criteria is sufficient by itself. For instance, there is no marked rhythmical difference between normal verse of Types B and C and the light verses here designated as Types d4 and d1 respectively.—no difference, at least, was detected by Sievers or any of his followers; yet the difference of distribution is very marked, since the normal verses are very much more frequent in the *b*-verse, and the light verses very much more frequent in the *a*-verse. Again, there is no difference of distribution between the varieties of Type A2b and Type D4 which have secondary stress, since both are found only in the *a*-verse, and both require double alliteration; yet the rhythmical difference between them is obvious. The basis of any valid classification, then, must be a combination of straightforward observation and statistical analysis.

89. Another requisite of a workable classification is that it should be sufficiently broad in its terms: a classification which is too detailed ceases to be a classification and becomes a mere description. For instance, the vast majority of verses in Old English verses consist of two 'feet' divided by a cæsura; it would be easy to devise a symbol for each of the possible varieties of foot, and to denote the verse by a combination of two symbols.[1]

---

[1] This was in fact attempted by Möller, *op. cit.*

Such a system would be quite useless, not only because the number of different types involved would be quite unmanageable, but also because symbols would be available for a vast number of types which never in fact occur. Furthermore, a workable classification should be flexible: that is, it should be possible to vary the degree of precision with which a verse is described. This is one of the great merits of Sievers' system: it is possible to describe a verse as belonging to Type A, Type A2 or Type A2b, according to the degree of precision required. The main reason why Kaluza's 90-type system was never widely adopted is its lack of this very flexibility; no adequate provision is made for grouping together any of the 90 types into more manageable units.

90. Still a further requisite of a successful classification of the Old English metrical forms is that it should not depart too widely from Sievers'. For better or worse, Sievers' system has dominated the field of Old English metrics for seventy years, and it has become so deeply ingrained into the minds of students that no entirely new system stands any chance of success. Moreover, Sievers' five types really do exist, as those who disagree with him so often come to recognize[1]; they really do represent the major rhythmical forms of Old English Verse. Any new classification, then, must incorporate as much as possible of Sievers' system, while eliminating its errors and anomalies and making provision for the notation of important differences which he overlooked.

91. The most important factor overlooked by Sievers was the position of the cæsura, which largely controls the proportion of *a*-verses and *b*-verses, the proportion of *a*-verses with double alliteration, and the presence or absence of anacrusis. Broadly speaking, verses in which the first breath-group is shorter than the second are more frequent in the *a*-verse than the *b*-verse; many varieties are found only in the *a*-verse. In these verses double alliteration is compulsory or quasi-compulsory, and anacrusis is permissible.[2] Verses in which the two breath-groups

[1] See, for instance, P. F. Baum, 'The Character of Anglo-Saxon Verse', *MPh* xxviii (1930-1) 144: 'The five types unquestionably occur in Anglo-Saxon verse.'

[2] There are, of course, exceptions to this general rule: the varieties of Type D with tertiary stress, for instance, are more frequent in the *b*-verse than in the *a*-verse; double alliteration is not compulsory, and anacrusis is not permissible.

are of equal length, or in which the first is longer than the
second, are generally more frequent in the *b*-verse than in the
a-verse; double alliteration is never compulsory and often rare;
anacrusis, even when possible, is not permitted. Clearly, this
important distinction must somehow be recognized in any useful classification; and the simplest method seems to consist in
prefixing to Sievers' letters the numbers 1, 2 or 3, indicating that
the first breath-group is shorter than, equal to, or longer than
the second breath-group. To these three categories may be
added another to contain the light verses, in which the first
breath-group is altogether lacking. The result can be represented schematically as follows:

a ××_́×	1A _́|×_́×	2A _́×|_́×	
		2B ×_́|×_́	3B ×_́×|_́
		2C ×_́|_́×	
d ×_́××	1D _́|_́××		
e ×××_́		2E _́×|×_́	3E _́××|_́

Some of the positions in the pattern must necessarily remain
blank: no such type as 2D or 3D, for instance, is conceivable.
This is regrettable; but some such inconsistency is inevitable if
anything of Sievers' scheme is to be preserved.

92. In the subdivision of the types Sievers' notation must be
preserved as far as possible, but for the sake of simplicity and
consistency some modification must be admitted. Moreover,
some of Sievers' distinctions will have to be abandoned if the
whole system is not to become unwieldy; thus, it will not be
possible to indicate the presence or absence of resolution except
in special cases. Again, the introduction of a new and important
distinction between secondary and tertiary stress introduces a
complication. It will clearly not be possible to distinguish between secondary stress, tertiary stress, and normal lack of stress
without an enormous complexity of classification: since there
is a substantial difference of behaviour between secondary stress
and tertiary stress, and practically no difference of behaviour
between tertiary stress and normal lack of stress, tertiary stress
and normal lack of stress will have to be classed together.[1] In
accordance with Sievers' general plan, the main subdivisions of

---

[1] It will be shown in Appendix B that this solution, advocated here on
grounds of practical convenience, is susceptible of theoretical justification.

the types will be indicated by adding a number, further minor subdivisions by adding a small letter; special variations can be indicated by the use of an asterisk.

93. In Type 1A the main distinction must be between the normal variety and the variety with secondary stress in the second thesis; thus, 1A1 ´|×´× and 1A2 ´|×´`. Small letters may be used to indicate the number of syllables before the second stress: 1A1a ´|×´×, 1A1b ´|××´×, 1A1c ´|×××´×. Since Sievers uses the asterisk to distinguish D* ´×|´×× from D ´|´××, it seems reasonable to use it also to distinguish 1A* ´×|×´× from 1A ´|×´×. In Type 1A* the normal variety must be distinguished from the three varieties with secondary stress in various positions: thus, 1A*1 ´×|×´×, 1A*2 ´×|×´`, 1A*3 ´`|×´× and 1A*4 ´`|×´` (the last two varieties corresponding to Sievers' Type A*). Here again small letters may be used to indicate the number of syllables before the second stress. In Type 1D it is, of course, necessary to distinguish tertiary from secondary stress, and this involves a considerable and regrettable departure from Sievers' notation. However, a measure of consistency can be attained by grouping all the varieties with tertiary stress together under 1D1, on the analogy of Type 1A1, which includes all the varieties of Type 1A with tertiary stress; then Sievers' Type D1 becomes 1D2 and his Type D2 becomes 1D3 (his Type D3, for obvious reasons, never has secondary stress). Sievers' Type D4 may conveniently be divided into three varieties, according to the position of division of the compound: 1D4 ´|´:×`, 1D5 ´|´×:`, 1D6 ´|´×:×`. In Type 1D1 it will not be possible to indicate either the position or the quantity of the syllable bearing tertiary stress, but this represents no real loss; not only do all the varieties behave in exactly the same way, but it is questionable whether tertiary stress is really distinct from normal lack of stress. The subdivision of Type 1D* follows exactly the same lines. The various light verses, whose relationship to normal verse has been explained in Chapter Ten, may be subdivided in the same way as Types 1A and 1D; small letters may be used to indicate the number of unstressed syllables before the stress.

94. In Type 2A the varieties with secondary stress may be distinguished by the use of the numbers 2, 3 and 4 already used for this purpose in Type 1A*: 2A1 ⌣́×|⌣́×, 2A2 ⌣́×|⌣⌣́, 2A3 ⌣⌣́|⌣́×, 2A4 ⌣⌣́|⌣⌣́. Since the small letters are not required to indicate the number of unstressed syllables before either of the stresses, they may be used to distinguish 2A1a ⌣́×|⌣́× from 2A1b ⌣⌣|⌣̆×, and 2A3a ⌣⌣́|⌣́× from 2A3b ⌣⌣́|⌣̆×. In Type 2B secondary stress is never found, so that the numbers may be used to distinguish 2B1 ×⌣́|×⌣́ from 2B2 ×⌣́|××⌣́. The small letters may be used as usual to indicate the number of unstressed syllables before the first stress; if the Type ⌣́×|⌣́ is recognized (§ 85) it can be called 2B1 – . In Type 2C the numbers may be used to distinguish 2C1 ×⌣́|⌣́× from 2C2 ×⌣́|⌣̆× ; the small letters will indicate the number of syllables before the first stress. In Type 2E the numbers will be used to indicate the absence or presence of secondary stress: 2E1 ⌣́×|×⌣́ will include not only the verses discussed in § 84, but also such verses as *Hroðgar geseon* 396b with tertiary stress; 2E2 ⌣⌣́|×⌣́ will include only verses with secondary stress. The small letters may be used to indicate the number of unstressed syllables before the second stress.

95. In Type 3B secondary stress is never found, so that the numbers may be used to distinguish 3B1 ×⌣́×|⌣́ from 3B2 ×⌣́××|⌣́. By a kind of inverse analogy with Types 1A* and 1D*, the sequence ×⌣́×|×⌣́ may be denoted by 3B*1 (the theoretical Type 3B*2 ×⌣́××|×⌣́ is not found in *Beowulf*). The small letters may be used to indicate the number of sylla-bles before the first stress. In Type 3E the numbers will be used to distinguish the absence or presence of secondary stress in just the same way as in Type 1D: 3E1 ⌣́××|⌣́, 3E2 ⌣⌣́×|⌣́, 3E3 ⌣̆×|⌣́. The varieties of Type 3E which have an unstressed syllable before the second stress will be called 3E*1, 3E*2 and 3E*3 respectively. The classification thus obtained is set out in Appendix C, Tables I and II: Table I gives the main types in sufficient detail for all ordinary purposes, Table II includes full subdivisions of each type. Only the types which actually occur in *Beowulf* are listed, but additional varieties which may occur in other poems can easily be fitted in.

96. If it were not for the desirability of preserving the outline of Sievers' classification as far as possible, a more scientific and significant classification could be obtained in the following way. The most important factors of the distribution of any type of verse are the proportion of *a*-verses to the total number of verses, and the proportion of *a*-verses which have double alliteration; these two factors can easily be represented graphically by laying off one against a vertical co-ordinate and the other against a horizontal co-ordinate. Such a graphical representation is shown in the diagram below, which is based on the

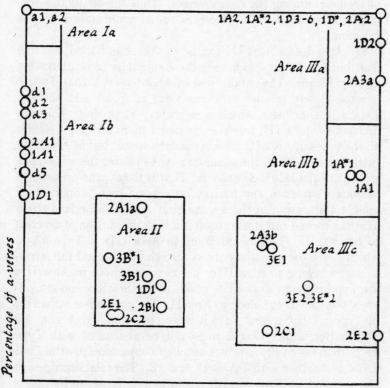

Percentage of a-verses with double alliteration

percentage figures given in Appendix C, Table IV.[1] In this diagram, the proximity of any two types means that their distributions are nearly the same, and hence, presumably, that they are in some way related to each other. It will be noticed that the various types are crowded into three disjunct areas,

---

[1] The figures in italics, based on an insufficient number of examples, have not been included in the diagram.

while the rest of the diagram is blank. The types in each of these areas have certain qualities in common. Area I contains only light verses, Area II contains only normal verses, and Area III (with few exceptions) contains either heavy verses or those varieties of normal verse which have secondary stress; these verses with secondary stress may loosely but conveniently be included among the heavy verses. Thus the distinction formulated in Chapter Two receives visual confirmation in this diagram.

97. Area I and Area III can be further subdivided, and the distribution of the types among these subdivisions is interesting and significant. The subdivision of Area I reveals that Type d is more closely related to Types 1*A*1, 1*D*1 and 2*A*1 than to Type a, a conclusion which is in no way surprising. The subdivision of Area III, however, is much more striking. Nearly all the types in Area III have secondary stress: but in Area IIIa (with one exception) the secondary stress *follows* the second full stress, in Area IIIc it *precedes* it. That is to say, the presence of secondary stress in any position requires a high proportion of double alliteration in the *a*-verse, but only a secondary stress *after* the second full stress requires a high proportion of *a*-verses to the whole. The one exception in Area IIIa is Type 2A3a, which, since the secondary stress precedes the second full stress, ought to belong to Area IIIc; the two exceptions in Area IIIc are Type 2C1 and Type 3E1, which, since they have no secondary stress, ought to belong to Area II. The presence in Area IIIc of Type 2A3b (Sievers' A2k) is interesting and significant. Its distribution shows that it must not be associated with Type 2A3a (Sievers' A2l), nor, as Campbell conjectured,[1] with Type 2A1a, but rather with Types 2E and 3E. The relationship with the varieties of Type E with resolution of the second stress is particularly clear: $\stackrel{\prime}{\_}\stackrel{\grave{}}{\_}|\smile\times$ does not diverge very greatly from $\stackrel{\prime}{\_}\stackrel{\grave{}}{\_}|\times\smile\times$ and $\stackrel{\prime}{\_}\stackrel{\grave{}}{\_}\times|\smile\times$.

98. The presence of Types 1*A*1 and 1A*1 in Area IIb is curious and interesting, since the distribution of these types seems to associate them with the types which have secondary stress either before or after the second full stress. There is, in fact, a linguistic analogy which might throw light on this association, but it is extremely remote and probably coincidental. In

---

[1] A. Campbell, *The Battle of Brunanburh* (1938) 21 note 3.

the vast majority of verses of Types 1A1 and 1A*1 the second
breath-group consists of a preposition and a noun; and in certain
Slavonic languages the preposition is so heavily stressed that in
certain circumstances the following noun becomes enclitic to it.[1]
If it could be assumed that in OE the preposition bore a secondary stress, the association of Types 1A1 and 1A*1 with the types
in Area IIIc would be explained, since the verses which do not
contain a preposition might owe their distribution to analogy
with those that do; but in the absence of confirmatory evidence
it is safer to postulate merely that the position of the cæsura
produces a rhythmical effect comparable to the presence of
secondary stress before the second full stress. Of course, arguing along such lines as these it would not be difficult to devise
a classification of OE metre based on the six distribution-areas
revealed by the diagram, but the departure from Sievers' classic
system would be complete.

[1] I am indebted to Professor A. S. C. Ross and Professor V. Kiparski for
advice on this point.

CHAPTER FOURTEEN

HYPERMETRIC VERSES

99. Among the verses which compose Old English poetry a few are conspicuously longer than the norm, and these are known as hypermetric verses; they usually occur in groups of lines, but single lines and even single verses are sometimes found. No satisfactory explanation of the reason for their appearance has yet been found.[1] The current metrical analyses of these verses are those of Sievers[2] and Kaluza,[3] but neither is really adequate. It is common ground that the vast majority of hypermetrical verses end with a group of syllables which is exactly equivalent to an ordinary verse.[4] According to Sievers, the hypermetric verse is equivalent to the running together of two ordinary verses; that is to say, the middle foot of the hypermetric verse serves as the second foot of the first ordinary verse and the first foot of the second. Unfortunately, this ingenious idea does not always work out in practice. Such a verse as

greteð gæst oþerne   Guth. 5a

is explained by Sievers as a running together of Type A and Type D; but no conceivable variety of Type A can have the sequence $\acute{} \times \acute{}\acute{}$. According to Kaluza, on the other hand, the part of the hypermetric verse which precedes the ordinary verse at the end must be looked on as an extended anacrusis which may share in the alliteration. This theory will not stand up to examination: anacrusis is by definition extrametrical and unstressed, yet in a very large number of hypermetric verses the

---

[1] For a recent attempt see B. J. Timmer, 'Expanded Lines in Old English Poetry', *Neophilologus* xxxv (1952) 226-30.

[2] E. Sievers, 'Der angelsachsische Schwellvers', *PBB* xii (1887) 454-82; *Altgermanische Metrik* (1893) 135-44.

[3] M. Kaluza, *A Short History of English Versification* (1911) 109-13. This view is accepted by Dickins and Ross, *The Dream of the Rood* (1934) 21, note on line 8.

[4] 'Fast jeder schwellvers enthält an seinem ende ein stück das einem normalvers gleichkommt'—Sievers, *Altgermanische Metrik* (1893) § 94.

first word, which according to Kaluza belongs to the anacrusis, is the most important word in the verse, and can hardly be unstressed. Such a verse is

wuldor weroda Dryhtne   Jud. 343a

in which *wuldor* cannot be described as an anacrusis without perverting the meaning of the word so far that the structure of the verse is left as obscure as ever.

100. Each of these theories has an element of truth in it, though neither is satisfactory as it stands. A more satisfactory explanation can be approached in the following way. Let the syllables ⏤́× be added to each of the main varieties of verse other than Types d and D:

a   × × ⏤́ × ⋮ ⏤́ ×

1A   ⏤́ | × ⏤́ × ⋮ ⏤́ ×

2A   ⏤́ × | ⏤́ × ⋮ ⏤́ ×

2B   × ⏤́ | × ⏤́ ⋮ ⏤́ ×

2C   × ⏤́ | ⏤́ × ⋮ ⏤́ ×

2E   ⏤́ × | × ⏤́ ⋮ ⏤́ ×

3B   × ⏤́ × | ⏤́ ⋮ ⏤́ ×

3E   ⏤́ × × | ⏤́ ⋮ ⏤́ ×

Each of these sequences of syllables ends with an ordinary verse, either of Type 2A or of Type 2C, and each is represented among the hypermetric verses, as the following examples show:

1A fah mid fotum sinum   *Gen.* 913a

a hwa þas fitte fegde   *Fates* 98a

2A halge heafdes gimmas   *Guth.* 1302a

2B begoten of þæs guman sidan   *Dream* 49a

2C geseoð sorga mæste   *Christ* 1208a

2E widlond ne wegas nytte   *Gen.* 156a

3B to hynþum heofoncyninge   *Christ* 1513a

3E wrætlicne wundurmaððum   *Beow.* 2173a

101. Instead of considering that the syllables ⏤́× have been added to the ordinary verse we can, however, consider that the final syllables of the ordinary verse have been *replaced* by a longer sequence. In Types a, 1A, 2A and 2C the final syllables ⏤́× have been replaced by the sequence ⏤́× ⋮ ⏤́×, equivalent to an ordinary verse of Type 2A; in Types 2B, 2E, 3B and 3E the final syllable ⏑́ has been replaced by the sequence ⏑́⫶⏑́×, equivalent to an ordinary verse of Type 2C, less the introductory syllables which are only exceptionally lacking from the ordinary verse. If, now, the final syllables are replaced by sequences equivalent to ordinary verses of other types, a much wider variety of hypermetric verses can be formed. In Types a, 1A, 2A and 2C the final syllables ⏑́× may be replaced by any of the types of ordinary verse which begin with a stressed syllable— that is, by Types 1A, 1D, 2A, 2E or 3E; in Types 2B, 2E, 3B and 3E the final syllable ⏑́ may be replaced by any one of Types 2B, 2C or 3B, less the introductory syllables which are only exceptionally lacking from the ordinary verse. The structure of the hypermetric verse can conveniently be indicated by the symbol appropriate to the corresponding ordinary verse, followed (in brackets) by the designation of the ordinary verse which replaces its final syllables. Thus, the sequence of syllables ⏑́⏑́|×⏑́⫶××⏑́× will belong to Type 1A*3(1A1b). The total number of possible varieties of hypermetric verse is very large, but nearly all of them are represented in Old English poetry; on the other hand, there are only six hypermetric verses in Old English which cannot be fitted into one or other of the available patterns.

102. This explanation of the structure of the hypermetric verse has features in common both with Sievers' theory and with Kaluza's. Sievers was right, in a sense, in considering the hypermetric verse as the running together of two ordinary verses; but he was wrong about the exact form of the junction. The verses of Type a, on the other hand, were correctly described by Kaluza as consisting of an ordinary verse preceded by an extended anacrusis; Sievers, by assuming an arbitrary stress in the first part of the verse, tried to force them into the same pattern as the normal hypermetric verse. The correctness of the present analysis is strongly supported by the occasional verses which have the form of a complete line—a sequence of two ordinary verses. The following is a clear example from *Beowulf*, which is equivalent to two ordinary verses of Types 3B1a and 1D1 respectively:

æt fotum sæt frean Scyldinga   *Beow.* 1166a

Verses of this kind cannot easily be fitted into the schemes of

Sievers and Kaluza: Sievers attempts no detailed explanation[1];
Kaluza merely includes the whole of the first part of the verse
in his 'extended anacrusis', thereby adding still further to the
difficulties of his theory, since we are now required to accept
the complete subordination of *two* full stresses. The explanation
of these verses is very simple: there have been two replacements
instead of the usual one. The verse quoted above is a verse of
Type 2C1a, in which the first stress is replaced by the sequence
´× ⦙´ (3B1) and the final syllables ´× are replaced by the
sequence ´⦙´×× (1D1); its full designation is therefore 2C1a
(3B1, 1D1). These verses are discussed at more length in § 109.

103. Hypermetric verses have a number of peculiarities of
distribution which distinguish them from ordinary verses, but
which can easily be explained in terms of the principles which
apply to ordinary verses. Chief among these peculiarities is
the distribution of weak verses of Type a: among the ordinary
verses these weak verses are found only in the *a*-verse, but
among the hypermetric verses they are found almost exclusively
in the *b*-verse; indeed, the vast majority of hypermetric *b*-verses
are weak verses of this type. It has long been recognized that
the structure of the *b*-verse is much more regular and less varied
than that of the *a*-verse; the majority of ordinary *b*-verses are
normal verses, and both light and heavy verses tend to be more
frequent in the *a*-verse. Now, apart from the light verses of
Type a, the vast majority of hypermetric verses are heavy
verses; that is, they consist of three stressed elements. Indeed,
in the looser sense of § 96, they are all heavy verses, since the
few verses which do not consist of three stressed elements contain a secondary stress in addition to the normal two stresses.
The only hypermetric verses which contain the normal quota
of two stresses are the light verses of Type a; and it is therefore
in complete accordance with the principles governing the distribution of ordinary verses that they should be preferred in
the *b*-verse.

104. Double alliteration in the *a*-verse is extremely frequent
among hypermetric verses; in the whole of Old English poetry
there are only four hypermetric verses which lack double alliteration, apart from the weak verses of Type a. This regularity of

---

[1] E. Sievers, *Allgermanische Metrik* (1893) § 96: 'Vierhebige schwellverse
sind . . . einige male überliefert.'

double alliteration is easy to understand: in ordinary verses the presence of a secondary stress after the second full stress requires a high proportion of double alliteration (§ 97); since all hypermetric verses (other than the weak verses of Type a) are heavy verses in the loose sense, they all necessarily require double alliteration. The frequency of double alliteration in the weak verses of Type a is less easy to explain; in fact, rather more than half the verses of this type have double alliteration. Strictly speaking, double alliteration should not occur here at all, since both the stresses belong to the same half of the verse; it is as unexpected as treble alliteration would be in other types of hypermetric verse. It is impossible to plead that these verses have been influenced by ordinary verses of similar types, which they resemble except for the introductory unstressed syllables, since the proportion of *a*-verses with double alliteration in Type a1d(2A1a), for instance, is 60 per cent, compared with a mere 33 per cent in the ordinary Type 2A1a. It is much more likely that the additional length of the hypermetric verse is felt to require the support of alliteration; and this view is confirmed by the frequency of non-functional alliteration in the hypermetric verses of Type a which lack double alliteration. Yet another peculiarity of hypermetric verses is the frequency of anacrusis, and this also is in accordance with the principles governing ordinary verses. It has been shown in § 49 that the two requirements for anacrusis are that the second half of the verse should be longer than the first, and that there should be double alliteration: both these requirements are fulfilled in all the types of hypermetric verse which allow of anacrusis.

105. It is often stated that the scansion of certain verses is ambiguous; they can be scanned either as ordinary or as hypermetric verses.[1] In the light of the more detailed analysis here proposed such a statement requires considerable modification. The number of possible ambiguities is in fact very small, and not all the theoretical possibilities actually occur. In theory, the hypermetric Types a(1A) × × ⌣́ ⋮ × ⌣́ ×, a(1A*) × × ⌣́ × ⋮ × ⌣́ ×, a(1D) × × ⌣́ ⋮ ⌣́ × × and a(1D*) × × ⌣́ × ⋮ ⌣́ × × might be confused with the ordinary Types 1A, 1A*, 1D and 1D* with anacrusis;

[1] 'Die grenzen zwischen normalvers und schwellvers sind nicht überall sicher zu ziehen. Die längeren formen des normalverses kommen den kürzeren formen des schwellverses nicht selten äusserlich gleich'—Sievers, *Altgermanische Metrik* (1893) § 90.

but in practice confusion is scarcely possible, since the hypermetric verses always begin with at least two unstressed syllables, whereas among ordinary verses disyllabic anacrusis is excessively rare. There is a real ambiguity between the hypermetric Types a(2E) and a(3E) and the ordinary Types 3B*1 and 3B2 respectively. In each of the following pairs of verses, the first is an ordinary verse and the second is hypermetric:

>   þæt wæs feohleas gefeoht   *Beow.* 2441a
>   him þæs grim lean becom   *Gen.* 46b

>   Ne bið þe [n]ænigre gad   *Beow.* 949b
>   Þær mon mæg sorgende folc   *Christ* 889b

There is also an ambiguity between hypermetric Type 3B(2C) and ordinary Types 1D*2 with anacrusis. In the following pair of verses the first is an ordinary verse and the second is hypermetric:

>   ne sohte searoniðas   *Beow.* 2738a
>   to hynþum heofoncyninge   *Christ* 1513a

It should be noticed, however, that such verses as the following would be objectionable as ordinary verses, since the cæsura would be in an impossible position:

>   cenned for cneomagum   *Elene* 587a
>   wlitige to woruldnytte   *Gen.* 1016a
>   ende ðurh insceafte   *Sol. & Sat.* 457a

These all belong to hypermetric Type 2E1(2C). The number of real ambiguities is very small, and the context is generally a sufficient guide to the correct scansion.

106. The number of hypermetric verses in *Beowulf* is quite insufficient to provide a basis for analysis, so the following brief survey of the varieties which occur is based on the hypermetric verses in the whole corpus of Old English poetry, with the exception of *Genesis B*, translated from the Old Saxon and therefore untrustworthy for our purpose. The list of hypermetric verses is based on that of Pope,[1] with certain additions and omissions made in the light of the analysis explained above.

---

[1] J. C. Pope, *op. cit.* 100-104.

Thus, in *Beowulf*, the following verses have been added, since they cannot be scanned as ordinary verses but are perfect hypermetric verses:

wrætlicne wundụrmaððum   2173a
ealne utanweardne   2297a

Similarly, the following verse has been omitted, since it cannot easily be scanned as a hypermetric verse but is a perfect ordinary verse:

þæt he hæfde mod micel   1167a[1]

The readings followed are those of Pope, but the titles of the various poems have been altered where necessary to conform with those of *The Anglo-Saxon Poetic Records*. A complete list of hypermetric verses, with the scansion of each, will be found on pages 162-8.

107. The number of preliminary unstressed syllables in Type a varies from one to eight; the most frequent numbers are three and four, followed by five, two, six, seven, eight and one in that order. There is only one example of one unstressed syllable:

mid synna fyrnum   *Order* 102a

This verse is probably corrupt, since two unstressed syllables should be the minimum number, as it is with ordinary verses of Type a. The most frequent configuration of the end of the verse is (2A1a), followed by (1A*1a) and (1A1a) in that order. The only verse which demands any special remark is the following:

genom him to wildeorum wynne   *Guth.* 741a

Here the end of the verse has the sequence $\acute{} \times \times \vdots \acute{} \times$ which is so scrupulously avoided by the *Beowulf* poet (§§ 4, 43), and it might seem better to read *wildrum* with Cosijn. However the same sequence recurs as the ending of a verse of Type 1A*1a, and three varieties of it occur in *Judith* and *Christ* expanded to hypermetric verses (§ 108), so it is wiser not to tamper with it; it may conveniently be designated Type 3A.

108. Hypermetric Type 1A1 differs from ordinary Type 1A1 in allowing a greater number of unstressed syllables before the

---

[1] A possible hypermetric scansion would be Type e(C2); but this interpretation seems rather strained.

second stress; whereas the ordinary type allows only three syllables, the hypermetric type allows up to five; the same is true of Type 1A*1a. In both these types the most frequent configuration of the end of the verse is, as before (2A1a), followed by (1A*1a) and (1A1a) in that order. There is one instance of Type 1A*1a(3A1):

> ealle ða yldestan ðegnas   *Jud.* 10a

Type 1A*3 is only sparsely represented. Type 2A1 is the most frequent type of all. The most frequent configuration of the end of the verse is (2A1a), followed by (1D1), (1A*1a) and (1A1a) in that order. Type 2A3 is considerably more frequent than Type 1A*3. The remaining types are all comparatively rare, and few of them require special comment. Hypermetric Type 2E allows a greater number of syllables before the second stress than the ordinary Type 2E: whereas the ordinary type allows only two syllables, the hypermetric type allows up to four. Type 3A, which is scrupulously avoided in *Beowulf*, occurs four times in all, three times in *Judith* and once in *Christ*:

Type 3A1(1A1a):

> nealæhte niht seo þystre   *Jud.* 34a
> haligre hyht geniwod   *Jud.* 98a

Type 3A2(2A1a):

> winhatan wyrcean georne   *Jud.* 8a

Type 3A*1a(2A1a):

> biwundenne mid wonnum claþum   *Christ* 1423a

109. In addition to the standard hypermetric verses there are a few verses in which both the beginning and the end of the verse have been replaced by sequences of syllables equivalent to ordinary verses (§ 102). These 'double hypermetric verses' are almost entirely restricted to *Maxims I* and *Maxims II*: of the thirteen examples in Old English poetry, nine are from *Maxims I*, one from *Maxims II*, and one each from *Beowulf*, *The Wanderer* and *Daniel*. The number of possible varieties of 'double hypermetric verse' is naturally very large indeed, and it is not surprising that only one of them is represented by more than a single verse. These verses are found only in the

a-verse, and double alliteration is compulsory: both these rules
are in accordance with the principles governing ordinary verses.

110. There are only six hypermetric verses in Old English
poetry which cannot be fitted into any of the types described
above; and the small number of remainders is surprising, since
in the absence of any completely satisfactory method of scansion hypermetric verses have been less emended by editors than
ordinary verses. What is still more surprising is the fact that
five of these six remainders are from *Maxims I*, the scansion of
which is notoriously difficult and idiosyncratic. The first group
of verses clearly belongs to a hypermetric type equivalent to
the ordinary type discussed in § 86, $\acute{-}|(\times)\times\times\times\acute{-}$, and confirms
the suggestion there made that the verses concerned are not
merely corrupt:

> Dol biþ se þe his dryhten nat   *Max. I* 35a
> Seoc se biþ þe to seldan ieteð   *Max. I* 111a

The remaining three verses from *Maxims I* seem to conform to
no intelligible pattern at all:

> ofercumen biþ he, ær he acwele   *Max. I* 113a
> Muþa gehwylc mete þearf   *Max. I* 124a
> þæt ece nið ælcum scod   *Max. I* 198a

The sixth remainder is from *Solomon and Saturn*:

> wunnon hie wið dryhtnes miehtum   *Sol. & Sat.* 329a

If it alliterated on *d* this verse would be a regular example of
the common Type aɪd(2Aɪa); but it alliterates on *w*. It is
possible that two verses have been lost from the text.

111. The distribution of hypermetric verses varies from poem
to poem. The general pattern is clear—normal and heavy verses
in the *a*-verse, light verses in the *b*-verse; and to this pattern
Beowulf, Guthlac B and *The Seafarer* conform completely. *Christ,
The Dream of the Rood, The Metres of Boethius* and *Guthlac A*
have a high proportion of light verses in the *a*-verse. *Solomon
and Saturn, Maxims I* and *Maxims II* have a high proportion
of normal and heavy verses in the *b*-verse, and this grouping is
particularly interesting, since all these three pieces are of the
gnomic type. *Maxims I* and *Maxims II* are further bound
together by the presence of 'double hypermetric verses' (§ 109),

and *Maxims I* is outstanding because of the high proportion of remainders it contains (§ 110). It seems clear that the gnomic poetry of the Anglo-Saxons belongs in some respects to a different tradition from the remainder of the poetry.

CHAPTER FIFTEEN

THE OLDEST ENGLISH VERSE

112. It has been shown that the verse of *Beowulf* is constructed according to rules and principles more elaborate than those formulated by Sievers, and that the hypermetric verses in Old English poems of all periods are constructed according to closely related principles. It is of some interest to determine whether the verse of the beginning and the end of the Anglo-Saxon period observes the same rules as *Beowulf*. There can be little doubt that the oldest English poetry is embedded in *Widsith*; *Beowulf* itself may claim to rank among the earliest compositions: but it is impossible to be sure that the metrical forms of such pieces have not been modified in the course of time by successive generations of scribes. The only early poems which have survived in early manuscripts are the three Northumbrian poems, *Cædmon's Hymn*, *Bede's Death Song* and *The Leiden Riddle*. Of these, *Cædmon's Hymn* was written in the seventh century and survives in two manuscripts of the eighth, and *Bede's Death Song* and *The Leiden Riddle* were written in the eighth century—no earlier than *Beowulf*—and survive in manuscripts of the ninth. The metrical forms of these three poems are briefly examined in the following paragraphs.[1]

113. The first point in which these early poems agree with *Beowulf* is the necessity of double alliteration in *a*-verses of Types IA, IA* and ID:

> heben til hrofe   *Cædmon* 6a
> hatan mith hęliðum   *Leiden* 12a
> Uundnae me ni biað ueflae   *Leiden* 5a
> Uyrmas mec ni auefun   *Leiden* 9a
> herum ðerh hehcraeft   *Leiden* 4a
> uerc uuldurfadur   *Cædmon* 3a

The following *b*-verse, which seems at first glance to belong to

---

[1] The edition used is that of A. H. Smith (1933).

Type 1D2 (very rare in the *b*-verse in *Beowulf*), rather belongs to Type 1D1, since the phonological development of *ælmihtig* in West Saxon shows that the first element was not directly associated with *eall*:

> frea allmectig　　*Cædmon* 9b

Type 2A1a has a higher proportion of double alliteration in the *a*-verse than it has in *Beowulf*, but the total number of examples is too small to be significant:

> metudæs maecti　　*Cædmon* 2a
> eci dryctin　　*Cædmon* 4a, 8a
> firum foldu　　*Cædmon* 9a

114. *The Leiden Riddle* contains an example of a variety of Type 2C which does not occur in *Beowulf*:

> ða ði geolu godueb　　*Leiden* 10a

There are only three examples in *Beowulf* of Type 2C with a long syllable after the second stress, and all of these have tertiary stress (§ 60): yet there seems to be no theoretical reason why the secondary stress which is permitted in Type 2A should not be permitted in Type 2C. There is one example of a long syllable with tertiary stress in the thesis of Type 3B:

> he aerist scop　　*Cædmon* 5a

Type 3E is restricted to the *b*-verse:

> hefaenricaes uard　　*Cædmon* 1b
> moncynnæs uard　　*Cædmon* 7b
> hygiðoncum min　　*Leiden* 4b

It must be admitted that the total number of verses in the three poems considered is not sufficient for any fair comparison with *Beowulf*: there are, for instance, no examples of anacrusis, so that it is impossible to determine whether the rules governing this important feature are the same or not. All that can be said is that there is no evidence in the early Northumbrian poems to show that the characteristics of the metre of *Beowulf* have undergone any substantial changes at the hands of the scribes.

CHAPTER SIXTEEN

LATE OLD ENGLISH VERSE

115. The poems most obviously suitable as a basis for the study of late Old English verse technique are *The Battle of Brunanburh*, which cannot be earlier than 937, and *The Battle of Maldon*, which cannot be earlier than 991.[1] These poems have the special interest that the first is reputed to be very strict in its metre, the second somewhat lax. The reputation of *The Battle of Brunanburh* is triumphantly vindicated by examination in the light of the stricter principles formulated in this study: there is only a single verse which fails to pass muster. Of the sixteen examples of Types 1A and 1A*, three lack double alliteration:

> cyning and æþeling 58a
>
> flotena and Sceotta 32a
>
> Engle and Seaxe 70a

The proportion is higher than in *Beowulf*, but all three examples are of a type familiar in *Beowulf*—a phrase consisting of two parallel words linked by *and*, which could not be used at all without breaking the rule of double alliteration; compare *nean ond feorran, dæges ond nihtes, sæla ond mæla* in *Beowulf*. It is often stated that there is no proof that front and back *g* still alliterate in the later poetry[2]; this statement must now be modified in the light of the following verses:

> garum ageted 18a
>
> giungne æt guðe 44a

Both these verses are of Type 1A*1a, and require double alliteration; if front and back *g* alliterate they have double alliteration; the only alternative is the assumption of coincidence, which might explain a single instance but hardly two. The only two

---

[1] The editions used are those of Campbell (1938), and Gordon (1937).
[2] cf. Campbell, *op. cit.* 33.

examples of anacrusis belong to Types 1A1a and 1A*1a respectively, and both have the double alliteration required by the rule:

> beslagen æt sæcce   42a
> geslogon æt sæcce   4a

116. The only examples of Type 1D in the *b*-verse belong to Type 1D1:

> land ealgodon   9b
> Feld dunnade   12b
> guma norþerna   18b
> hræ bryttian   60b

There are no examples of secondary stress in Types 2B, 2C or 3B, though there is one example of Type 3B1b with tertiary stress in the second thesis:

> swilce Scittisc eac   19b

The only verse which offers real difficulty is the following:

> grædigne guðhafoc   64a

This verse is a perfect example of hypermetric Type 3E1(2C2), but it is difficult to scan as an ordinary verse. It can hardly belong to Type 1D*, since a disyllabic thesis is unknown in this type; perhaps it is best to scan it as Type 3A2, $\acute{-}\_\times|\acute{-}\grave{\smile}\times$, with resolution of the half stress; this type is not found in *Beowulf*, though its equivalent occurs among the hypermetric verses (§§ 107, 108).

117. *The Battle of Maldon* emerges rather creditably from a fresh examination. Inevitably the same glaring faults of defective alliteration are still present, but there are few new faults to be observed; and in some respects the usage is more regular than that of *The Battle of Brunanburh*. Out of 81 instances of Types 1A and 1A* in the *a*-verse, only six lack double alliteration—a proportion which does not differ much from that of *Beowulf*—and of these six one may be illusory:

> reaf and hringas   161a
> eard gesecan   222a
> Ælfnoð and Wulmær   183a
> Offa gemælde   230a
> Leofsunu gemælde   244a
> Offa þone sælidan   286a

In the first instance it is possible that initial *hr-* had already become *r-* in pronunciation, so that double alliteration is actually present. The second instance is easily paralleled from *Beowulf*: compare *rand geheawe, wræc adreog*an. The third instance must be corrupt, since the line alliterates neither on a vowel nor on *w*. The fourth and fifth instances are excusable, since it would be unreasonable to restrict the useful verb *gemælde* to proper nouns beginning with *M-*. The last instance, however, is quite inexcusable, since the verse has a half stress after the second stress, a structure which absolutely demands double alliteration. In no instance are front and back *g* linked together by the alliteration; on the contrary, in two instances the alliteration of front and back *g* would mean double alliteration in the *b*-verse:

mid gafole forgyldon   32b
guþe ne gymdon   192b

It would seem that the two varieties of *g* had ceased to alliterate in the course of the tenth century.

118. Anacrusis is frequent in *The Battle of Maldon*. The following are regular instances in Types 1A and 1A*:

Gemunaþ þara mæla   212a
forwegen mid his wæpne   228a
To lang hit him þuhte   66b
Þa flotan stodon gearowe   72b
Se eorl wæs þe bliþra   146b

Gegremod wearð se guðrinc   138a
He bræc þone bordweall   277a

and begen þa beornas   182a
forheawen æt hilde   223a
on wlancan þam wicge   240a
his ealdre gelæstan   11b
mid gafole forgyldan   32b
to heanlic me þinceð   55b
mid prasse bestodon   68b
and georne gesawon   84b
for wætere ne murnon   96b
Abreoðe his angin   242b

ac wendon fram þam wige   193a

There are no instances of irregular anacrusis. In Type 1D5 there is one apparent instance of single alliteration in the *a*-verse:

wis ealdorman 219a

Here we must assume that the composition of the word was no longer felt by the writer, as is indeed probable, since the meaning had developed far from the etymological meaning; in this case the verse belongs to Type 1D1. All the instances of Type 1D in the *b*-verse belong to Type 1D1:

grið fæstnian 35b

bord hafenode 42b, 309b

wigan unforhte 79b

hand wisode 141b

hyse unweaxen 152b

ham siðie 251b

119. The only instances of Type 2A1a which require comment are those which have resolution of a long syllable in the first thesis:

stiðlice clypode 25b

heardlice feohtan 261b

geornlice fylstan 265b

These verses offend against the rule established in § 37, which forbids a long vocalic ending in the second of two resolved syllables in the thesis, and it seems to follow that the traditional quantities of final syllables had at last been forgotten. The only example of Type 2A3a with resolution in the thesis does not offend against the rule:

wælspere windan 322a

Of the three examples of Type 3B1 with a long syllable in the thesis, none has secondary stress:

Þa Byrhtnoð bræd 162a

Hwæt, þu, Ælfwine, hafast 231a

þe her ricost eart 36b

The second of these, which has resolution of the long syllable in the thesis, does not offend against the rule.

120. There are some dozen verses in *The Battle of Maldon* which offer special difficulty. The instances of postponed alliter-

H

ation are well known: they must be divided into two groups,
those in which the alliterating word is preceded by a word which
should bear a stress, and those in which it is not. The following
are the verses in which the alliterating word is not preceded by
a word which should bear a stress:

> þa he ætforan his frean   16a[1]
> Þa he hæfde þæt folc   22a
> ða onemn hyra frean   184a
> þæt hi moston gewrecan   263a

All these verses can easily belong to Type e: the proportion is
much higher than the proportion of Type e verses in *Beowulf*,
but otherwise there is no irregularity. The assumption of con-
traction in verses 16a and 184a (*frêan*) would remove them to
Type a1; but the remaining verses cannot be so treated. The
following are the verses in which the alliterating word is preceded by a word which should bear a stress:

> Ælfere and Maccus   80a
>
> hwæt þis folc segeð   45b
> se wæs haten Wulfstan   75b
> þe ahte his hlaford   189b
> Offa forheawen   288b

The first three of these verses could be improved by inverting
the order of the words: *Maccus and Ælfere, hwæt segeð þis folc,
se Wulfstan wæs haten*. Since, however, the remaining two
verses cannot be so treated it seems better to accept irregularity
of alliteration as a characteristic of the poem.

121. The following two verses must be considered next:

> ærænde to þam eorle   28a
> oþerne bylde   234b

These verses must be scanned as Types 3A*1b and 3A1 respectively; both these types are avoided in *Beowulf*. The following
two verses offer considerable difficulty:

> Se flod ut gewat   72a
> abeod eft ongean   49b

---

[1] The alliteration of *ætforan* is, of course, accidental; a preposition cannot be
stressed unless it is displaced from its normal position as a proclitic.

These seem to be heavy verses of Type 2E2a with anacrusis: yet there are no examples of anacrusis with Types 2E or 3E in *Beowulf*. All alternative scansions seem to be ruled out. Type 1D4 is impossible because it requires double alliteration in the *a*-verse and is not found at all in the *b*-verse; Type 3B*a is impossible because secondary stress is never present in this Type. There remain three difficult verses:

> he let him þa of handon   7a
> þæt wære hit ure hlaford   240b
> and swiðe manig oþer   282b

The first of these alliterates on *l*, and no scansion is possible; compare § 22. The only remedy for this verse is to emend *handon* to *landon*[1]: the verse is then exactly parallel to *ne geweox he him to willan* (*Beowulf* 1711a), and belongs to Type a1e with non-functional alliteration of *let*. Verses 7-8a will then read as follows:

> he let him þa of landon   leofne fleogan
> hafoc wið þæs holtes

In this context it is clear that *land* is contrasted with *holt*, and has the common meaning 'agricultural land, cultivated land'[2]; the presence of *handum* in line 4 may have contributed to the error. The second of the three verses quoted above presents the same kind of difficulty as the first, but no simple emendation will put it right. The third verse seems to be a heavy verse of Type 1D*2 with anacrusis; but Type 1D* is not found at all in the *b*-verse.

---

[1] For the opposite error see Hickes' transcript of *The Fight at Finnsburh* 11a.
[2] See Bosworth-Toller (especially the *Supplement*) s.v.

CHAPTER SEVENTEEN

TOWARDS AN INTERPRETATION

122. The purpose of this study is to provide an adequate statistical basis for an interpretation, not a detailed interpretation itself; but it is within its scope to point out the direction in which a successful interpretation must be sought. A number of general points must be emphasized to begin with. It is not intrinsically likely that the interpretation of Old English verse will be satisfyingly simple: it is not to be hoped that a single all-embracing theory will explain all the peculiarities of a verse form which we approach for the first time after perhaps a thousand years of unrecorded history. The distribution of the same alliterative metre among all the Germanic peoples proves that it must have had its origin before the dispersal of the tribes; and the wide divergence of the manifestations of the metre in the different Germanic languages is further evidence of a long independent history. Conservative though the Anglo-Saxon poets undoubtedly were, the differences of usage between *Beowulf* and *The Battle of Maldon,* separated by three hundred years at the most, hint at the obsolescences and innovations that must have preceded our earliest extant poetry. It is to be expected, then, that Anglo-Saxon verse should retain vestigial forms of obsolete features; it is to be expected that it should give evidence of contrary tendencies and developments yet to come.

123. It should hardly be necessary to observe that the investigator should be free from preconceived opinions, that he should allow the facts to speak for themselves; yet recent interpretations of Old English verse show that this warning is only too much needed. The current interpretation of modern English verse is that it is chronometric: that is, that its stresses recur at equal intervals irrespective of the amount of speech-material that separates them. This theory has the advantage that it is susceptible of verification, though it does not appear that the verification has ever been done.[1] Recent interpreters of Old English verse, notably Heusler and Pope,[2] have attempted to apply this theory to Old English, on the explicit assumption that the fundamental structure of Old English verse is the same as that of modern English verse; there is absolutely no evidence for this assumption, and in fact the widespread and deepseated changes which the English language underwent during the Middle English period render it exceedingly implausible. Moreover, the chronometric theory is even more difficult to apply to Old English than to modern English verse, because of the greater variety of speech-material which the former allows; some of the difficulties involved have already been discussed in §§ 2-3.

124. The first difficulty, that of equalizing the duration of the two feet of such a verse as *wis welþungen* without introducing either an intolerable drawl or a rest which interrupts the sense, has been recognized by the exponents of the chronometric theory, who try to evade it by insisting that Old English verse was not spoken but sung; Pope devotes a substantial section of his study to a consideration of the Anglo-Saxon harp.[3] It is indeed highly probable that Old English poetry was sung, since references in the verse itself to the activities of the *scop* commonly make use of the verb *singan* or its equivalent, and the harp is frequently mentioned; but the tacit assumption that Anglo-Saxon music, like modern music, was isochronous is difficult to defend. It must be regretfully admitted that we know nothing at all of Anglo-Saxon music, and the only contemporary music of which we have any detailed knowledge, the Gregorian chant, is certainly not isochronous: its rhythm is variable, and is entirely dependent on the natural prose rhythm of the words sung; any such arbitrary lengthening of words and syllables as is required by the chronometric theory is quite alien to its nature.[4] It is still possible, of course, that Anglo-Saxon music was entirely different from the Gregorian chant, and was in fact isochronous, but we are certainly not entitled to assume it, still less to base an elaborate theory on the assumption.

---

[1] It would not be difficult to record the reading of an experienced verse-speaker ignorant of prosodic theory, and to measure the actual interval between the stresses.

[2] For references see § 1.   [3] J. C. Pope, *op. cit.* 88-95.

[4] This important observation was made by P. F. Baum, 'The Metre of the *Beowulf*', *MPh* xlvi (1948-9) 74-75.

125. Assuming for want of evidence that Anglo-Saxon music is more likely to have resembled the Gregorian chant than any modern isochronous music, is it possible to base an interpretation on the ordinary prose rhythm of the words used? The attempt is at least worth making. It is common ground that poetic rhythm depends for its effect on variations from a norm which appears often enough unvaried to provide a mental background against which the variations form a counterpoint; and there can be no doubt that the norm of Old English verse is the rhythm ´×(×)´×, which underlies nearly 40 per cent of the verses in *Beowulf*. If now, abandoning the chronometric theory, we assume that the stresses in the verse may be *displaced* forwards or backwards in time, the following rhythms result: if the first stress is displaced forwards the result is ×(×)´´×, Type C; if the second stress is displaced forwards the result is ´××(×)´, Type E; if both stresses are displaced forwards the result is ×(×)´×´, Type B; if the second stress is displaced backwards the result is ´(×)´××, Type D. These are the only possible displacements, and the displacement theory thus explains the five types which actually occur and no others.[1] The interval between successive stresses is no longer constant, but the *average* interval between stresses is approximately so. Instead of being displaced, the first of the two stresses in a verse may be subdued, or even disappear altogether: the result is what is here termed a 'light' verse. It has been shown in § 69 that the disappearance of one of the stresses results in an increase in the number of syllables in a verse; and the process of compensation there hinted at can now be more accurately defined. It is a well-known law of sound-change that a short syllable which acquires a stress tends to be lengthened, and that a long syllable which loses its stress tends to be shortened; there is, then, a certain correlation between stress and duration.[2] It follows that if the average interval between stresses is to remain constant the loss of a stress must be accompanied by an increase in the total number of syllables.

[1] It cannot, for instance, account for the hypothetical type ××´´, which has always invalidated previous attempts to derive the five types from a single pattern: see J. Routh, 'Anglo-Saxon Meter', *MPh* xxi (1923-4) 429-34; W. W. Greg, 'The "Five Types" in Anglo-Saxon Verse', *MLR* xx (1925) 12-17.

[2] It has been shown in Chapter Three that the contrary of this proposition is false: stress may induce lengthening, but length cannot induce a stress for which there is no other justification.

126. So far we have been concerned with *rhythm*; now, to continue the musical terminology, we must consider *phrasing*. Phrasing in music consists in the division of a sequence of notes into articulated groups by the introduction of minimal pauses; and it is the executant's skill in phrasing which largely distinguishes a good from a bad performance. In music, the correct phrasing can only be determined by a careful examination of the conventions of the period at which the piece concerned was written, the composer's personal idiosyncrasies, and his musical intentions as revealed by the structure of the piece as a whole; in metre the phrasing is dictated by syntactical considerations, but it is none the less important. The cæsura may divide the verse into two equal or two unequal sections; light verses represent the ultimate case in which the cæsura moves to the beginning of the verse, so that the first of the two theoretical sections has no existence. Verses in which the first section is shorter than the second are more frequent in the *a*-verse, verses in which the first section is equal to or longer than the second are more frequent in the *b*-verse: in fact, verses of the former kind account for 65 per cent of the *a*-verses, and verses of the latter kind account for 70 per cent of the *b*-verses. The standard structure of a complete line follows the following pattern, as far as the phrasing is concerned:

$$\times \mid \times \times \times \parallel \times \times \times \mid \times$$

The standard line is roughly symmetrical, with two substantial phrases in the middle rounded off by a shorter phrase at each end; and these shorter phrases not only give the line greater stability, but also serve to mark the division between the lines, a division which tends to be obscured by the characteristic Old English *enjambement*. At the same time, the disparity between the two sections of the verse must not be too great: Type 1A*, with the division 2/3, is more frequent than Type 1A, with the division 1/3, and in all the verses of Type 1 anacrusis may be introduced to lessen the disparity between the two sections.

127. The stability of the line depends not only on the length of the sections of the verses, but also on their weight. Verses with a secondary stress in the second section are allowed only in the *a*-verse, but verses with a secondary stress in the first section (Types 2A3, 2E2 and 3E2) are allowed freely in the

b-verse: in other words, the extra weight of secondary stresses
tends to accumulate in the middle of the verse rather than at
the ends. It is possible that the distribution of the alliteration
follows the same kind of system, in so far as alliteration directs
the attention to the section of the verse in which it occurs, and
therefore in a sense adds to the weight of that section. In the
b-verse the alliteration always falls in the first section (except,
of course, in light verses where the first section is reduced to
zero); in the *a*-verse, although the alliteration always falls in
the first section except in light verses, it often falls in the second
section as well. It is often stated that the alliterating letter of
the *b*-verse (Old Norse *hofuðstafr*, German *Hauptstab*) is the
most important, and that it dictates the alliteration of the rest
of the line: this is a convenient fiction in so far as the alliteration of the *b*-verse is more stable than that of the *a*-verse, but
it is obvious that for the hearer or reader the first alliterating
word of the *a*-verse is the most important, since it gives the
first clue to the alliteration of the line. This is the reason why
the first stress of the *a*-verse always alliterates; it is also the
reason for the comparative frequency of non-functional alliteration in light verses—the reader is warned of the alliteration of
the coming line as early as possible. What is not clear is the
reason why double alliteration is so often lacking in verses of
Types 2 and 3: it might have been expected that double alliteration would be compulsory in these verses, so as to compensate
for the defective length and weight of the second section.

128. The interpretation of hypermetric verses presents a special
and separate problem. Attempts have been made, by Kaluza
and Heusler among others, to treat the hypermetric verses as
special cases of the standard pattern, to consider them as exceptionally heavy examples of the ordinary verse: Kaluza treats
the first part of the verse as an extended anacrusis, Heusler
crams the lengthened ending into a measure of normal duration;
neither treatment is at all convincing. Pope assumes a transi-
tion from 4/8 time to 4/4 time, a procedure whose implications
are far from clear. However, a glance at a printed page of verse
shows that the distinction between hypermetric and ordinary
verses is too substantial to be avoided in this way: the introduction of hypermetric verses involves an unmistakable change
of rhythm. The nearest comparison is with the Alexandrine at

the end of a Spenserian stanza; in each case the fundamental rhythm remains unchanged, but the movement of the verse is slowed down.

129. The interpretation of Old English verse here outlined is necessarily fragmentary. Further investigation may solve some of the remaining problems, but it is likely that a number of loose ends will remain forever untied. It is to be hoped, however, that even this brief sketch will be sufficient to show that our understanding of Old English verse is likely to be considerably increased by a more intensive and detailed study of actual metrical forms: there is no profit to be found in arguing in a vacuum, without a sound basis of statistical information.[1]

[1] For a further discussion of some of the points raised in this chapter see Appendix E.

SECONDARY AND TERTIARY STRESS

1. It has been shown in § 31 that there is metrical evidence of a distinction between secondary stress and tertiary stress, and in § 92 that there is no metrical evidence of a distinction between tertiary stress and normal lack of stress: it remains to see what light is thrown on the question by purely phonological considerations. The nature of tertiary stress cannot be determined on metrical grounds, and unless there are serious phonological objections it will obviously be more convenient to ignore it altogether; this has in fact been done, on grounds of practical convenience, in the classification here adopted. A certain degree of stress on formative and derivative syllables has been invoked by the phonologists to explain two distinct phenomena, the survival of certain medial syllables where others are lost, and the lengthening of a short stem syllable when it is followed by a long medial or final syllable. These two phenomena will be discussed in turn in this appendix.

2. The development of medial vowels in Old English is quite clear (references are to K. Luick, *Historische Grammatik der englischen Sprache*). In medial syllables, prehistoric *æ* and *e* are always lost, irrespective of the quantity of the stem syllable (Luick § 303); prehistoric *i* and *u* are lost after a long stem syllable but retained after a short stem syllable (Luick § 306). Prehistoric long vowels other than *ī* and *ū* were shortened and retained, but prehistoric *ī* and *ū* were shortened and subsequently lost (Luick §§ 312.5, 314). The retention of the shortened long vowels is explained as due to the survival of a *Nebenakzent* after a long stem syllable, the loss of shortened *ī* and *ū* as due to the loss of the *Nebenakzent* (Luick § 314).

3. A number of objections can be made to the hypothesis adopted by Luick. Firstly, it seems unnecessary to invoke *Nebenakzent* at all: quite apart from any question of stress, an originally long vowel might be expected to survive longer than an originally short vowel. The introduction of *Nebenakzent* seems to be a concession to Sievers' erroneous belief that there was metrical evidence of secondary stress on formative and derivative syllables. Secondly, it is impossible to understand how the quality of a vowel can affect the survival of *Nebenakzent*; in other words, although there is plenty of analogy for the earlier shortening of the close vowels $\bar{i}$ and $\bar{u}$, there is none for the earlier loss of *Nebenakzent*.

4. There is a simpler and more satisfactory explanation of the facts, suggested by the chronology of the loss of short vowels. Luick shows (§ 309) that the loss of *æ* and *e* was earlier than the loss of *i* and *u*, and it is probable on phonetic grounds that $\bar{i}$ and $\bar{u}$ were shortened before the other long vowels.[1] The following combined chronology explains all the facts, without invoking any kind of *Nebenakzent*:

(1) Loss of *æ* and *e*;
(2) Shortening of $\bar{i}$ and $\bar{u}$;
(3) Loss of *i* and *u*;
(4) Shortening of long vowels other than $\bar{i}$ and $\bar{u}$.

There is so far no ground for assuming that tertiary stress differs from normal lack of stress.

5. *Nebenakzent* has also been invoked to explain the lengthening of short stressed vowels in certain words both native and borrowed. In native compounds whose first element ends in a short vowel, and whose second element 'retains its stress unchanged', the short final vowel of the first element is lengthened (Luick § 104) just as short final vowels are lengthened in stressed monosyllables (Luick § 103): *twī-feald, twī-wintre*, etc. It should be noticed that Luick's association of these two sound-changes implies that the stress on the second element of the compound was at least secondary stress rather than tertiary stress, and probably even 'level stress', which would allow the first element to be pronounced almost as a separate word. So far there is no objection to be made.

[1] Professor C. E. Bazell tells me that the long close vowels are actually undergoing shortening in present-day Hungarian. 'As a curiosity it may be noted that while the literary language maintains the graphic distinction in printed works, the good folk who provide typewriters have profited from the shortening in order to economize by presenting no special letters for long *i* and *u* (or *ü*) on the typewriter. For all other vowels the distinction between long and short is essential' (Letter of 1.3.55).

6. But the same lengthening before a *Nebenakzent* is also in-voked to explain the lengthening of the stressed vowel in such Latin loanwords as *sācerd, māgister*, etc. (Luick § 218), and here we are upon much more debatable ground: for in native words the lengthening occurs only in compounds, and these borrowed words can by no stretch of the imagination be considered as compounded. The stress on the second syllable is presumably due not to its length alone, but to the survival in a reduced form of the original Latin tonic stress; and if this is so we have no direct means of comparison either with native compounds or with native formative and derivative syllables. Yet there remains some certainty in spite of these doubts: it is clearly impossible that the lengthening of the stressed vowel can be due to tertiary stress. We have seen that the lengthening in native compounds presupposes at least secondary, or more prob-ably level stress; on the other hand native words of the type *cyning, cyningas*, which may be presumed to have borne tertiary stress on the derivative ending,[1] show no lengthening. It seems impossible to avoid this conclusion: in the borrowed words, either so strong an accent survived on the original stressed syllable that it was equivalent to secondary or even level stress, or the lengthening of the stressed syllable has nothing to do with the stress on the second syllable.

7. It is unfortunately impossible to determine the degree of stress on these borrowed words with any certainty on metrical grounds, since they occur only rarely in Old English verse. The only word of this type which occurs in Beowulf is *gīgant*, and all three instances are inconclusive. The only verse I have noted which seems at all significant is the following from *Christ*:

sacerd soðlice   Christ 137

It has been shown in §§ 64 and 65 that there are no instances in *Beowulf* of secondary stress in the first thesis of Type 1D*1 (Sievers' Type D*2), and the long vocalic ending of *soðlice* makes it impossible to scan the verse as Type 2A1a (Sievers' Type A2ab) with resolution of the second thesis; it appears, then, that *sācerd* has only tertiary stress. If this is so (and admittedly

---

[1] Luick's statement (§ 314) that *Nebenakzent* survived only after a long stem-syllable is entirely *ad hoc*, and seems to be designed to evade this very difficulty.

one instance is hardly conclusive) the lengthening in words of this type cannot be due to any stress on the second syllable; so that, in default of any native analogy, the lengthening must have its origin in Latin rather than in Old English. It may be tentatively suggested that a short countertonic vowel in an open syllable would tend to be lengthened in plainsong, in which (apart from certain cadences) all syllables are of equal duration[1]; and it is noteworthy that all the words concerned are of ecclesiastical origin. However, the important result from the present point of view is that there is still no ground for assuming that tertiary stress differs from ordinary lack of stress.

8. *Nebenakzent* has also been invoked to explain the name of the river Severn, Old English *Sæfern*, from British **Sabrina* or **Sabrena* with ultimate *a*-affection; compare modern Welsh *Hafren*. This place-name bears a recognizable likeness to the Latin loanwords discussed above, in so far as the stress has been shifted in the course of its transference into Old English, but there are many important differences: the borrowing was very much earlier; the stem vowel appears as *æ* instead of the *a* which is usual in the later borrowings; the second syllable was short, not long, in the language of origin; and the quantity of the stressed vowel in Old English is not known. Of these differences the most important by far is the last: since the word does not occur at all in verse, and since the vowel in Modern English is short, we have no evidence that any lengthening ever took place, let alone that it was due to *Nebenakzent*.

9. The supposition that the first vowel of Old English *Sæfern* was long[2] seems designed to explain Modern English *Severn* instead of **Savern*: OE *Sǽfern* > ME *Sę́uern* > MnE *Sĕvern* just as OE *ǽfre* > ME *ę́uere* > MnE *ĕver*. To this view there are two powerful objections. The development of OE *ǽfre* is exceptional, and the shortening of the long vowel must be due to lack of stress, since the combination *v* + liquid is not one which favours shortening. Moreover, it is impossible to imagine that an Old English place-name *Sǽfern*, referring to what is, at

---

[1] It is true that Jackson has shown (*Language and History in Early Britain* (1953) 269 § 2(3)) that in British Latin, at least, long countertonic vowels were shortened before the general redistribution of quantity in Vulgar Latin; but this is true of early spoken Latin, and the OE words were borrowed much later.

[2] Cf. E. Ekwall, *English River Names* (1928) 360.

least in its lower reaches, a large expanse of water, should not have been associated with the common noun *sǣ*; and this association would certainly be sufficient to frustrate any incipient shortening.

10. It is much easier to defend the alternative view, that the first vowel of Old English *Sǣfern* was short.[1] It is true that the normal development of Old English *æ* in Modern English is *a*; but in Kentish and in certain varieties, at least, of Mercian *æ* was early raised to *e*. If it is true that the Middle English dialect of the *Ancrene Wisse* is to be located in the Worcester-Herefordshire area, it is clear that those who lived on the banks of the Severn must have called it **Sefern* rather than *Sǣfern*[2]; and there is no difficulty in believing that the local pronunciation of a place-name may become accepted as the standard form.

11. It must further be pointed out that there are many other place-names of Celtic origin in which exactly the same phonetic conditions are present, but in which lengthening has certainly not occurred: if lengthening in the name of the Severn could be demonstrated, it would be unique. In fact, the general absence of lengthening in Celtic names of this type throws further doubt on the supposed lengthening in Latin loanwords. There is, indeed, no evidence, either metrical or phonological, that tertiary stress differs in any way from normal lack of stress. In every case in which *Nebenakzent* has been called in to explain a phonological phenomenon, the explanation proves upon closer examination to be either insufficient or unnecessary. The omission from the classification suggested in Chapter Thirteen of any distinction between tertiary stress and normal lack of stress (§ 92) is in fact not only practically convenient but also theoretically justifiable. Yet those who feel that tertiary stress as a distinct degree of stress is a useful concept are free to retain it if they please, without invalidating any of the metrical conclusions reached in this study.

[1] Cf. M. Förster, *Der Flussname Themse* (1942) 245-6; K. Jackson, *op. cit.* 271-2 § 3.

[2] This hypothesis may throw light on the date of the *zweite Aufhellung*; but it must be remembered that the name of such an important river as the Severn is likely to have been known to the invaders before they reached its banks.

VOCALIC ENDINGS IN OLD ENGLISH

1. It has been shown in § 37 that metrical evidence leaves no doubt that there was in Old English a clear-cut distinction between two types of vocalic ending, and it is of considerable interest to try and determine the nature of the distinction. There are two main possibilities. On the one hand, the distinction may have been phonological; that is, it may have depended on some difference in the sound of the endings—not necessarily in historic Old English, but recent enough to be within reach of poetic tradition. On the other hand, the distinction may have been morphological; that is, it may have depended on a difference in the usage of the endings. It is, of course, also possible that the distinction was both phonological and morphological. Whatever it was, it must have been easily accessible to the poets, whom we must not credit with too much philological acumen.

2. Inflectional endings in Primitive Germanic were of three types: the first type was always lost in Old English, the second type was lost after a long stem-syllable but retained after a short stem-syllable, the third type was retained irrespective of the quantity of the stem-syllable. For obvious reasons, it is only the second and third types with which we are concerned here. It is generally agreed that the distinction between the second and third types was one of quantity: in Primitive Old English endings of the third type were longer than those of the second. Fortunately we need not concern ourselves here with the origin of this quantitative distinction; it is usually attributed to the presence of *Schleifton* on endings of the third type,[1] but recent work has tended to discredit this view. It is at least clear that no distinction of quantity can have survived into historic Old English, since the early coalescence of final -æ and -i clearly implies that the original long vowels had been shortened.

---

[1] Luick, *op. cit.* § 312; Sievers-Brunner, *Altenglische Grammatik*, § 150.

3. It has already been pointed out (§ 37) that there is a close correlation between the vocalic endings which permit resolution and those which are lost after a long stem-syllable, and between the vocalic endings which prohibit resolution and those which are retained after a long stem-syllable. We must now examine how close this correlation is. In the list of endings which permit resolution (§ 35) there are only four types which are retained after a long stem-syllable, the feminine ō-stem accusative singular, the masculine i-stem dative singular, the masculine i-stem nominative plural, and the masculine u-stem accusative plural; there are two instances of the first type and one of each of the others, a total of five out of 56 instances in all. Of these four types of ending, the last three must be considered doubtful. The Old English dative combines the functions, and presumably the endings, of two cases, the dative and the instrumental; of these, the first should be retained after a long stem-syllable and the second should perhaps be lost. Since it is impossible to be certain that the single example in *Beowulf* of the masculine i-stem, dative singular, does not represent a survival of the old instrumental, this instance must be considered doubtful. The ending of the masculine i-stem, nominative plural, preserved mainly in tribal names such as *Engle*, *Mierce*, etc., is retained after a long stem, but this retention appears to be analogical. The normal ending of the masculine u-stem, accusative plural, is -a in Old English, and it is retained after a long stem-syllable; but the single instance in *Beowulf* (*bordwudu beorhtan* 1243a) retains the older ending -u, which is lost after a long stem-syllable. The only certain instances, therefore, of a final vowel which is retained after a long stem-syllable are the two instances of the feminine ō-stem, accusative singular:

> modceare micle   1778a
> modceare mændon   3149a

The fact that both these verses contain the same word *modceare* is suspicious; possibly it replaces an obsolete word of a different declension.

4. In the list of endings which prohibit resolution (§ 36) there are no instances of endings which are lost after a long stem-syllable, except for the single instance of the neuter a-stem, accusative plural, which has already been explained in § 37.

I

Since there are at most two certain anomalies in the first list, the correlation is very close indeed. This correlation is not, as we shall see, the only one which can be discerned, but it has the great advantage of being one which would have been easily discernible to the poet. It has already been pointed out that there is a very obvious analogy between morphological and metrical equivalences: nominative plural *scipu* and *hus* and genitive plural *scipa* and *husa* are equivalent both in grammar and in metre.

5. Yet there is another and equally striking correlation. Even a cursory glance at the list of verses in § 35 reveals that none of the words in which resolution occurs ends in -*a*,[1] although final -*a* is frequent in the list in § 36. A more searching examination reveals that, apart from the feminine *ō*-stem accusative singular and perhaps the masculine *i*-stem dative singular, all the endings in § 35 had -*i* or -*u* in Primitive Old English, while all the endings in § 36 had -*æ* or -*a*[2]; particularly striking is the instance of the masculine *u*-stem, accusative plural, which retains the primitive ending in -*u*. Here we have a distinction which, as late as the early seventh century, was still purely phonological.

6. It is of course possible that the phonological and morphological correlations are interrelated: it is possible that after a long syllable the close vowels *i* and *u* are more readily lost than the open vowels *æ* and *a*. Yet it is of some importance to try and determine which of the two correlations was the origin of the metrical distinction, since, apart from the light thrown on the mental processes of the Anglo-Saxon poet, the origin of the metrical distinction may suggest its probable date. If the metrical distinction originated from the morphological distinction with which it is correlated, it cannot have existed before the loss of -*i* and -*u* after a long stem-syllable in the seventh century; but if it originated from the phonological distinction we can put no date to it, since we must not assume that it necessarily depended on the precise phonological repartition of the various endings in Primitive Old English.[3]

---

[1] There is one apparent instance of final -*a* in *morðbeala mare* 136a, but the -*a* is here a late spelling for -*u*.

[2] Apart from the neuter *a*-stem, accusative plural, explained in § 37.

[3] A study of the metrical forms of the other Germanic dialects, which might throw light on the date of the origin of this distinction, is outside the scope of this study.

7. In favour of a morphological origin for this distinction is the fact that it relies less on the force of poetical tradition: the morphological analogy is one which survived unchanged to the end of the Old English period and beyond it, so that poets of any period could make the same observation for themselves. Against a morphological origin is the fact that the distinction is in fact less carefully observed by the later poets than the author of *Beowulf* (§ 120); and it is easier to imagine a poetic tradition in decay than a generation of poets incapable of drawing a simple morphological analogy. We may perhaps reach a compromise by suggesting that the distinction was preserved primarily by a poetic tradition which had its origin in the tendency of the close vowels *i* and *u* to disappear after a long stem-syllable.

THE SCANSION OF *BEOWULF*: STATISTICAL INFORMATION

TABLE I

[This Table gives the distribution of the main types of verse. Of the three columns at the right of the page the first gives the number of *a*-verses with double alliteration, the second the number of *a*-verses with single alliteration, and the third the number of *b*-verses.]

			(1)	(2)	(3)
1.	Type a1:	(× × × ×) × × ́×	0	330	0
2.	Type a2:	(× × × ×) × × × ́ ̀	0	26	0
3.	Type d1:	(× × ×) × ́× × ×	0	178	49
4.	Type d2:	(× × ×) × ́ ̀×	0	125	42
5.	Type d3:	(× × × ×) × ́ ̌×	0	161	61
6.	Type d4:	(× ×) × × × ́ : × ̀	0	7	4
7.	Type d5:	(× × ×) × ́ × : ́ ̀	0	36	28
8.	Type e1:	(× × ×) × × ́	0	7	0
9.	Type 1A1:	́ ̀ : × ́×	0	48	31
10.	Type 1D1:	́ ̀ ́ ̀ × ×	0	50	51
11.	Type 2A1:	́× : ́×	0	79	44
12.	Type 3E1:	́× × : ́ ̀	0	0	1
13.	Type 1A1:	́ |(× ×) × ́×	223	12	187
14.	Type 1A2:	́ |(×) × ́ ̀	40	0	0
15.	Type 1A*1:	́× |(× ×) × ́×	308	25	261
16.	Type 1A*2:	́× |(×) × ́ ̀	20	0	0
17.	Type 1A*3:	́ ̀ | × ́×	1	0	0
18.	Type 1A*4:	́ ̀ | × ́ ̀	2	0	0
19.	Type 1D1:	́ | ́× ×	30	46	220
20.	Type 1D2:	́ | ́ ̀×	22	0	2
21.	Type 1D3:	́ | ́ ̌×	40	0	0
22.	Type 1D4:	́ | ́ : × ́	3	0	0
23.	Type 1D5:	́ | ́× : ́	58	0	0
24.	Type 1D6:	́ | ́× : × ́	5	0	0

TABLE I (*cont.*)		(1)	(2)	(3)
25. Type 1D*1:	$\underline{\prime}\times\mid\underline{\prime}\times\times$	22	0	0
26. Type 1D*2:	$\underline{\prime}\times\mid\underline{\prime}\underline{\prime}\times$	45	0	0
27. Type 1D*3:	$\underline{\prime}\times\mid\underline{\prime}\smile\times$	47	0	0
28. Type 1D*4:	$\underline{\prime}\times\mid\underline{\prime}:\times\underline{\prime}$	9	0	0
29. Type 1D*5:	$\underline{\prime}\times\mid\underline{\prime}\times:\underline{\prime}$	23	0	0
30. Type 1D*6:	$\underline{\prime}\times\mid\underline{\prime}\times:\times\underline{\prime}$	1	0	0
31. Type 2A1:	$\underline{\prime}\times\mid\underline{\prime}\times$	160	315	550
32. Type 2A2:	$\underline{\prime}\times\mid\underline{\prime}\underline{\prime}$	26	0	0
33. Type 2A3:	$\underline{\prime}\underline{\prime}\mid\underline{\prime}\times$	138	7	67
34. Type 2A4:	$\underline{\prime}\underline{\prime}\mid\underline{\prime}\underline{\prime}$	5	0	0
35. Type 2B1:	$(\times\times\times\times\times)\underline{\prime}\mid\times\underline{\prime}$	14	20	140
36. Type 2B2:	$(\times\times\times\times)\underline{\prime}\mid\times\times\underline{\prime}$	3	2	9
37. Type 2C1:	$(\times\times\times\times\times)\underline{\prime}\mid\underline{\prime}\times$	27	12	247
38. Type 2C2:	$(\times\times\times\times\times)\underline{\prime}\mid\smile\times$	13	35	215
39. Type 2E1:	$\underline{\prime}\times\mid(\times)\times\underline{\prime}$	1	3	18
40. Type 2E2:	$\underline{\prime}\underline{\prime}\mid(\times)\times\underline{\prime}$	12	0	79
41. Type 3B1:	$(\times\times\times\times)\times\underline{\prime}\times\mid\underline{\prime}$	59	108	438
42. Type 3B2:	$(\times)\times\times\underline{\prime}\times\times\mid\underline{\prime}$	0	0	4
43. Type 3B*1:	$(\times\times\times\times)\times\underline{\prime}\times\mid\times\underline{\prime}$	12	39	104
44. Type 3E1:	$\underline{\prime}\times\times\mid\underline{\prime}$	30	11	77
45. Type 3E2:	$\underline{\prime}\underline{\prime}\times\mid\underline{\prime}$	51	16	189
46. Type 3E3:	$\underline{\prime}\smile\times\mid\underline{\prime}$	0	0	5
47. Type 3E*1:	$\underline{\prime}\times\times\mid\times\underline{\prime}$	2	1	8
48. Type 3E*2:	$\underline{\prime}\underline{\prime}\times\mid\times\underline{\prime}$	8	2	29
49. Type 3E*3:	$\underline{\prime}\smile\times\mid\times\underline{\prime}$	1	0	0
50. Remainders, Defective, Hypermetric		13	7	22
	TOTAL	1474	1708	3182

TABLE II

[This Table gives the more detailed information of which Table I is a summary.]

		(1)	(2)	(3)
1. Type a1b:	$\times\times\underline{\prime}\times$	0	7	0
Type a1c:	$\times\times\times\underline{\prime}\times$	0	113	0
Type a1d:	$\times\times\times\times\underline{\prime}\times$	0	140	0
Type a1e:	$\times\times\times\times\times\underline{\prime}\times$	0	57	0
Type a1f:	$\times\times\times\times\times\times\underline{\prime}\times$	0	13	0

TABLE II (*cont.*)		(1)	(2)	(3)
2. Type a2c:	× × × ´ `	o	5	o
Type a2d:	× × × × ´ `	o	13	o
Type a2e:	× × × × × ´ `	o	6	o
Type a2f:	× × × × × × ´ `	o	1	o
Type a2g:	× × × × × × × ´ `	o	1	o
3. Type d1a:	× ´ × ×	o	17	6
Type d1b:	× × ´ × ×	o	121	33
Type d1c:	× × × ´ × ×	o	33	6
Type d1d:	× × × × ´ × ×	o	7	4
4. Type d2a:	× ´ ` ×	o	17	15
Type d2b:	× × ´ ` ×	o	79	17
Type d2c:	× × × ´ ` ×	o	22	8
Type d2d:	× × × × ´ ` ×	o	7	2
5. Type d3a:	× ´ ˘ ×	o	35	14
Type d3b:	× × ´ ˘ ×	o	94	39
Type d3c:	× × × ´ ˘ ×	o	22	7
Type d3d:	× × × × ´ ˘ ×	o	8	1
Type d3e:	× × × × × ´ ˘ ×	o	2	o
6. Type d4b:	× × ´ : × ´	o	5	1
Type d4c:	× × × ´ : × ´	o	1	3
Type d4d:	× × × × ´ : × ´	o	1	o
7. Type d5a:	× ´ × : ´	o	4	5
Type d5b:	× × ´ × : ´	o	26	20
Type d5c:	× × × ´ × : ´	o	5	2
Type d5d:	× × × × ´ × : ´	o	1	1
8. Type e1b:	× × ´	o	1	o
Type e1c:	× × × ´	o	2	o
Type e1d:	× × × × ´	o	3	o
Type e1e:	× × × × × ´	o	1	o
9. Type 1*A*1:	´ : × ´ ×	o	48	31
10. Type 1*D*1:	´ : ´ × ×	o	50	51
11. Type 2*A*1:	´ × : ´ ×	o	79	44
12. Type 3*E*1:	´ × × : ´	o	o	1
13. Type 1*A*1a(i):	´ | × ´ ×	150	11	151
Type 1*A*1a(ii):	´ | × ´ ˘ ˘	2	o	2
Type 1*A*1b(i):	´ | × × ´ ×	68	1	32
Type 1*A*1b(ii):	´ | × × ´ ˘ ˘	1	o	o
Type 1*A*1c:	´ | × × × ´ ×	2	o	2

Table II (*cont.*)

	(1)	(2)	(3)
14. Type 1A2a(i): ´|×´`	27	0	0
Type 1A2a(ii): ´|×´`◡	4	0	0
Type 1A2b(i): ´|××´`	8	0	0
Type 1A2b(ii): ´|××´`◡	1	0	0
15. Type 1A*1a(i): ´×|×´×	270	25	251
Type 1A*1a(ii): ´◡◡|×´×	1	0	0
Type 1A*1b: ´×|××´×	35	0	9
Type 1A*1c: ´×|×××´×	2	0	1
16. Type 1A*2a(i): ´×|×´`	18	0	0
Type 1A*2a(ii): ´×|×´`◡	1	0	0
Type 1A*2b: ´×|××´`	1	0	0
17. Type 1A*3: ´`|×´×	1	0	0
18. Type 1A*4: ´`|×´`	2	0	0
19. Type 1D1: ´|´××	30	46	220
20. Type 1D2: ´|´`×	22	0	2
21. Type 1D3: ´|´◡×	40	0	0
22. Type 1D4: ´|´:×´	3	0	0
23. Type 1D5: ´|´×:´	58	0	0
24. Type 1D6: ´|´×:×´	5	0	0
25. Type 1D*1(i): ´×|´××	21	0	0
Type 1D*1(ii): ´◡◡|´××	1	0	0
26. Type 1D*2: ´×|´´×	45	0	0
27. Type 1D*3(i): ´×|´◡×	46	0	0
Type 1D*3(ii): ´◡◡|´◡×	1	0	0
28. Type 1D*4: ´×|´:×´	9	0	0
29. Type 1D*5: ´×|´×:´	23	0	0
30. Type 1D*6: ´×|´×:×´	1	0	0
31. Type 2A1a(i): ´×|´×	146	289	533
Type 2A1a(ii): ´×|´◡◡	0	25	1
Type 2A1a(iii): ´◡◡|´×	12	0	4
Type 2A1b: ´_|◡×	2	1	12
32. Type 2A2(i): ´×|´`	20	0	0
Type 2A2(ii): ´×|´`◡	1	0	0
Type 2A2(iii): ´◡◡|´`	5	0	0

TABLE II (*cont.*)

		(1)	(2)	(3)
33. Type 2A3a(i):	́`|́×	63	0	19
Type 2A3a(ii):	́⌣⌣|́×	58	0	7
Type 2A3a(iv):	́⌣⌣|́⌣⌣	1	0	0
Type 2A3b:	́`|⌣×	16	7	41
34. Type 2A4(i):	́`|́`	3	0	0
Type 2A4(ii):	́⌣⌣|́`	2	0	0
35. Type 2B1-:	́|×́	0	1	0
Type 2B1a:	×́|×́	3	0	7
Type 2B1b:	××́|×́	10	16	92
Type 2B1c:	×××́|×́	0	3	34
Type 2B1d:	××××́|×́	0	0	7
Type 2B1e:	×××××́|×́	1	0	0
36. Type 2B2-:	́|××́	0	0	1
Type 2B2a:	×́|××́	1	1	1
Type 2B2b:	××́|××́	2	1	4
Type 2B2c:	×××́|××́	0	0	2
Type 2B2d:	××××́|××́	0	0	1
37. Type 2C1-:	́|́×	0	2	1
Type 2C1a:	×́|́×	14	1	114
Type 2C1b:	××́|́×	11	8	81
Type 2C1c:	×××́|́×	2	1	44
Type 2C1d:	××××́|́×	0	0	6
Type 2C1e:	×××××́|́×	0	0	1
38. Type 2C2-:	́|⌣×	0	0	1
Type 2C2a:	×́|⌣×	4	6	28
Type 2C2b:	××́|⌣×	7	24	131
Type 2C2c:	×××́|⌣×	1	5	47
Type 2C2d:	××××́|⌣×	1	0	7
Type 2C2e:	×××××́|⌣×	0	0	1
39. Type 2E1a:	́×|×́	1	2	17
Type 2E1b:	́×|××́	0	1	1
40. Type 2E2a:	́`|×́	11	0	75
Type 2E2b:	́`|××́	1	0	4
41. Type 3B1a(i):	×́×|́	10	24	33
Type 3B1a(ii):	×́⌣⌣|́	0	0	1
Type 3B1b:	××́×|́	41	61	256
Type 3B1c(i):	×××́×|́	4	21	131
Type 3B1c(ii):	×××́⌣⌣|́	0	0	1
Type 3B1d:	××××́×|́	4	2	15
Type 3B1e:	×××××́×|́	0	0	1
42. Type 3B2b:	××́××|́	0	0	3
Type 3B2c:	×××́××|́	0	0	1

Table II (cont.)		(1)	(2)	(3)
43. Type 3B*1a:	×´×|×´	1	7	2
Type 3B*1b:	××´×|×´	9	22	49
Type 3B*1c:	×××´×|×´	2	9	36
Type 3B*1d:	××××´×|×´	0	1	10
Type 3B*1e:	×××××´×|×´	0	0	7
44. Type 3E1:	´××|´	30	11	77
45. Type 3E2:	´`×|´	51	16	189
46. Type 3E3:	´◡×|´	0	0	5
47. Type 3E*1:	´××|×´	2	1	8
48. Type 3E*2:	´`×|×´	8	2	29
49. Type 3E*3:	´◡×|×´	1	0	0
50. Remainders		1	2	8
Defective		0	5	3
Hypermetric		12	0	11
	TOTAL	1474	1708	3182

TABLE III

[This Table gives the distribution of all verses with anacrusis. The figures are included in, not additional to, the figures in Tables I and II.]

Verses with monosyllabic anacrusis

	(1)	(2)	(3)
Type 1A1a(i):	6	0	8
Type 1A1b(i):	5	0	0
Type 1A*1a(i):	5	0	0
Type 1A*1b:	1	0	0
Type 1D1:	2	0	0
Type 1D2:	4	0	0
Type 1D3:	3	0	0
Type 1D5:	7	0	0
Type 1D*2:	7	0	0
Type 1D*3(i):	2	0	0
Type 1D*5:	2	0	0
TOTAL	44	0	8

Verses with disyllabic anacrusis

	(1)	(2)	(3)
Type 1A1b(i):	1	0	0
Type 1A2a(i):	1	0	0
Type 1D*5:	1	0	0
TOTAL	3	0	0

TABLE IV

[This Table converts the distribution figures given in Table I into percentages. The first percentage opposite each type represents the proportion of *a*-verses with double alliteration to the total of *a*-verses; the second represents the proportion of *a*-verses to the whole. Figures which are unreliable because the number of examples is very small are printed in italics. These figures form the basis of the diagram on page 85.]

	(1)	(2)		(1)	(2)
Type a1:	0	100	Type 2A1a:	33	47
Type a2:	0	100	Type 2A1b:	*67*	*20*
			Type 2A2:	100	100
Type d1:	0	78	Type 2A3a:	100	82
Type d2:	0	75	Type 2A3b:	70	36
Type d3:	0	72	Type 2A4:	*100*	*100*
Type d4:	*0*	*64*			
Type d5:	0	56	Type 2B1:	39	20
			Type 2B2:	*60*	*36*
Type e1:	*0*	*100*			
			Type 2C1:	69	14
Type 1A1:	0	61	Type 2C2:	27	18
Type 1D1:	0	50			
Type 2A1:	0	64	Type 2E1:	25	18
Type 3E1:	—	*0*	Type 2E2:	100	13
Type 1A1:	95	56	Type 3B1:	35	28
Type 1A2:	100	100	Type 3B2:	—	0
Type 1A*1:	92	56	Type 3B*1:	24	33
Type 1A*2:	100	100			
Type 1A*3-4:	*100*	*100*	Type 3E1:	73	35
			Type 3E2:	80	26
Type 1D1:	39	26	Type 3E3:	—	0
Type 1D2:	100	92			
Type 1D3-6:	100	100	Type 3E*1:	*67*	*27*
			Type 3E*2:	80	26
Type 1D*:	100	100	Type 3E*3:	*100*	*100*

HYPERMETRIC VERSES: STATISTICAL INFORMATION

TABLE I

[This Table gives the distribution of the main types of verse. Of the three columns at the right of the page the first gives the number of *a*-verses with double alliteration, the second the number of *a*-verses with single alliteration, and the third the number of *b*-verses.]

		(1)	(2)	(3)
1. Type a(1A):	(× × × × ×) × × ´:(×) × ´ ×	7	5	76
2. Type a(1A*):	(× × × × ×) × × ´:(×) × ´ ×	15	8	98
3. Type a(1D):	(× × ×) × × ´:´ × ×	1	1	16
4. Type a(2A):	(× × × × × × ×) × ´ × :´ ×	25	29	200
5. Type a(2E):	(× ×) × × ´ × :× ´	0	0	2
6. Type a(3A):	× × × × ´ × × :´ ×	1	0	0
7. Type a(3E):	(× × ×) × × ´ × × :´	0	1	15
8. Type a(3E*):	(×) × × × × ´ × × :× ´	1	0	1
9. Type 1A(1A):	´|(× ×) × ´:× ´ ×	4	0	1
10. Type 1A(1A*):	´|(× × × ×) × ´ × :× ´ ×	16	0	4
11. Type 1A(1D):	´|(×) × ´:´ × ×	3	0	0
12. Type 1A(2A):	´|(× ×) × ´ × :´ ×	38	2	14
13. Type 1A(2E):	´|× ´ × :× ´	0	0	1
14. Type 1A(3E):	´|× ´ × × :´	2	0	1
15. Type 1A(3E*):	´|× × ´ × × :× ´	1	0	1
16. Type 1A*(1A):	´ × |(× × ×) × ´:(×) × ´ ×	10	0	0
17. Type 1A*(1A*):	´ × |(× × × ×) × ´ × :× ´ ×	24	0	4
18. Type 1A*(1D):	´ × |(×) × × ´:´ × ×	3	0	0
19. Type 1A*(2A):	´ × |(× × × ×) × ´ × :´ ×	76	1	6
20. Type 1A*(2E):	´ × |× × × ´ × :× ´	1	0	0
21. Type 1A*(3A):	´ × |× ´ × × :´ ×	1	0	0
22. Type 2A(1A):	´ × |´:(×) × ´ ×	7	0	1
23. Type 2A(1A*):	´ × |´ × :× ´ ×	12	0	1
24. Type 2A(1D):	´ × |´:´ × ×	17	1	1
25. Type 2A(2A):	´ × |´ × :´ ×	61	0	0
26. Type 2A(2E):	´ × |´ × :× ´	1	0	0
27. Type 2A(3E):	´ × |´ × × :´	4	0	0
28. Type 2A(3E*):	´ × |´ × × :× ´	2	0	0

		(1)	(2)	(3)
TABLE I (*cont.*)				
29. Type 2B(2C):	(×)́|× × ́:́ ×	2	0	1
30. Type 2B(3B):	́|× × ́× :́	1	0	0
31. Type 2C(1A):	× × ́|́:× ́ ×	1	0	0
32. Type 2C(1A*):	× ́|́× :× ́ ×	1	0	0
33. Type 2C(2A):	(× × ×)́|́× :́ ×	7	0	1
34. Type 2C(2E):	× ́|́× :× ́	1	0	0
35. Type 2C(3E):	× × × ́|́× × :́	0	0	1
36. Type 2E(2B):	́×|× ́:× ́	1	0	0
37. Type 2E(2C):	́×|(×)× ́:́ ×	7	0	0
38. Type 2E(3B):	́×|(× × ×)× ́×(×):×	6	0	0
39. Type 3A(1A):	́× ×|́:× ́ ×	2	0	0
40. Type 3A(2A):	́× ×|́× :́ ×	1	0	0
41. Type 3A*(2A):	́× ×|× ́× :́ ×	1	0	0
42. Type 3B(2C):	× ́×|́:́ ×	1	0	0
43. Type 3B*(2C):	× × ́×|× ́:́ ×	1	0	0
44. Type 3E(2C):	́× ×|́:́ ×	1	0	0
45. Remainders, Double Hypermetric Verses:		18	1	0
	TOTAL	385	49	446

TABLE II

[This Table gives the more detailed information of which Table I is a summary.]

		(1)	(2)	(3)
Type a1a(2A1a):	× ́×:́ ×	0	1	0
Type a1b(1A1a):	× × ́:× ́ ×	0	1	7
Type a1b(1A1b):	× × ́:× × ́ ×	0	1	0
Type a1b(1A*1a):	× × ́×:× ́ ×	2	2	8
Type a1b(1D1):	× × ́:́ × ×	0	0	5
Type a1b(1D2):	× × ́:́ ́ ×	1	0	0
Type a1b(2A1a):	× × ́ ×:́ ×	2	2	27
Type a1b(2A1b):	× × ́:⌣ ×	0	0	2
Type a1b(2E2a):	× × ́×:× ́	0	0	1
Type a1b(3E1):	× × ́× ×:́	0	0	2
Type a1b(3E2):	× × ́ ×:́	0	0	1
Type a1c(1A1a):	× × × ́:× ́ ×	6	1	28
Type a1c(1A1b):	× × × ́:× × ́ ×	0	0	1
Type a1c(1A*1a):	× × × ́×:× ́ ×	6	0	30
Type a1c(1D1):	× × × ́:́ × ×	0	0	1
Type a1c(2A1a):	× × × ́×:́ ×	5	6	65

TABLE II (*cont.*)

Type	Scansion	(1)	(2)	(3)
Type aic(2Aib):	x x x ´⌣:◡ x	o	o	2
Type aic(2A3a):	x x x ´¯:´ x	o	o	1
Type aic(2A3b):	x x x ´¯:◡ x	o	1	o
Type aic(3Ei):	x x x ´ x x:´	o	o	6
Type aic(3E2):	x x x ´¯ x:´	o	o	1
Type aid(iAia):	x x x x ´:x ´ x	1	1	18
Type aid(iAib):	x x x x ´:x x ´ x	o	o	2
Type aid(iA*ia):	x x x x ´ x:x ´ x	3	3	37
Type aid(iA*ib):	x x x x ´ x:x x ´ x	o	o	1
Type aid(iDi):	x x x x ´:´ x x	o	o	8
Type aid(iD2):	x x x x ´:´¯ x	o	o	1
Type aid(2Aia):	x x x x ´ x:´ x	13	8	58
Type aid(2A3a):	x x x x ´¯:´ x	o	o	1
Type aid(2Eia):	x x x x ´ x:x ´	o	o	1
Type aid(3A2):	x x x x ´¯ x:´ x	1	o	o
Type aid(3Ei):	x x x x ´ x x:´	o	1	2
Type aid(3E2):	x x x x ´¯ x:´	o	o	1
Type aid(3E*i):	x x x x ´ x x:x ´	o	o	1
Type aie(iAia):	x x x x x ´:x ´ x	o	o	17
Type aie(iA*ia):	x x x x x ´ x:x ´ x	2	o	17
Type aie(iDi):	x x x x x ´:´ x x	o	1	1
Type aie(2Aia):	x x x x x ´ x:´ x	3	6	31
Type aie(2A3a):	x x x x x ´¯:´ x	o	o	1
Type aie(2A3b):	x x x x x ´¯:◡ x	1	o	1
Type aie(3Ei):	x x x x x ´ x x:´	o	o	2
Type aie(3E*2):	x x x x x ´¯ x:x ´	1	o	o
Type aif(iAia):	x x x x x x ´:x ´ x	o	o	3
Type aif(iA*ia):	x x x x x x ´ x:x ´ x	1	3	3
Type aif(2Aia):	x x x x x x ´ x:´ x	1	4	9
Type aif(2Aib):	x x x x x x ´¯:◡ x	o	o	1
Type aig(iAia):	x x x x x x x ´:x ´ x	o	1	o
Type aig(iA*ia):	x x x x x x x ´ x:x ´ x	1	o	2
Type aig(2Aia):	x x x x x x x ´ x:´ x	o	1	o
Type aih(2Aia):	x x x x x x x x ´ x:´ x	o	o	1
Type iAia(iAia):	´|x ´:x ´ x	2	o	o
Type iAia(iA*ia):	´|x ´ x:x ´ x	5	o	3
Type iAia(iDi):	´|x ´:´ x x	1	o	o
Type iAia(2Aia):	´|x ´ x:´ x	22	2	7
Type iAia(2Eia):	´|x ´ x:x ´	o	o	1
Type iAia(3Ei):	´|x ´ x x:´	2	o	1

TABLE II (*cont.*)

		(1)	(2)	(3)
Type 1A1b(1A1a):	´|× × ´:× ´×	2	0	0
Type 1A1b(1A*1a):	´|× × ´×:× ´×	6	0	1
Type 1A1b(1D1):	´|× × ´:´× ×	2	0	0
Type 1A1b(2A1a):	´|× × ´×:´×	13	0	7
Type 1A1b(3E*2):	´|× × ´´×:× ´	1	0	1
Type 1A1c(1A1a):	´|× × × ´:× ´×	0	0	1
Type 1A1c(1A*1a):	´|× × × ´×:× ´×	2	0	0
Type 1A1c(2A1a):	´|× × × ´×:´×	3	0	0
Type 1A1d(1A*1a):	´|× × × × ´×:× ´×	1	0	0
Type 1A1e(1A*1a):	´|× × × × × ´×:× ´×	2	0	0
Type 1A*1a(1A1a):	´×|× ´:× ´×	5	0	0
Type 1A*1a(1A1b):	´×|× ´:× × ´×	1	0	0
Type 1A*1a(1A*1a):	´×|× ´×:× ´×	11	0	2
Type 1A*1a(2A1a):	´×|× ´×:´×	36	1	3
Type 1A*1a(2A3a):	´×|× ´´:´×	1	0	0
Type 1A*1a(3A1):	´×|× ´× ×:´×	1	0	0
Type 1A*1b(1A1a):	´×|× × ´:× ´×	3	0	0
Type 1A*1b(1A*1a):	´×|× × ´×:× ´×	7	0	0
Type 1A*1b(1D1):	´×|× × ´:´× ×	1	0	0
Type 1A*1b(2A1a):	´×|× × ´×:´×	26	0	2
Type 1A*1c(1A*1a):	´×|× × × ´×:× ´×	5	0	1
Type 1A*1c(1D1):	´×|× × × ´:´× ×	2	0	0
Type 1A*1c(2A1a):	´×|× × × ´×:´×	4	0	1
Type 1A*1c(2A3b):	´×|× × × ´´:◡×	1	0	0
Type 1A*1c(2E1a):	´×|× × × ´×:× ´	1	0	0
Type 1A*1d(1A1a):	´×|× × × × ´:× ´×	1	0	0
Type 1A*1e(1A*1a):	´×|× × × × × ´×:× ´×	1	0	0
Type 1A*1e(2A1a):	´×|× × × × × ´×:´×	1	0	0
Type 1A*3a(2A1a):	´´|× ´× ×:´×	5	0	0
Type 1A*3b(2A1a):	´´|× × ´×:´×	2	0	0
Type 2A1(1A1a):	´×|´:× ´×	5	0	0
Type 2A1(1A1b):	´×|´:× × ´×	1	0	0
Type 2A1(1A*1a):	´×|´×:× ´×	8	0	1
Type 2A1(1D1):	´×|´:´× ×	17	1	1
Type 2A1(2A1a):	´×|´×:´×	47	0	0
Type 2A1(2A1b):	´×|´´:◡×	1	0	0
Type 2A1(2A3b):	´×|´´:◡×	1	0	0
Type 2A1(2E1a):	´×|´×:× ´	1	0	0
Type 2A1(3E1):	´×|´× ×:´	2	0	0
Type 2A1(3E2):	´×|´´×:´	2	0	0
Type 2A1(3E*1):	´×|´× ×:× ´	1	0	0
Type 2A1(3E*2):	´×|´´×:× ´	1	0	0

TABLE II (*cont.*)

		(1)	(2)	(3)
Type 2A3(1A1a):	´´|´:×´×	1	0	1
Type 2A3(1A*1a):	´´|´×:×´×	4	0	0
Type 2A3(2A1a):	´´|´×:´×	12	0	0
Type 2B2–(2C1):	´|××´:´×	1	0	1
Type 2B2–(3B1):	´|××´×:´	1	0	0
Type 2B2a(2C1):	×´|××´:´×	1	0	0
Type 2C1–(2A1a):	´|´×:´×	1	0	0
Type 2C1a(1A*1a):	×´|´×:×´×	1	0	0
Type 2C1a(2A1a):	×´|´×:´×	5	0	0
Type 2C1a(2E1a):	×´|´×:´	1	0	0
Type 2C1b(1A1a):	××´|´:×´×	1	0	0
Type 2C1b(2A1a):	××´|´×:´×	0	0	1
Type 2C1c(2A1a):	×××´|´×:´×	1	0	0
Type 2C1c(3E1):	×××´|´××:´	0	0	1
Type 2E1a(2B1):	´×|×´:×´	1	0	0
Type 2E1a(2C1):	´×|×´:´×	3	0	0
Type 2E1a(3B1):	´×|×´×:´	1	0	0
Type 2E1a(3B2):	´×|×´××:´	2	0	0
Type 2E1b(2C1):	´×|××´:´×	2	0	0
Type 2E1b(3B1):	´×|××´×:´	1	0	0
Type 2E1d(3B1):	´×|××××´×:´	1	0	0
Type 2E2a(2C1):	´´|×´:´×	1	0	0
Type 2E2b(2C2):	´´|××´:◡×	1	0	0
Type 2E2b(3B1):	´´|××´×:´	1	0	0
Type 3A1(1A1a):	´××|´:´×	2	0	0
Type 3A2(2A1a):	´´×|´×:´×	1	0	0
Type 3A*1a(2A1a):	´××|×´×:´×	1	0	0
Type 3B1a(2C1):	×´×|´:´×	1	0	0
Type 3B*1b(2C1):	××´×|×´:´×	1	0	0
Type 3E1(2C1):	´××|´:´×	1	0	0
Remainders:		5	1	0
Double Hypermetric Verses:		13	0	0
	TOTAL	385	49	446

TABLE III

[This Table gives the distribution of all verses with anacrusis. The figures are included in, not additional to, the figures in Tables I and II.]

	(1)	(2)	(3)
Type 1A1a(2A1a):	2	0	0
Type 1A1b(1A1a):	1	0	0
Type 1A1b(1A*1a):	2	0	0
Type 1A*1a(1A1b):	1	0	0
Type 1A*1a(2A1a):	6	0	2
Type 1A*1b(1A1a):	1	0	0
Type 1A*1b(1A*1a):	4	0	0
Type 1A*1b(2A1a):	5	0	0
Type 1A*1c(2E1a):	1	0	0
Type 2A1(1A1a):	2	0	0
Type 2A1(1A*1a):	1	0	0
Type 2A1(1D1):	4	0	1
Type 2A1(2A1a):	8	0	0
Type 3A*1a(2A1a):	1	0	0
TOTAL	39	0	3

Verses with disyllabic anacrusis

	(1)	(2)	(3)
Type 1A*1a(2A1a):	1	0	0
Type 1A*1b(2A1a):	1	0	0
Type 2A1(2A1b):	1	0	0
TOTAL	3	0	0

TABLE IV

[This Table lists the twelve types of double hypermetric verse which actually occur. All are *a*-verses and all have double alliteration. Each occurs only once, except for the first, which occurs twice.]

Type 1A1a(3B1,2A1a):	´×:´|×´×:´×
Type 1A1b(3B1,2A1a):	´×:´|×××´×:´×
Type 2A1(1A1a,2A1a):	´:×´×|´×:´×
Type 2A1(2E1c,2E1a):	´×:×××´|´×:×´
Type 2A1(3E2,1A1a):	´´×:´|´:×´×
Type 2B1–(3B1,2C1):	´×:´|×´:´×
Type 2B2–(2B1,2B1):	´:×´|×××´:×´
Type 2C1–(2B2,1A*1a):	´:×××´|´×:×´××
Type 2C1–(3B1,2A1a):	´×:´|´×:´×
Type 2C1a(3B1,1D1):	×´×:´|´:´××
Type 2E1b(1A*1a,2C1):	´×:×´×|×××´:´×
Type 2E1b(3E1,2C1):	´×××:´|××´:´×

THE COMBINATION OF VERSES INTO LINES

1. All students of Old English metre have accepted as the basis of their analysis the verse or half-line; and their example has been followed in this study, except for a brief mention of the structure of the line in § 126. There can be no question that the analysis of the verse instead of the line is fully justified, since despite differences of frequency precisely the same metrical patterns are found in the a-verse and in the b-verse[1]; the line is made up of two sections of similar pattern, linked together by alliteration. However, this linking together of verses into pairs shows that their combination into lines is a reality of Old English metre, and it is therefore of some interest to examine the various ways in which they are combined. In particular, it is important to determine whether the combination of two verses is due solely to chance, or whether it is dictated by some sense of poetic propriety in the mind of the poet; since any such discernible tendency may throw further light on the vexed question of the aesthetics of Old English mtere.

2. All the material for this examination is readily available in the Index to the Scansion of *Beowulf*, and this material is summarized in Table I,[2] in which the a-verses are listed at the left-hand side, and the b-verses along the top; the number of combinations of each pair of types is to be found at the intersection of rows and columns, and totals to the rows and columns are given at the right-hand side and along the bottom. There is room only for a very summary classification, and for convenience the rare Type e, found only in the a-verse,[3] is included under Type a. If the combination of verses into lines were due solely to chance, the figures in each column would be

---

[1] A number of metrical patterns appear only in the a-verse, but these are all variants of patterns which appear also in the b-verse. The exclusion of verses of Type a from the b-verse is counterbalanced by their great frequency in this position among the hypermetric verses (§ 103).

[2] For obvious reasons it is impossible to take account of the 31 lines which include anomalous, defective or hypermetric verses: remainders, 183, 186, 1792, 2093, 2420, 2435, 2488, 2717, 2721, 2728, 3056; defective, 62, 2226-31; hypermetric, 1163-8, 1705-7, 2173, 2297, 2995-6. All the remaining 3151 lines are included.

[3] 262 e—1A*, 459 e—2A, 779 e—2A, 1514 e—1A*, 1728 e—2A, 2048 e—3B, 3027 e—1D.

K

TABLE I

	d	1A	1D	2A	2B	2C	2E	3B	3E	Total
a	30	26	68	74	15	65	8	33	44	363
d	7	162	31	221	1	38	4	21	15	500
1A	48	17	49	42	34	134	40	191	119	674
1D	22	111	18	124	14	46	4	48	14	401
2A	59	31	50	43	71	131	32	214	101	732
2B	1	16	2	12	1	4	0	0	2	38
2C	7	17	5	32	1	6	4	9	5	86
2E	1	1	1	2	1	3	1	5	2	17
3B	4	67	36	78	0	17	0	7	8	217
3E	6	32	10	32	10	17	4	10	2	123
Total	185	480	270	660	148	461	97	538	312	3151

proportional to the totals for the rows, and the figures in each row would be proportional to the totals for the columns; but the most cursory inspection shows that this is far from being so. So marked is the discrepancy that there is no call for elaborate statistical methods, and the simplest analysis will suffice.

3. The smallness of the figures in some of the squares makes it difficult to evaluate with any accuracy the extent to which the observed values diverge from chance expectation, and for this purpose it is convenient to compress the Table still further. There are two ways in which this compression can be carried out: it was pointed out in § 126 that metre comprises two distinct elements, *rhythm* and *phrasing*, and we can carry out the compression to illustrate one or the other. Table II gives the values for the five main types of rhythm, Type A (including a, 1A and 2A), Type B (including 2B and 3B), Type C (including only 2C), Type D (including d and 1D), and Type E (including e, 2E and 3E). Table III gives the number of combinations of each pair of types to be expected as the result of pure chance: these values are easily calculated from the totals for rows and columns. Table IV gives the difference between the observed and expected values, expressed as percentages of the expected values: thus a positive figure implies that a given

TABLE II

	A	B	C	D	E	Total
A	228	557	330	303	344	1762
B	173	8	21	43	10	255
C	49	10	6	12	9	86
D	618	84	84	78	37	901
E	72	27	20	19	9	147
Total	1140	686	461	455	409	3151

combination occurs *more* frequently than can be explained by chance, a negative figure that it occurs *less* frequently.

TABLE III

	A	B	C	D	E
A	638	384	258	255	229
B	92	55	37	37	33
C	31	19	13	12	11
D	326	196	132	130	117
E	53	32	21	21	19

TABLE IV

	A	B	C	D	E
A	−64	+45	+28	+19	+50
B	+88	−85	−43	+16	−70
C	+58	−47	−54	0	−18
D	+90	−57	−36	−40	−68
E	+36	−16	−5	−10	−53

4. The interest of Table IV is considerable, since (apart from the small positive value + 16 for the combination B-D) all the positive values are for combinations including one, and only one, verse of Type A, either in the *a*-verse or in the *b*-verse.[1] With the same exception, all the negative values are for combinations of two verses of Type A, or of two verses not of Type A. It follows that the poet tends, consciously or unconsciously, to combine a verse of Type A with a verse of a different type, to an extent far beyond what can be accounted for by chance. This Table provides clear statistical confirmation of the conjecture made in § 125, that the norm of Old English metre is the falling rhythm of Type A, and that the variety of the metre is achieved by variations from this norm. The tendency to include one verse of Type A in as many lines as possible ensures that the norm shall not be obscured by the variations[2]; and the avoidance of the combination of two verses of Type A, though a necessary concomitant of the previous tendency, also serves to ensure variety.

5. If instead of illustrating rhythm we compress Table I so as to illustrate the phrasing of the verse, we obtain quite different results. The four main varieties of phrasing, which depend on the position of the cæsura, are conveniently displayed in § 91, and the four columns there shown may be designated Groups 0, 1, 2 and 3, Group 0 standing for those verses in which the first stress is suppressed, so that there is no cæsura. Table V gives the values for these four groups, Group 0 (including Types a, d and e), Group 1 (including Types 1A and 1D), Group 2 (including Types 2A, 2B, 2C and 2E), and Group 3 (including Types 3B and 3E). Table VI gives

---

[1] It must be emphasized that this peculiarity has nothing to do with the intrinsically greater frequency of Type A (56 per cent of *a*-verses, 36 per cent of *b*-verses), which has been allowed for in the calculations.

[2] If the combination of verses into lines were due to mere chance, the number of lines including at least one verse of Type A would be 72 per cent; in fact no less than 85 per cent of the lines in *Beowulf* include at least one verse of Type A.

the number of combinations of each pair of groups to be expected as the result of pure chance; as before, these values are calculated from the totals for rows and columns. Table VII gives the differences between the observed and expected values, expressed as percentages of the expected values.

TABLE V

	0	1	2	3	Total
0	37	287	426	113	863
1	70	195	438	372	1075
2	68	123	344	338	873
3	10	145	158	27	340
Total	185	750	1366	850	3151

6. Once again the results are interesting, for the distribution of positive and negative values is exactly symmetrical. If we consider Groups 0 and 3 as extreme groups, and Groups 1 and 2 as central groups, we find that without exception all the positive values are for combinations of extreme with central groups, and all the negative values are for combinations of extreme with extreme or central with

TABLE VI

	0	1	2	3
0	51	205	374	233
1	63	256	466	290
2	51	208	379	235
3	20	81	147	92

TABLE VII

	0	1	2	3
0	− 27	+40	+14	− 52
1	+11	− 24	− 6	+28
2	+33	− 41	− 9	+44
3	− 50	+79	+ 7	− 71

central groups. The poet tends, either consciously or unconsciously, to seek variety of phrasing by avoiding lines in which both the verses are of the extreme or of the central groups. This distinction cuts right across the distinction to which attention was called in § 126 between on the one hand Groups 0 and 1, which together account for 65 per cent of the *a*-verses, and on the other hand Groups 2 and 3, which together account for 70 per cent of the *b*-verses.

7. To sum up, the analysis of the combinations of pairs of verses into lines reveals that the combinations are not the result of mere chance. The poet combines his pairs of verses in such a way as to achieve greater variety, both of rhythm and of phrasing, than chance would dictate; and at the same time to ensure that the falling rhythm of Type A, the norm of Old English metre, is maintained in as many lines as possible.

INDEX TO THE SCANSION OF *BEOWULF*

1	d3b	d3a	41	2A1a	2C1b	81	1A1a	1D1
2	1D1	1A1a	42	3B1a	1A1a	82	1A2a	3E2
3	d1b	2A1a	43	a1e	2A1a	83	2A1a	3B*1c
4	2C1a	2A1a	44	1A1	2C2a	84	d3b	2A1
5	2A1a	3E*2	45	d2d	1A1a	85	d2b	2A1a
6	2A1a	3B1b	46	1A*1b	1D1	86	d5b	2A1
7	2A1a	3B*1b	47	a1e	1D1	87	1A*1a	3B1c
8	1A1b	3E2	48	1A1b	2C2b	88	3B*1b	1A1a
9	a1c	1D1	49	1A*1a	2C2b	89	1A*1a	3B1b
10	d2b	2A1a	50	3E1	1A1a	90	1D3	1A*1b
11	2A1a	2C2b	51	1A*1a	1D1	91	2A1a	2A1a
12	3B1a	2A1a	52	1A1b	3B*1b	92	d2c	2A1a
13	1A1a	2C1b	53	a1c	1D1	93	3E2	1A1a
14	1A*1a	3E*2	54	1D3	2A1a	94	1D*2	1A*1a
15	2C2b	2A1	55	1A*1a	3E2	95	1A*1a	1D1
16	2A1a	d2b	56	1A*1a	2B1c	96	d1b	2A1a
17	2A1a	3E*2	57	1D1	1A1b	97	1A1a	2E2a
18	1A*1a	3E2	58	1A2a	1D1	98	1A*1a	2C1c
19	2A1a	3E1	59	3B1a	1A1	99	d3b	2A1a
20	2C2b	1A*1a	60	2C1a	2A1a	100	2A1	2B1b
21	1D2	2C1a	61	1A*1a	3B1a	101	2A1a	1A1a
22	a1d	1A1a	62	def.	3B1a	102	3B1b	2A1a
23	1A1	2C2b	63	1D1	1A1	103	1D*3	3B1b
24	1A*1a	3E2	64	d1b	2A3b	104	1A1a	3E2
25	3B*1a	1A1a	65	2A2	d2c	105	3E2	2A1a
26	2B1b	d2b	66	2A1a	2B1c	106	a1c	2C1a
27	2A3a	2C1a	67	2A3b	2B1b	107	2C1a	2B1b
28	a1e	2C1a	68	d3a	2A1a	108	2A1a	3B1c
29	1A*1a	3B1b	69	2A3b	1A1a	109	a1f	2B1a
30	3B1b	1D1	70	3B1b	1A*1a	110	1A1b	3E2
31	1D3	2A1a	71	a1c	1A1a	111	d1b	1A*1a
32	3B1b	2A1	72	1A*1a	2C1a	112	1A*1a	d1a
33	1A*2	3E1	73	d3b	2C1a	113	d1b	2C1b
34	3B1a	2A1a	74	3B*1b	1A1a	114	2A1a	2B1c
35	2A1a	2C2a	75	2A1a	d5c	115	d1c	2B1b
36	1A*1a	3B1b	76	2A3a	3B*1b	116	2A1a	d3b
37	d3a	1A*1a	77	1A*1a	d3c	117	d2b	2C1a
38	d1d	1A1a	78	3E2	2C2b	118	a1c	3E*1
39	2A1	d2a	79	3B*1c	2A1a	119	1A1b	1A*1a
40	1A*1a	3B1b	80	2B2a	2A1a	120	2A1b	1D1

139

121	1A1a	3E2	169	1A*1a	2C1b
122	1A1a	3B*1b	170	2C2b	1D1
123	2A1a	2E2a	171	2A1a	2E2a
124	2A1a	2C2a	172	1A*1a	1D1
125	d2c	2A1a	173	d2a	2A1a
126	a1c	d2a	174	d3a	d1b
127	2A2	1D1	175	1A*1b	d3a
128	a1d	2E2a	176	1D1	2A1a
129	1D5	2A1a	177	d3b	1A*1a
130	2A1a	3E1	178	d2a	2C2b
131	2A2	3E2	179	3E1	1A*1a
132	a1d	1D1	180	d3a	1A1b
133	2A1a	2B1c	181	2A1a	3B1d
134	1A1a	3B1b	182	3B1d	1A*1a
135	3B1b	1A1a	183	2A1a	*rem.*
136	2A3a	2C2b	184	3B1a	1A*1a
137	1A*1a	2B1b	185	3B1a	1A*1a
138	d2b	3B1b	186	1A*1a	*rem.*
139	d1a	2A1a	187	d3b	2A1a
140	1A1b	3B1c	188	2C1b	1D1
141	1D1	2A1a	189	d3b	1D1
142	3E2	2A3a	190	3E1	2C2c
143	1A1a	3B*1b	191	1A1a	2B1c
144	d1a	3B1b	192	1A1a	3B*1c
145	1A*1a	3B1b	193	2A4	3E2
146	2A1a	2C2b	194	2B1b	3E1
147	3E2	1A1a	195	1A1a	2A1a
148	1D1	1A*1a	196	d2b	2A1a
149	2A1a	3B1b	197	2C2a	2A1a
150	2A1a	3E1	198	1A*1a	d3b
151	2A1a	3B1b	199	1A*1a	d3b
152	1A*1a	3E2	200	d2b	2A1a
153	1A*1a	1D1	201	2A1a	3B1c
154	3E1	1A*1a	202	3B1b	2A1a
155	3B1a	2A1a	203	2A1a	2C1c
156	2A3a	1D1	204	1D*2	1D1
157	a1d	2A1a	205	a1c	2A1a
158	2A1a	2C1a	206	1A*1a	d1d
159	d1b	3E1	207	2A1a	3E1
160	1D3	1A*1a	208	2A3a	1D1
161	1A*1a	3E1	209	3E2	1*A*1
162	2A1a	1A1a	210	1D4	1A1b
163	d2b	2A1a	211	1A1b	2A1a
164	2C1a	1D2	212	2C2a	2A1a
165	1D2	1A1a	213	1A1a	2A1a
166	2A1a	1D1	214	2C2a	2A1a
167	3E2	2A1a	215	2A3a	2A3b
168	a2d	2A1a	216	1A2a	1D1

217	a2e	1A*1a
218	1D5	1A*1a
219	a1c	2A1a
220	2*A*1	2C1a
221	d1b	1A1a
222	2A3a	2A1a
223	1D*2	2C2b
224	1A*1a	2C2b
225	2A1a	2C2a
226	2A3a	2A1a
227	1*A*1	1D1
228	d2c	2A1a
229	3B*1b	1D1
230	d2b	2A1a
231	1A1b	2A1a
232	2A3a	3B1b
233	1*A*1	2C1b
234	a1e	2A1a
235	1D1	2A1a
236	2A3a	3E2
237	3B1a	1D1
238	2A1a	3B1b
239	d2b	2A1a
240	1A1b	3B1b
241	2*A*1	3E2
242	2C2b	2A1a
243	d2a	1A*1a
244	d1b	1A1a
245	1D1	d5b
246	1D1	1A*1a
247	1A*1a	3B*1c
248	1A*1b	3B1c
249	1A1a	d3b
250	1A*1a	2C1d
251	2A1a	3B1b
252	2A3b	2C2b
253	1D1	2C2a
254	2A1a	d2b
255	1D1	1A*1a
256	3E*1	1A1a
257	d1b	2C1d
258	d1b	1D1
259	2A1a	2E2a
260	d2b	2A1a
261	d1a	1*A*1
262	e1b	1A*1a
263	1D*3	2A1a
264	3B1b	2C1c

#			#			#		
265	1A1a	3B*1b	313	1A1a	2C1c	361	a1d	2A1a
266	2A1a	1A*1a	314	2A1a	3E2	362	3B*1b	2A1a
267	3B1b	2A1a	315	1A1a	3E2	363	d1b	2*A*1
268	1D1	2A1a	316	a1d	1D1	364	2A1a	3B1a
269	1*A*1	3B1c	317	d3a	1A*1a	365	3B1b	2C1a
270	a1e	1D1	318	1A*1a	2C1b	366	2A1a	3B*1c
271	2A1a	3B1c	319	2C2a	2A1a	367	d3b	2A3a
272	1A1b	2B2a	320	1A2a	1D1	368	d4b	2A1a
273	d1b	2A1a	321	1A1a	3E2	369	1A*1a	3B1c
274	d1b	2A1a	322	1D3	3E2	370	d2b	1D1
275	1D*3	2A1a	323	1A1a	2C1c	371	2A1a	1D1
276	1A*1a	3E1	324	d2c	2A1a	372	a1c	1D1
277	1A*2	3B1b	325	1D*2	2A1a	373	d3b	2A1a
278	3B1a	1A1a	326	1D*2	3B1b	374	2B1b	2A1a
279	2B1b	1A1b	327	a1d	2A1a	375	2A1a	3B1b
280	d1b	2A1a	328	2A3a	2A1a	376	1D3	3B1b
281	2A1a	2A3b	329	3E2	1A1a	377	3B1b	1D1
282	d2b	2A1a	330	2A4	d5b	378	d2b	2A1a
283	2C1b	2*A*1	331	1A*1a	2C2b	379	1A1a	d1b
284	2A3b	2C2b	332	2*A*1	3B1b	380	2A2	d3b
285	d3a	2A1a	333	3B1b	2A1a	381	2A3a	3B1b
286	1D1	3B1b	334	2A1a	d2a	382	d3a	1A1a
287	2A1a	3E1	335	3E2	d1b	383	d3a	2C1b
288	1D3	2C2a	336	1A1a	d2c	384	3B1a	3B1b
289	1A*1a	2C1b	337	3B1a	2*A*1	385	d3b	2A1a
290	a1c	2C2c	338	a1e	d2c	386	a1c	2C1a
291	1D1	2C2c	339	d2b	2A1a	387	1D6	1A1a
292	1A*1b	d1b	340	d5b	1D1	388	a1e	d1c
293	d2c	2A1a	341	1D5	3E2	389	2A1a	2C1b
294	3B*1a	1D1	342	1A1b	d1b	390	2A3b	3E*2
295	1D1	1A1a	343	1*A*1	2E1b	391	a1b	3E2
296	2A1a	2C2b	344	a1d	1D1	392	1D*3	3B1d
297	d2b	2A1a	345	2A1a	1D1	393	a1c	d2b
298	1D5	d2a	346	2A1a	3B1d	394	1D1	1D1
299	1D1	3B1b	347	a1e	2A1a	395	a1d	d4c
300	d5c	1A1a	348	2A1a	3B1b	396	d2b	2E1a
301	a1a	3E2	349	d3b	1A*1a	397	d5b	1A1a
302	1A*1a	3E2	350	1A1a	2C1b	398	1D2	1A*1a
303	3B1a	2A3b	351	1D1	2A1a	399	a1d	2C2c
304	d2b	2C1a	352	2A1a	3B1b	400	1D*5	2C2b
305	1A2a	3E2	353	2A1a	3B1a	401	2A3a	3B*1c
306	2A3a	1D1	354	d1c	1A*1a	402	1A*1a	1D1
307	1A1a	2C1c	355	a1c	2C1a	403	3B1b	2A3a
308	1A*2	2C1a	356	d1b	3B1a	404	1A1a	3B*1c
309	d2b	1D1	357	1A1a	3B*1b	405	2A1a	3B1b
310	1A*1b	3B1c	358	1D*5	3B*1c	406	2A3b	1D1
311	1A*1a	3B1b	359	2A1a	3B1c	407	3B1b	d1b
312	d5b	1D1	360	2A1a	d2b	408	1A2a	3B1c

409	1A*1a	3B1b	457	3B1b	2A3a	505	1A*1b	2C1ł
410	d5c	3E1	458	d1b	2A1a	506	a1c	2C1c
411	1D*2	2C1b	459	e1c	2A1a	507	3B1a	2C2a
412	1D1	1A*1a	460	d1b	d3a	508	a1c	1D1
413	1A*1a	d5b	461	d1a	3B1c	509	d2b	2C2a
414	3B1b	2C1a	462	d2a	1A*1a	510	2A1a	3B1b
415	a1d	2A1a	463	a1d	3E3	511	2B1a	2C1a
416	d1a	2A1a	464	3B*1b	1D1	512	3E1	2C1c
417	2A1a	2C1b	465	3B1b	2A1a	513	d5b	2A1a
418	3B1c	2A1a	466	3B1b	2A1a	514	1D*2	2A1a
419	1A*1b	3B1c	467	2A3a	3B1b	515	1A1b	3E2
420	1A1a	3B*1b	468	3B1a	1D1	516	2A1a	3B1b
421	1D*5	3B1b	469	1D1	3B*1b	517	2A3a	2B2c
422	2A1a	3E2	470	a1c	1D1	518	3B1b	d5d
423	1D5	1D1	471	d1c	3B1b	519	d1a	2E2a
424	2C2a	3B1c	472	2A1a	3B1b	520	a1d	2A1a
425	d1b	1A*1a	473	1A1c	2C1a	521	1A1a	1D1
426	1A1a	2C1a	474	2A1a	2C2b	522	2A3a	2C1b
427	1D1	2A1a	475	1A*1a	d2b	523	1A1a	2E2a
428	1D1	2A1a	476	3E*2	d3b	524	1D1	1A*1a
429	a1e	3E1	477	2E2a	2B1a	525	3B*1b	1A*1a
430	2A3a	3B1c	478	3B1a	3E2	526	d2b	2C1a
431	a1d	3B*1c	479	d3b	1A*1a	527	2A1a	3B1b
432	3B1a	1D1	480	d1c	2A1a	528	3E2	2A1a
433	a1e	d1b	481	d2b	2*A*1	529	2A1a	1D1
434	d2b	1A*1a	482	d3c	2A1a	530	2C2b	2A3a
435	a1e	3B1b	483	2A1a	2C1a	531	2A1a	2C1a
436	1D2	2A1a	484	a2d	d5a	532	1A*1b	1A1a
437	2C2b	3B1b	485	2A4	2C1b	533	d2b	2A1a
438	1A*3	3B1c	486	d3a	1A*1a	534	1A*1a	3B1d
439	1A1a	2C2b	487	1D2	3B*1c	535	a1c	1*D*1
440	1A1a	3B1b	488	2A1a	2B1b	536	d1b	3B*1b
441	2A1a	2C2a	489	a1d	2C2b	537	d2a	3B1c
442	a1d	3B1b	490	2A3a	2C1b	538	2A1a	3B1c
443	d3b	2A1a	491	d2b	1A1a	539	2C2b	2C1c
444	1D1	2C2b	492	d3a	1A1a	540	1A1a	d2c
445	1D1	3B1b	493	d2a	2A1a	541	2A1a	2B1b
446	2A1a	3B1c	494	2A1a	3E*2	542	3E2	2A1a
447	2A1a	2C2b	495	3B1c	1D2	543	1A1a	2C1c
448	1D5	2A1a	496	1D*3	3E2	544	a1c	2C1a
449	1D1	1*D*1	497	1A*1a	3B1b	545	3E2	2B1c
450	1D*3	3B*1c	498	1D1	1A1a	546	1D1	2A1a
451	2A1a	1D1	499	2A1a	3E1	547	3E1	d5a
452	d1b	2C2b	500	3B1b	1D1	548	2E2a	1A1b
453	3E2	2C2c	501	1D2	3B2b	549	d2a	1A1a
454	2A1a	3B1b	502	2A2	1D1	550	a1c	3E2
455	3E*1	2B2b	503	a1e	3B1c	551	1D3	1A*1a
456	2A1a	1D1	504	3B*1b	2*A*1	552	2A3a	3B1a

553	1A*1a 3B1b	601	d3a 3B1c	649	d1b 1A1b
554	1D3 2A1a	602	1A1a 3E1	650	3E*2 2A1a
555	1A1a 3B1c	603	1A*1a 2E2b	651	1A1b 2E2a
556	d1b 1A*1a	604	2C1a d5b	652	3B1a 1D1
557	2A1 2E2a	605	3B1b 2A1a	653	2A1a 2B1b
558	2A2 3B1a	606	1D*3 2A1a	654	3E*2 2B1b
559	a1c 1A1	607	a1c 2A1a	655	3B1c 1A1a
560	2A1a d3b	608	1A*4 1A*1a	656	2B1a 2A1a
561	2A1a 3B1c	609	1D1 d1d	657	2A3b 2C1b
562	a1d 2C1a	610	2A1a 3E*2	658	2E2b 2A1a
563	1A1 2C1b	611	3B1b 1D1	659	2C1a 3E2
564	1A*1a 3E2	612	1A1b 3B1b	660	1A1a 3B1c
565	d1b 2A1a	613	1D1 1A*1a	661	d5c 1A*1a
566	d2a 2A1a	614	1D*3 1A1a	662	3B*1b 3B*1b
567	1A*1a 3B1a	615	3B1b 1A1a	663	1D1 1A1a
568	3B1a 1D1	616	1D*3 2A1	664	d3b 2A1a
569	1A*1a 3E2	617	a1c d3c	665	1A1b d2b
570	1D3 1D1	618	2A1a 2B1b	666	1A*1a 1A1a
571	d2b 2C1a	619	1A*2 2A3b	667	2E2a 3E*2
572	2A1a 2A3b	620	3B1a 1D1	668	2C2a 2E2a
573	3E1 3B1c	621	1A*1a 1D1	669	3B1b 2A1a
574	a1e 3B*1c	622	2A3a 2B1b	670	2A1a 2A1a
575	2A1a 2B1c	623	d1b 3E3	671	2C2c 2A1
576	3B1b 2A1a	624	1A*1a 2E2a	672	1A1a 3B1c
577	d2b 2A1a	625	1D*5 1D1	673	3E1 2A1
578	3B1d 1A*1a	626	2A1a 3B*1e	674	3B1b 2A1
579	2A1a 2B1b	627	d1c 1A1a	675	a1d 3E2
580	1A1b 3B1a	628	2A1a 2B1b	676	2A1a 2C2c
581	1D1 2B1b	629	2A3b d1a	677	d2d 2A1a
582	1D*2 2A1a	630	d1b 1A*1a	678	1A1 2C2b
583	2A1a 3E2	631	2A1a 1D1	679	a1e 2A1a
584	d2a 2C1b	632	a1b 2B1c	680	1A*1a 2C2b
585	d1a 1A1a	633	2E2a 3B*1c	681	a1d 2C1d
586	2A1a 2C1c	634	d1b 2A1a	682	1A1a 2C1c
587	a1d 2C1a	635	1A*1a 2C1c	683	1A1 2C2c
588	2A1 3B1c	636	3E2 3B1b	684	1A*1b 3B1c
589	2A1a 2C2b	637	2A1a d5b	685	1A1b 3B1c
590	a1e 1D1	638	d2c 1A*1a	686	3B1b 2A1a
591	3B*1c 1A1a	639	2B1a 1D1	687	2A1a 2C1a
592	1D1 2A1a	640	2A3a d3b	688	a2e 3E*2
593	1A*1a 2C1b	641	2A2 2C1c	689	1D*1 2C2c
594	1A2a 2C2b	642	2B1b 1A*1a	690	2A2 3E*2
595	a1e 3B*1c	643	2A3b 1A1a	691	a1d 2C1b
596	1D*3 2A1a	644	3E2 d1b	692	1D3 1A*1a
597	1A*1a 1D1	645	1D1 2A1a	693	1A2b 3B1c
598	1D2 2A1a	646	2A1 d1c	694	a1e 2C1d
599	2A1a 2C2b	647	d3b 1A*1a	695	d3b 2E2a
600	1A1a 1A*1a	648	3B1c 2C1a	696	2A1a 3B*1b

697	3E*2	2A1a	745	1A1a	2E2a	793	d3b	2A1a
698	1A*1a	2C2b	746	a1c	1D1	794	2A1a	3B1b
699	3B1a	1A*1b	747	1A1a	2E1a	795	1D1	2A1a
700	2A1a	1A1b	748	1A1a	2C2b	796	d2b	1D1
701	3B1a	2A1a	749	2A1	2B1b	797	2A1a	3B1b
702	1D5	3B1b	750	a1d	2A1a	798	a1c	2C2c
703	1D*2	2A1a	751	a1c	2A1	799	1D1	2A1
704	d3b	2A1a	752	2A1a	3B1a	800	3B*1b	2A1a
705	1A*1b	3B1b	753	2A3a	3B1b	801	2A1a	d3b
706	a1c	2C1a	754	1A1a	2C1c	802	1A*1b	3E1
707	d3a	2C1b	755	1A1b	3B1c	803	3E2	2A1a
708	d1b	1A*1a	756	3B*1b	3B1c	804	d2b	2C1a
709	1D5	1A*1a	757	d3d	1A1a	805	1A*1a	d4c
710	a1c	d3b	758	a1e	1D1	806	2C2a	2A1a
711	2A1a	3E2	759	2A1	2E1a	807	2A1a	d5b
712	d3c	2A1a	760	3B*1b	2A1a	808	3B*1a	1D1
713	1A*1a	2B1a	761	1A1a	3E2	809	a1c	2C1b
714	1A1b	d3d	762	a1c	3B1b	810	2A1a	2A1a
715	2A3a	2A1a	763	1A*1a	2C2b	811	1A*1a	2B1b
716	2A1a	3B1c	764	1A2a	3B*1c	812	d3c	2A1a
717	d1b	1A1a	765	2C1a	3B1b	813	a1d	1D1
718	d3d	1A1a	766	d3b	3B*1a	814	1A*1a	2C1b
719	2A1a	3E2	767	2A3a	3E2	815	3E1	2E2a
720	a1c	1D1	768	1D1	1A*1a	816	1D1	3B1b
721	1A*1a	3E*2	769	1D*2	1A*1b	817	2A3b	1A*1a
722	3E2	3B*1e	770	1D*2	1D1	818	1D*3	3E1
723	d2c	3B1c	771	2C2b	d3b	819	2A3a	2C2b
724	2A1a	2B2–	772	1D*2	3B*1c	820	2A3a	d3b
725	3B1a	1D1	773	2A2	3B1c	821	3B1b	1A*1a
726	1D*5	3B1b	774	1A*1a	2A1	822	3B1b	1A*1a
727	1A*1a	1D1	775	3E*2	3B*1b	823	2A2	3E2
728	a1d	2A1a	776	2A3b	1A*1a	824	d2c	1A*1a
729	1D6	1A1a	777	1A*1a	2C1b	825	a1d	3B1c
730	3E2	2B1b	778	3B1b	1D1	826	1A2a	1D1
731	a1e	2C1b	779	e1e	2A1a	827	1A1a	3E*2
732	1D1	1A*1a	780	1A*2	2C1a	828	2A1	d3b
733	1A1a	3B1c	781	1A*1a	3B1b	829	3E1	1A1a
734	3E2	2B1c	782	1A*1a	2E2a	830	d1b	1A*1a
735	2C1c	2A1a	783	1A*1a	3E3	831	2A1	2C2b
736	1A*2	2E2a	784	2A1a	1A*1a	832	d2b	2A1a
737	1D1	d3b	785	a1d	1A1a	833	1D1	2C2b
738	d3b	2C1a	786	2A3b	1D1	834	d5b	1A1a
739	d1c	2A1a	787	3E1	1D1	835	1A1a	2C2b
740	2C2c	2A1a	788	2A1a	2A3a	836	2A1a	3B1b
741	3E1	1D1	789	3B1b	2A1a	837	a1c	1A*1a
742	1D3	3E2	790	2C2a	2A1a	838	2A3b	3E1
743	3E2	2A1a	791	3B1b	2A1a	839	1D*3	1A*1a
744	1D1	1A1a	792	d3b	1A*1a	840	d3a	1D1

841	2A1a	d4b	889	2A1a	3B1c	937	a1d	d5b
842	2A1a	2A1a	890	a1d	2B1b	938	1D*4	1A*1a
843	d1c	1D1	891	3E1	3B*1c	939	1A*1a	2C2a
844	d5b	2C2a	892	2A1a	3E2	940	3B1a	1A1a
845	2E1b	3B1a	893	d1b	1A*1a	941	a1b	1A1a
846	1A*1b	3E2	894	d2b	2A1a	942	1A*1a	3B1b
847	a1c	1D1	895	2A1a	2E2a	943	a1d	2C1c
848	1D6	1A1a	896	1A2a	2A1a	944	d2b	2C2b
849	2A1a	3E2	897	2A1a	2E2a	945	d3c	2A1a
850	3E2	3B1b	898	d1b	2A1a	946	1*A*1	3B1b
851	d3a	1A1a	899	d2b	3E1	947	2C1-	2C1b
852	2A1a	2B1b	900	2*A*1	2B1b	948	1A*1a	2C2a
853	2B1b	1*A*1	901	d1b	1D1	949	2A1a	3B2c
854	2C2b	d2a	902	1A1a	3B1b	950	2A1a	2C1c
855	2C1a	2A1a	903	3B*1a	1A1a	951	a1d	1D1
856	1A*1a	d1b	904	1A*1a	d2b	952	1D1	2A1a
857	2A1a	2E2a	905	1A*1a	3B1b	953	1A*1a	2C2b
858	2B1b	2C1a	906	1D*1	d3a	954	2E1a	2C2b
859	d5b	2A1a	907	2B1b	2A1a	955	1A*1a	3E1
860	3B*1b	2A1a	908	3E2	2A3b	956	1A*1a	2C2c
861	1D1	2A1a	909	3B1c	1A*1a	957	2A1a	1D1
862	d2d	1A1a	910	3B1b	2C1a	958	d5b	2A1a
863	2A1a	2C2c	911	3E*2	1A1a	959	2A1a	1A*1a
864	1D*2	2A1a	912	1A2a	2A1a	960	1D1	2A1a
865	2C2b	2A1a	913	1D1	3B1b	961	a1d	2C1a
866	d3b	2A1a	914	1D1	2A1a	962	1A1a	1D1
867	2A1a	3B1b	915	1A*1a	2B1b	963	d1c	2A1a
868	1D3	1A*1a	916	d1b	2A1a	964	d2a	2A1a
869	d1b	1*A*1	917	2A1a	d5b	965	d3c	2A1a
870	1A1a	3E2	918	1A1a	2C2b	966	1D*3	2C2c
871	1A*1a	2E2a	919	1D1	2B1a	967	a1d	2C1a
872	1D1	2A1a	920	3E2	2C2b	968	1A*1a	3B*1a
873	2C2b	1A1a	921	d2a	3E2	969	1*A*1	d1b
874	2A1a	2E1a	922	2A2	2C1a	970	1A1a	3B*1e
875	d1c	2A1a	923	1A*1a	2B1b	971	d3a	1D1
876	2*A*1	3E1	924	3E2	2A1a	972	1A1a	3B*1b
877	3E*1	2A1a	925	2A1a	3B1b	973	2A1b	1A*1a
878	3B1c	1A*1a	926	1A1a	3B1b	974	2C2b	1*A*1
879	1A*1a	3B*1b	927	2A1a	3B1a	975	1A*1a	2C2c
880	3B1c	2A1a	928	d1b	3E2	976	d3a	1A*1a
881	2E1a	2C1b	929	1A*1a	3B*1c	977	2A1a	3B1b
882	3B*1a	1*A*1	930	1A*1a	2C1b	978	1D5	2A1a
883	d1b	2A1a	931	1A*1b	2A1a	979	2C2b	2A1a
884	1A*1a	3E*1	932	d1b	3B2b	980	3B1b	1D1
885	d3b	1D1	933	1A*1a	3B1a	981	d2a	1*A*1
886	3B1b	1A1a	934	1A*1a	3B1b	982	d1b	2A1a
887	2A1a	3B1c	935	2A1a	3E2	983	3B1b	1D1
888	3E1	1A*1a	936	1D3	1A*1a	984	2A1a	3E2

985	3E*2	1A*1a	1033	2A3a	d3b	1081	2A1a	2C1b
986	1D*3	2*A*1	1034	2C2a	2A1a	1082	a1c	d3b
987	1A*1	2E1a	1035	3B1b	2A1a	1083	1D1	1A1a
988	3B1b	2A1a	1036	2*A*1	2C1a	1084	d2b	1A*1a
989	2A2	d1b	1037	1A1b	3B1b	1085	2A1a	3B1d
990	1D*2	2C1a	1038	1D5	1A*1a	1086	3B1c	1A1a
991	3B1b	1D1	1039	d5b	1*D*1	1087	1A*2	3B*1b
992	1A*1a	3E2	1040	3B*1b	1D1	1088	3B1a	2A1a
993	1A1a	d3b	1041	2A1a	3B1c	1089	d2b	3E1
994	2A3a	2A3b	1042	3E2	2C1b	1090	1A*1a	1D1
995	1A1b	3E2	1043	d1b	1A*1a	1091	3E1	2A1a
996	1A*1a	2C2	1044	1D1	2E1a	1092	a1c	1*A*1
997	3B1b	2C1a	1045	1A*1a	2C1c	1093	2A1a	3B1b
998	1D1	3E2	1046	d1a	2A1a	1094	d3a	2A1a
999	1A*1a	3E*2	1047	2A3a	3E2	1095	a1c	2C1a
1000	2A1a	d1b	1048	1A*1a	2C1d	1096	1D*2	1D1
1001	3E2	2B1a	1049	3B1b	1A1b	1097	1D*1	1A*1a
1002	1D*1	3B1b	1050	d1b	2A1a	1098	d2c	2A1a
1003	d1b	1A*1b	1051	d1d	3E2	1099	2A1a	3B1b
1004	3B1b	1*D*1	1052	d2c	1A*1a	1100	1A*1a	1A*1a
1005	1A*1a	2A1a	1053	2*A*1	3B1c	1101	d5b	1A*1a
1006	1*D*1	2A1a	1054	1A*1a	3B1c	1102	d3d	1D1
1007	d3b	3E2	1055	1A*1a	2C1d	1103	2*A*1	3B1d
1008	1A1b	2B1b	1056	3B1c	1A1a	1104	3B1c	2A1a
1009	3B1b	3E1	1057	3B1b	3E2	1105	d3a	2A1a
1010	2C2b	2A1a	1058	2A1a	2C1a	1106	3B1c	2A1a
1011	a1f	2A1a	1059	a1c	2A1a	1107	1A1b	3B1a
1012	d3c	1A1a	1060	2A2	1A1b	1108	1A1a	1D1
1013	a1d	1D1	1061	1A*1a	3B1b	1109	1D2	2C2b
1014	1A*1a	1A*1a	1062	d3c	2A1a	1110	3B1b	1*A*1
1015	2A3b	2A1a	1063	2B1b	1A1a	1111	2A3a	2A3a
1016	1*D*1	2B1a	1064	d1b	2*A*1	1112	1D5	2A3b
1017	1A*1a	3E2	1065	2A3a	2A3b	1113	1A*1a	2C1c
1018	1A*1a	d3b	1066	d3b	3E1	1114	d1b	2C1a
1019	1D1	2A1a	1067	d2b	2A1a	1115	3B1b	1A*1a
1020	d1c	1D1	1068	2A1a	2B1c	1116	2A3a	2C1b
1021	1D1	1A*1a	1069	1D1	1D1	1117	1A*1a	1D1
1022	1D5	1A1a	1070	d3a	2A1a	1118	2A1a	2E2a
1023	1D*5	1A*1a	1071	d1c	2A1a	1119	1A1a	3E2
1024	2C2c	2E1a	1072	2A1a	3E1	1120	1A*1a	2A1a
1025	1A1a	d2d	1073	2C1a	d3b	1121	2A3a	2B1b
1026	d1a	2A1a	1074	1A*1a	2C2c	1122	2A3a	3E*2
1027	d1d	2A1a	1075	2A1a	3B1b	1123	2A1a	2B1d
1028	1A*1a	3E2	1076	d1b	2A1a	1124	2A1a	2C2c
1029	d2a	1A*1a	1077	2E2a	3B1b	1125	a1e	2A1a
1030	3B1b	2*A*1	1078	a1d	2C1a	1126	1A*1a	2E1a
1031	1A*1a	3E2	1079	2A3a	3B1c	1127	1A*2	2E1a
1032	3B1b	1A*1a	1080	2A1a	3E*2	1128	3E2	1A*1a

1129	1D1	1A1a	1177	2A3a	1A1c	1225	2A1a	2C2b
1130	a1c	2C1a	1178	2A1a	3B1c	1226	1*A*1	2C1b
1131	2*A*1	3E2	1179	1A1a	2C2c	1227	1A*1a	1D1
1132	1A1a	3E*2	1180	2A1a	3B1a	1228	3B1b	1A*1a
1133	1*A*1	3B1b	1181	2A1a	3B1c	1229	2A1a	3E2
1134	1A1a	2C1b	1182	2A1a	2B2b	1230	1A*1c	2A3b
1135	d1b	1A1a	1183	1D1	1A1a	1231	1D*3	1A1b
1136	3E2	2C2b	1184	a1f	2A1a	1232	a1d	3B1b
1137	1D5	2A1a	1185	2A1a	2B1c	1233	2C2b	1A1a
1138	1A1a	d3b	1186	a1c	d2b	1234	2A3a	3B1c
1139	2A1a	d2c	1187	3E2	1A*1a	1235	2A1a	3B1b
1140	d4b	2C1a	1188	a1c	2C1c	1236	3B*1b	2C1a
1141	3B1b	1A*1a	1189	1A*1a	3B1a	1237	1A*1a	1D1
1142	a1d	1D1	1190	1A1a	3B1b	1238	2A1a	2C2c
1143	a1c	2*A*1	1191	2A1a	3B1c	1239	2A3a	3B1b
1144	2A1a	2C2a	1192	2C2b	d3a	1240	1A*1a	3E2
1145	a1d	2A1a	1193	1A*1a	3B1a	1241	1A1a	3E*2
1146	d3b	2E2a	1194	1A*1a	3E2	1242	a1d	2*A*1
1147	2A3a	3B1b	1195	1A1a	3E2	1243	2A3a	3B1b
1148	3B1b	1A*1a	1196	a1e	2C1a	1244	d1b	1*A*1
1149	d2b	2A1a	1197	a1f	2A1a	1245	3E2	2A1a
1150	1D5	3B1c	1198	2A3a	3B*1b	1246	2A3a	2C2a
1151	1A*1a	2C2b	1199	3B1c	3E1	1247	a1c	2C1a
1152	2A1a	2C2b	1200	1A*2	3E2	1248	1A1b	2C1b
1153	1A1a	2C2b	1201	2*A*1	3B1b	1249	a1d	d2c
1154	1D*1	2C1a	1202	2C1b	2A1a	1250	1A1a	2C2b
1155	1D4	1D1	1203	1D1	2A1a	1251	a1d	3B*1a
1156	3B1d	2A1a	1204	a1e	1D1	1252	2*A*1	2B1c
1157	1D*2	d2b	1205	2A3a	2B1b	1253	d3b	2A1a
1158	3E1	2C1a	1206	a1d	1D1	1254	2A1a	3B*1b
1159	1A*1a	1A1b	1207	1A*1a	3B1b	1255	1A1b	3B1b
1160	3E2	2E2a	1208	2*A*1	3B1b	1256	2A3a	2B1b
1161	2A2	2A1a	1209	2A1a	3B*1c	1257	1A*1b	2A1a
1162	1A2a	3B1b	1210	3B1d	1D1	1258	d3b	2A1a
1163	*hyp.*	*hyp.*	1211	1*A*1	2C2b	1259	1D5	1A*1a
1164	*hyp.*	*hyp.*	1212	1D*3	1D1	1260	d2b	2A1a
1165	*hyp.*	*hyp.*	1213	d3b	2A1a	1261	2A1a	3B1b
1166	*hyp.*	*hyp.*	1214	2A3a	3E*2	1262	d3a	2A1a
1167	2C2d	*hyp.*	1215	2A1a	3B1d	1263	2*A*1	2B1b
1168	*hyp.*	*hyp.*	1216	1A1b	2A1a	1264	1A*1a	2A3a
1169	1A1b	3E2	1217	1A1a	3B1c	1265	2A1a	2C2b
1170	2A1a	3B1b	1218	1*A*1	2C2b	1266	2*A*1	3B1c
1171	2A3a	3B1b	1219	a1c	3B1c	1267	2A3a	3B1b
1172	2A1a	2C1b	1220	2A1a	2B1c	1268	3E1	2A1a
1173	3B1b	1A*1a	1221	a1d	2B1b	1269	d1b	3E1
1174	1A1a	2C2a	1222	d5b	1D1	1270	a1d	2A1a
1175	a1b	2C1c	1223	a1c	1A1a	1271	3E1	2C1b
1176	2A3a	1A1b	1224	2A3a	1A1c	1272	d1c	1A*1a

1273	1A*1a	2B2d	1321	2A1a	1D1	1369	1D5	2A3a
1274	1D*5	2B1b	1322	a1e	1A1b	1370	1A*1a	2C2b
1275	1A*1a	2A3a	1323	2A1a	1A1a	1371	1A*1a	2C1b
1276	3E2	3B*1b	1324	*2A1*	2A1a	1372	2A1a	3B1b
1277	1A*2	2C1a	1325	d3a	d3b	1373	d4b	1A1a
1278	3E1	2A3b	1326	*1A1*	d1d	1374	1A1a	2C2b
1279	a1c	d3a	1327	2A1a	2C1b	1375	1A1a	2C1b
1280	2C1b	3B1b	1328	2A1a	2C2c	1376	2A1a	2B1c
1281	2A1a	3B1b	1329	2A1a	3B1a	1377	1A1b	2E2a
1282	2A1a	2C1b	1330	a1c	d3a	1378	2A1a	3B1b
1283	a1c	3B1b	1331	2A3a	2C2b	1379	3E1	1A1b
1284	2A3a	d5a	1332	1D5	3E2	1380	a1c	1D1
1285	2C1b	1A*1a	1333	1A*1a	3B1b	1381	*1A1*	2C2b
1286	1D5	1A1b	1334	3B1b	2A1a	1382	2A1a	2C2c
1287	2A1a	2A1b	1335	3B1a	2A1a	1383	2A1a	1D1
1288	a1c	2A3b	1336	a1d	2A1a	1384	1D*3	1A*1a
1289	1A1b	2A3b	1337	1A*1a	3B*1b	1385	2C2c	2C1c
1290	1D5	1A1b	1338	2A1a	3B1b	1386	3B1b	1A*1a
1291	2A1a	3B*1d	1339	1D*3	2C2d	1387	2A1a	1A*1b
1292	a1c	2C2b	1340	2C2a	1A*1a	1388	1A*1a	d3b
1293	2A1a	3B1c	1341	3B1b	2A1a	1389	*1D1*	2A1a
1294	d1c	2A1a	1342	d3d	2C1a	1390	1D5	2C1b
1295	1A*1a	3B1c	1343	2A3a	2C2b	1391	2A1a	1D1
1296	d1b	2A1a	1344	d1c	2A1a	1392	a1d	2C2c
1297	3B1b	2C1a	1345	d2b	2A1a	1393	3B1b	d5b
1298	1D*3	3B*1e	1346	*1D1*	2A1a	1394	3B1b	1A1b
1299	3E2	3B1a	1347	a1c	2A1a	1395	3E2	2C2a
1300	3B1b	1A1a	1348	1D*3	2A1a	1396	1A*1a	3B1c
1301	d3b	2A1a	1349	*2A1*	3B1b	1397	a1d	1D1
1302	1A1b	3B*1c	1350	d1d	2C1a	1398	2A1a	2B1b
1303	2A1a	1A1b	1351	1D*1	d3b	1399	d1b	1A1a
1304	1A*1a	3B1d	1352	2C1a	3E2	1400	1D5	2A1a
1305	2C1c	2A1a	1353	a1d	2C1d	1401	2A1a	3E2
1306	2A1a	2C2b	1354	d3c	2A1a	1402	1D1	2A1a
1307	1D5	2C1a	1355	*1D1*	2C1b	1403	d3b	1A*1a
1308	d5c	*1D1*	1356	3B1c	1A1a	1404	1A1b	3B1a
1309	d1b	2A1a	1357	2A1a	3B1a	1405	3B1b	3E2
1310	a1d	2A1b	1358	1D*3	2A1a	1406	d1b	*2A1*
1311	3E2	1D1	1359	1D*4	d5a	1407	d1d	1D1
1312	1D*5	2A1a	1360	3B*1b	1A1a	1408	3B1b	3E1
1313	1A1b	3B1b	1361	1A1b	2C2b	1409	1D3	2A1a
1314	d2c	2A1a	1362	*1A1*	2C1b	1410	1D*3	2E1a
1315	d2b	1A*1a	1363	d1c	2A1a	1411	2A1a	3E2
1316	a1d	3E2	1364	1D5	1A1b	1412	3B1a	2C1a
1317	d3b	2A3a	1365	3B*1b	3E2	1413	2A1a	1D1
1318	a1d	2A1a	1366	1A1a	2C2b	1414	d1c	*2A1*
1319	1D1	1A1b	1367	2A1a	2C2c	1415	3B1b	2A1a
1320	d2b	1A1a	1368	d3b	1A*1a	1416	3E1	3E2

1417	1A*1b	3E2	1465	a1d	1D1	1513	d3c	3E1
1418	1D1	1A*1a	1466	2A1a	2B1b	1514	e1d	1A*1a
1419	d1b	2A1a	1467	2A1a	3B*1c	1515	d3c	1A*1a
1420	1D*6	d1b	1468	1D*3	1A*1a	1516	2A3a	2E2a
1421	d3b	2A1a	1469	3B*1b	1A*1a	1517	2A1a	2A1a
1422	3E2	2A3a	1470	2A1a	3B*1b	1518	a1d	1D1
1423	2A1a	3E2	1471	2A1	3B1c	1519	2A3a	2E2a
1424	2A2	2E2a	1472	a1f	2C1a	1520	2A1	2E2b
1425	a1f	3E2	1473	2A1a	1D1	1521	a1d	2E2a
1426	1D*3	1D1	1474	a1d	1D1	1522	2A2	2B1b
1427	d3c	2A1a	1475	2A1a	3B1c	1523	d2b	2A1a
1428	d5b	1A1a	1476	2A3a	2C1b	1524	2A1a	2B1b
1429	3E1	d2a	1477	a1c	2A1a	1525	1A*1a	2A3b
1430	1A*2	2C2b	1478	2A1a	2C1c	1526	1A1	2E2a
1431	1A*1b	1A1a	1479	1A1	2C1a	1527	2A2	3B1b
1432	2A3b	3B1b	1480	d3b	d2b	1528	2A1a	2B1b
1433	d3a	1A*1a	1481	1A1	2C2b	1529	1A1a	3B1b
1434	1A1	3B1c	1482	a1d	2C1b	1530	1A*1a	1D1
1435	2A3a	3B1b	1483	2A1a	3E*1	1531	d5b	1A*1a
1436	1A*1a	2B1c	1484	2B1e	2A1a	1532	1D*1	3B1c
1437	a1d	d2a	1485	1D2	2C2e	1533	1A2a	1A*1a
1438	1D1	1A*1a	1486	d2b	2A1a	1534	2A3a	2C1b
1439	1A*1a	2C2b	1487	2A1a	1A1b	1535	a1d	2C1a
1440	1D*3	1D1	1488	3B1b	2A1a	1536	3E1	2C2c
1441	3E1	2A3a	1489	2A2	3E2	1537	a1d	3B1c
1442	1A1	3B1c	1490	2A3a	d1c	1538	3E1	2A1a
1443	d2b	1A*1a	1491	1A1a	2C2c	1539	3B1b	3B1c
1444	1A2a	1D1	1492	a1c	3E1	1540	1A1	2B1c
1445	d3b	2A1a	1493	1A*1a	d1b	1541	2C2b	2E1a
1446	d5b	1A*1a	1494	2A1a	2E2a	1542	2A1a	3B1c
1447	1D*5	1A*1a	1495	2A1	2C2b	1543	d5d	2A1a
1448	3B1b	2A1a	1496	a2d	2C1a	1544	2A1	3B1c
1449	d2b	2A1a	1497	a1d	3B*1b	1545	a2e	2B1c
1450	1D*4	1A*1a	1498	3E*2	1D1	1546	1A2a	2C2d
1451	1D*2	d3c	1499	1A1a	3B1b	1547	2A1a	3B1b
1452	1D*5	2A1a	1500	3E2	1D1	1548	2A3a	2C1b
1453	1D*2	3B1c	1501	a1c	2E2a	1549	1A1b	2E2a
1454	1D*2	1A*1a	1502	2A1a	2B1c	1550	a1d	1D1
1455	a1d	1D1	1503	2A1a	3E*2	1551	3B1b	2A1a
1456	3B1c	1D1	1504	a2d	1A1a	1552	d2c	1A*1a
1457	d2b	2A1b	1505	1D*2	2A1a	1553	2A3a	3B1a
1458	2C2b	1A1	1506	a2c	3B1c	1554	1D3	2A1a
1459	1A1a	3E2	1507	2A1a	2C1a	1555	2A1a	2B1b
1460	1D*2	3B*1d	1508	a1c	3B1c	1556	2A1	2B1c
1461	2A1a	3B*1e	1509	1A*1a	3B*1c	1557	a1d	3E2
1462	d2b	2C1a	1510	1A*1a	2A3b	1558	2A3a	2A1a
1463	2A3a	3B1b	1511	2A1	3E2	1559	2A2	3B1b
1464	d5b	2A1a	1512	1D*1	2B1b	1560	a1d	2C1a

1561	d2a 2C1a	1609	3B1b 1A1a	1657	2A1 3E1
1562	1A1a 3E*1	1610	1D*2 2C2b	1658	1A1a 2C1c
1563	1A2a 1D1	1611	1A*1a 2C2b	1659	a1e d1a
1564	1A2a 2E2a	1612	a1e 3E1	1660	1A1a 2C2b
1565	1D*1 3E1	1613	3E2 2B*1c	1661	a1c 2A1a
1566	a1d 1D1	1614	a1d 2C2b	1662	3B*1c 1D1
1567	3E2 2E2a	1615	2A1a 2E2a	1663	2A3a 1D1
1568	1D*3 2B1b	1616	1D5 2B2b	1664	2A1a 3B*1c
1569	1A1a 3E*2	1617	1D*5 3B1b	1665	a1f 2B1b
1570	1A*1a 3E2	1618	1A*1b 3B*1d	1666	2A1a d5b
1571	a1d 2A1a	1619	2A3a 2E2a	1667	1D5 2B1b
1572	2A1a 3B1c	1620	d4b 1A1a	1668	1D*2 2C2b
1573	a1c 2A1a	1621	2A1a d5b	1669	1A*1a 3E2
1574	1A1a 3E1	1622	1D3 3B*1a	1670	2A3a 3B1c
1575	1A*1a 2C2b	1623	a1c 3E2	1671	a1f 3B1c
1576	2A1 2C1b	1624	2A3a 3E*2	1672	2A1b 3B*1c
1577	1A*1a 3E2	1625	1D1 2C1e	1673	3B*1a 2A1a
1578	a1e d3a	1626	a1e 1D1	1674	1A*1a 3B*1d
1579	2A1a 3B1c	1627	1D*5 1A*1a	1675	1D1 2C1a
1580	d1c 1A1	1628	a1f 2C1a	1676	2A3a 2C2b
1581	1A1a 3E1	1629	a1d 1A1a	1677	3B1b 2A1a
1582	2A1a 3E1	1630	1A*1a 1D1	1678	1D*3 2C2a
1583	3B1a 1A1a	1631	1A1b 3E2	1679	1D*4 2B1b
1584	3E1 2B1c	1632	1D*3 2A1	1680	3B1b 2A1a
1585	2A1a 3B*1e	1633	2A1a 2A3a	1681	3E*3 2B1c
1586	1D1 2A1a	1634	2A1a 3E2	1682	2A3b 1D1
1587	2A1 2B1b	1635	d3b 2A1a	1683	2A1a 3B1b
1588	1A1a 3E2	1636	2A1 d1b	1684	2B1b 1D1
1589	a1e 1D1	1637	1D1 2A1a	1685	d1a 2C1a
1590	2A3a 3B*1d	1638	d2b 1A*1a	1686	d1d 2A1a
1591	1A*1b 2A1a	1639	d3b 2A1a	1687	2A1a 1D1
1592	d1c 2C2a	1640	d1b 2C1a	1688	2A1a 2C2c
1593	d4b 1A1a	1641	1D3 2A1	1689	2A1 2B1b
1594	1D5 2A1	1642	2A1a 3E2	1690	1D1 3E1
1595	1A*1a 2C1a	1643	1A*1b 3E2	1691	1A*1a 3B1b
1596	d1c 1A1a	1644	2C1b 2A1a	1692	2A1a d5b
1597	d2b 2A1a	1645	3E2 1A*1a	1693	3B1a 2A1a
1598	2A1a 3B*1b	1646	1D5 2A1a	1694	a1d 2A1a
1599	a2d 2C1a	1647	a1c 2C2a	1695	d3a 1A*1a
1600	2C2b 1A1a	1648	2A1a 2C1a	1696	2B2a 2B1b
1601	1D1 2C2c	1649	1A*1a 3B1c	1697	3E1 2A1a
1602	2A3a 2A1a	1650	2A3a 2A3a	1698	1A*4 3B1b
1603	2A1a 2C1b	1651	2A1a 1D1	1699	1D1 2A1a
1604	1A*1b d2d	1652	a2d 1D1	1700	a1c 2B1b
1605	1A*1a 2B1b	1653	1D1 2A1a	1701	1A1a 2E2a
1606	d2b 2A1	1654	1A*1a 2C1c	1702	1D5 2C1b
1607	2A3a 3B1b	1655	d1b 1A*1a	1703	2C1a 1A1b
1608	2B1b 1A*1a	1656	1A*1b 1A1a	1704	d3a 2A3a

1705	hyp.	hyp.	1753	d5b	1A1a	1801	2C2b	2A1a
1706	hyp.	hyp.	1754	d3b	1A*1a	1802	2A3a	2C2b
1707	hyp.	hyp.	1755	1A*1a	3E2	1803	1A*1b	1D1
1708	d2a	2A1a	1756	d1c	2A1a	1804	d1b	1A1a
1709	1A*1a	3B1b	1757	1D*4	1A*1a	1805	1A*1a	2C2b
1710	1D*1	1D1	1758	a2e	2A1a	1806	1D5	2A1a
1711	a1f	d2b	1759	2C1-	3B*1c	1807	a1c	2A1b
1712	d3b	2A1a	1760	2A1a	3E*1	1808	1D1	2C2b
1713	1D5	1A1	1761	2A1a	3B1d	1809	2A1a	3B1d
1714	1A1	3B1c	1762	2A1a	3E2	1810	d3d	2A1a
1715	2A1a	3E2	1763	2B2b	1A*1a	1811	1D1	3B1b
1716	3B1d	2A1a	1764	3B1b	3B1b	1812	2A1a	3B1b
1717	2A1a	3B1b	1765	2C1b	3B1b	1813	d3b	2A1a
1718	1A1a	3B1e	1766	2C1b	3B1b	1814	2A1a	2C2b
1719	2A4	3B1b	1767	1A1b	3E1	1815	1A*1a	3B1b
1720	1A1b	2E1a.	1768	d3b	1A1b	1816	1D5	2A1a
1721	a1d	1D1	1769	d3b	1D1	1817	2A1a	1D1
1722	2A3a	2B1b	1770	1A1b	3B*1b	1818	d1b	2A1a
1723	3E*2	2B1b	1771	2A1a	d5c	1819	2A1a	d1b
1724	1D5	1A*1b	1772	1A*1a	d1c	1820	2A1a	2C2b
1725	3B1a	2A1a	1773	3B*1b	1A1a	1821	1A*1a	2C1b
1726	3B1a	2A1a	1774	a1d	3E1	1822	a1e	3E1
1727	1A1a	3B*1b	1775	1A1b	3B1b	1823	d3b	2C2c
1728	e1d	2A1a	1776	1A1	3E2	1824	2A1a	2A1a
1729	1D*4	2A1a	1777	a1c	3E1	1825	1A1	2C1b
1730	a1d	2A1a	1778	2A3a	3B1b	1826	a1d	3B*1b
1731	d1a	2A3b	1779	2A1a	3B*1d	1827	d2b	2A1a
1732	a1e	2A1a	1780	a1e	1D1	1828	d1b	2A1a
1733	2A1a	3B*1c	1781	2B1b	2A1a	1829	d1b	2A1a
1734	d1a	1A*1a	1782	a1c	3E2	1830	1A*1a	3B2b
1735	a1d	2C2c	1783	1A1	2C2b	1831	2A1a	2C1c
1736	1A1a	d5b	1784	1A*1a	3B1b	1832	2A1a	3B1c
1737	2C1a	2C1b	1785	1A2a	3E2	1833	1A*1a	2C1c
1738	2A3a	2C2b	1786	2A1a	3B1b	1834	a1c	2A3b
1739	1A*1a	3B*1b	1787	2B1b	2A1	1835	2A1a	3B1c
1740	a1d	3E1	1788	1D1	1A*1a	1836	a1d	2C1a
1741	1A*1a	2C2c	1789	2A1a	2E2a	1837	1D*5	2C2b
1742	2A1a	2B1b	1790	1A2b	2E2a	1838	2A1a	3E2
1743	1A*1a	3E2	1791	d5b	2A1a	1839	1A*1a	3B1c
1744	d3c	2A1a	1792	2A1a	rem.	1840	2A1a	1A1a
1745	a1d	2C2b	1793	1D*3	2A1a	1841	d3b	2A1a
1746	2A1a	3B*1b	1794	a2c	2A1a	1842	2C1a	d1d
1747	1D4	2A1a	1795	2A1	1D1	1843	3B1b	1D1
1748	a1d	3B1b	1796	d1b	1A*1a	1844	3B1b	3B1b
1749	1D*2	2C2c	1797	2A1a	2C1b	1845	1D3	1A1a
1750	2A1a	d4c	1798	1D1	2A1a	1846	a1c	2C2b
1751	1A1b	2C1d	1799	a2e	1D1	1847	1D2	2A1a
1752	2A1a	3E2	1800	1A2a	3E2	1848	1A1b	2A1a

L

1849	2A1a	2C2c	1897	1D2	2A1	1945	1D1	2A1a
1850	d2b	2A1a	1898	1A*1a	1D1	1946	d2b	1A1a
1851	d1b	1D1	1899	d1b	1A1	1947	2A1	3B1b
1852	2A3a	3B1b	1900	d2b	2A1a	1948	1D3	2A1a
1853	2A1a	d3b	1901	1A1a	3B1b	1949	2A1a	3B1c
1854	1D*4	2A1a	1902	d2a	1A*1a	1950	3B1b	2C1a
1855	a1d	3B1b	1903	2A1	2C2c	1951	1A*1a	3B1b
1856	2A1a	d3a	1904	1D*3	2E2a	1952	d2a	2A1a
1857	1A1a	2C1a	1905	a1c	3E2	1953	1A1	3E1
1858	2A1	2C2b	1906	1D5	2A3a	1954	1D3	3B1a
1859	1A1c	2A1a	1907	d3b	1A1b	1955	d2b	1A*1a
1860	1A*1a	1D1	1908	1A*1a	3E2	1956	d1b	2C1a
1861	1A*1a	3B1b	1909	1D5	1A1b	1957	2A1	3B1b
1862	d3a	2C1b	1910	2A1	d2b	1958	1A1a	3E2
1863	1A2a	3B1b	1911	3B1b	2C1a	1959	1A*1a	3E1
1864	2B2b	1A*1a	1912	2A1a	2E2a	1960	2A1a	3B1b
1865	1D*1	2A1a	1913	1A1	3B1a	1961	1A*1a	3E1
1866	3B1c	1A*1a	1914	1A1b	2A3b	1962	1D1	2A1a
1867	1D1	2A1a	1915	3B1c	2A1a	1963	a1e	d3b
1868	a1e	2A1a	1916	1A1a	1D1	1964	1A1b	2A3b
1869	1A*1b	2A3b	1917	1A*1a	3E2	1965	2A1a	3E2
1870	3B1a	3E2	1918	3E2	3B1c	1966	1D5	2C2a
1871	1D1	2C1-	1919	1D1	2C1a	1967	1A*1a	3B1c
1872	3B*1b	2A1a	1920	2C2b	3E*1	1968	1D1	1A*1a
1873	2A1	3B1b	1921	1A*2	2C2b	1969	1D*3	1A*1a
1874	1D*1	2A1a	1922	d1b	2A1a	1970	2A1a	3E1
1875	3B1b	2C1a	1923	2A1a	2C2b	1971	1D1	1A*1a
1876	1A*1a	2B2c	1924	1A*1b	3E2	1972	a1c	3E1
1877	a2d	1A1a	1925	1A1a	2A3b	1973	1A1	3E1
1878	a1c	3E2	1926	1A1a	3E2	1974	3E2	2C1a
1879	3B1b	2A1a	1927	1D2	3B1b	1975	1A1b	3B*1b
1880	1A1a	3B1a	1928	d3b	2C1a	1976	2A1	1D1
1881	2A4	3E2	1929	2A1a	2B1b	1977	a1d	3B*1b
1882	2A1a	3E2	1930	2C2b	2A1a	1978	1A1a	d2b
1883	2A1	3B1c	1931	1A1	3E1	1979	d3a	1A*1a
1884	a1c	1D1	1932	1D5	1D1	1980	2A1a	3E2
1885	1A1a	2C2b	1933	a1c	1A1a	1981	d3b	2A1a
1886	1D*1	3B*1c	1934	1A*1a	d2b	1982	1A*1a	3E2
1887	2A1a	3B1c	1935	2C2c	2A1a	1983	1A*1a	2E1a
1888	a1c	1D1	1936	d2b	2A1a	1984	1A*1a	2B1a
1889	3E2	2A3a	1937	1A1	3E2	1985	2A1a	3B1b
1890	1D*2	2E2a	1938	d3b	1A*1a	1986	d2b	2A1a
1891	2A3a	2C2b	1939	d5b	2A1a	1987	a1d	2A1a
1892	a1c	2C1a	1940	2A3a	3B1c	1988	d1b	1A1a
1893	2A1a	3B1c	1941	1A*1a	3B1c	1989	2A1a	2C2b
1894	d1b	2A1a	1942	d2b	1A*1a	1990	1A*1a	d1b
1895	1D3	2C1a	1943	d2b	2A1a	1991	3E2	1A*1a
1896	a1c	2A3b	1944	d1d	3E1	1992	2A1a	d3b

1993	3E2	1A*1a	2041	a1d	2B1b
1994	2A1a	3B1b	2042	1D3	2B1b
1995	a2d	1A*1a	2043	2A3a	2C2b
1996	d3b	1A*1a	2044	d5c	2A1a
1997	1A*1a	2A3a	2045	3B*1a	1D1
1998	a1e	2C1a	2046	2A3a	2B1b
1999	2A1a	1D1	2047	2C2b	1A*1a
2000	a1c	2A1a	2048	e1c	3B1b
2001	1A1a	2A1a	2049	d2b	2A1a
2002	d5a	2A1a	2050	2A1a	2C1c
2003	1A1b	3B1b	2051	1D*2	3B1b
2004	1D1	1A*1a	2052	3B1b	1D1
2005	1A*1a	2B1b	2053	a1d	1D1
2006	3B*1b	2A1a	2054	2A1a	2C1a
2007	1A*1b	2A3b	2055	2A1a	2C2c
2008	3B1b	2A1a	2056	a1e	2A1a
2009	1A*1a	3B1b	2057	a1d	1A*1a
2010	d3b	2A1a	2058	2A1a	2C2b
2011	a1d	1D1	2059	3B1b	2C1b
2012	d3c	2A1a	2060	3B1b	2A3b
2013	3B1b	1A1a	2061	2A1a	2C2b
2014	1A1b	3B1c	2062	1D1	2C2b
2015	3B1b	1D1	2063	a1d	2C1a
2016	2A3b	3B1b	2064	2A3a	d1b
2017	2A3a	2E2a	2065	1D*2	d3b
2018	1D*2	d3b	2066	d2b	2A1a
2019	2A1a	3B1c	2067	d1b	1A*1a
2020	a1c	1D1	2068	3E2	1D1
2021	1A*1a	3E2	2069	2A1a	2C2b
2022	d1b	1D1	2070	1A1b	2C1b
2023	2A1a	3B1b	2071	2A1a	3B1b
2024	2A1a	3B1b	2072	2A3a	3B1b
2025	1D3	2A3a	2073	1A1b	3E2
2026	a1d	1D1	2074	1D5	2A1a
2027	2A1a	2C2b	2075	a1c	1D1
2028	a1d	3E2	2076	d1b	1D1
2029	1A*1a	3B1a	2077	2A3a	3B1a
2030	d3b	2A1a	2078	2A1a	3B1a
2031	2A3a	2C2b	2079	1D*2	d3a
2032	a1e	1D1	2080	2A1a	2E2a
2033	3B*1a	2A1a	2081	2B1c	2A1
2034	a1d	2C1a	2082	1D5	1A*1a
2035	2A3b	1A*1a	2083	d3b	2A1a
2036	a1b	2A1a	2084	3B1b	1D1
2037	1A2a	3E*1	2085	2A2	1D1
2038	a1d	2A1a	2086	1A1a	3E2
2039	a1d	d3b	2087	d1b	1A1a
2040	1A*1a	3B1c	2088	2A1a	2C1a

2089	a1d	1D1
2090	1D3	2C1a
2091	2A1a	3B1b
2092	a1d	2E1a
2093	*rem.*	d3c
2094	1A*1a	2E1a
2095	3B1b	2A1a
2096	2A1a	2C1b
2097	2A1a	3E2
2098	a1d	1D1
2099	1A1a	2C2b
2100	2A1a	2E2a
2101	a2c	1D1
2102	2A1a	1D1
2103	2A1a	3B1b
2104	a1c	2C1a
2105	2B1b	2A1a
2106	1D1	2A1a
2107	1D*5	2A1a
2108	2A3a	2B1b
2109	1A1a	3B1b
2110	1A*1b	2A3b
2111	2B1b	1A*1a
2112	1D3	2A1a
2113	2A1	3E2
2114	3B1c	1A1a
2115	a1c	3E1
2116	2A1a	2B1b
2117	1A*1a	2C2b
2118	1D3	2A1a
2119	2A1a	2E2a
2120	2A3a	1D1
2121	2B1b	1A1a
2122	2A1	d1b
2123	1D*3	1D1
2124	a1f	3B1b
2125	1D1	2A1a
2126	1A*1a	2C2b
2127	2A1a	2B1b
2128	2A1a	d5b
2129	d1b	2A1a
2130	d3c	1A*1a
2131	3B1b	2A1a
2132	2A2	3B*1c
2133	2A1a	1A*1a
2134	2A1a	3B*1b
2135	a1c	3B1b
2136	1D*1	3E2

L *

2137	3B1b	1A1a	2185	d2d	2A1a	2233	d3c	2A1a
2138	1D5	3B*1b	2186	2A1a	2C1a	2234	2*A*1	2A1a
2139	d3b	2A1a	2187	2A1a	2C1b	2235	1*D*1	1A1a
2140	2A1a	3E1	2188	2A1a	3E1	2236	2A1a	2B1c
2141	1A1a	3B*1b	2189	3E2	1A*1a	2237	2A1a	2B1b
2142	3B1b	1A1a	2190	3B1b	1A1a	2238	2A1a	3B1b
2143	2A1a	1D1	2191	2A3b	2A1a	2239	1D2	1A*1a
2144	d3b	2A1a	2192	1A*1a	3B1b	2240	3B1b	1*A*1
2145	a1d	2C1a	2193	2A3a	3B1a	2241	2A1a	2A3b
2146	2A1a	3B1c	2194	d1c	1A1a	2242	1A*1a	3E2
2147	1D1	3B1c	2195	a1c	1D1	2243	1A*1a	3E2
2148	d3c	2A1a	2196	1A2a	2C2b	2244	3B1b	1*A*1
2149	1A*1a	2B1b	2197	d1b	1A1a	2245	2A1a	3E2
2150	2E1a	2C2a	2198	1D5	2A1a	2246	2A1a	3E2
2151	2*A*1	3B1b	2199	2A1a	3B1b	2247	a1c	1A1a
2152	2C2b	3*E*1	2200	1A1b	2A1a	2248	2A1a	2B1b
2153	3E2	2A1a	2201	2*A*1	3B1b	2249	1A*1a	2E2a
2154	2A3a	3E2	2202	d1a	2*A*1	2250	2A3a	1A*1a
2155	d5b	2A1a	2203	d2b	2C1a	2251	2A1a	2B1d
2156	2A1a	3E2	2204	a1d	d2a	2252	2A2	2C2b
2157	3B1c	1A1a	2205	1D*4	1*D*1	2253	d1b	2A1a
2158	a1c	2A1b	2206	1A*1a	1*D*1	2254	2A3a	3E2
2159	1D1	2A1a	2207	d1b	2A1a	2255	3B1b	2*A*1
2160	2C1c	2A1a	2208	2B1a	2C2b	2256	1A*1a	2A1b
2161	1D1	2C1c	2209	2A1a	2C2b	2257	d2b	2A1a
2162	1*A*1	3E2	2210	1D5	2B1b	2258	a2d	3B*1b
2163	a1e	2A1a	2211	2A1a	1D1	2259	3B*1b	1D1
2164	1A*1a	1D1	2212	2C1c	1A1a	2260	1A*1b	3B1b
2165	2*A*1	2B1b	2213	2A3a	3E2	2261	d3b	2A1a
2166	1A*1a	2C1b	2214	2A1a	3B1b	2262	1A*1a	3B1a
2167	d5b	2A1a	2215	2A1a	2B1b	2263	1D2	2C2a
2168	2A1a	1D1	2216	2A1a	3E2	2264	2C1a	3B1b
2169	1*A*1	3E1	2217	1D5	3B*1c	2265	2A3a	2A3b
2170	2A1a	3E2	2218	d1c	2C1a	2266	1D2	1A1a
2171	2C1b	1A*1a	2219	2A1a	2B1b	2267	d5a	2A1a
2172	a2g	1A*1a	2220	2A1a	3B1c	2268	1A1b	3E1
2173	*hyp.*	3B1d	2221	a1d	2E2a	2269	1A1a	3B1b
2174	2A1a	2A3b	2222	2A1a	3B*1c	2270	1A1a	3E2
2175	1A*2	3B1b	2223	d2b	1D1	2271	1D3	2A1a
2176	d3b	1A1a	2224	2A1a	3E2	2272	d1b	2A1a
2177	d1a	1D1	2225	2A1a	3B1b	2273	1D3	2A1a
2178	1D5	2A1a	2226	1D3	*def.*	2274	1A*1a	d2b
2179	1A1b	3B1b	2227	*def.*	3E2	2275	1A*1a	3B1b
2180	1*A*1	2C2b	2228	d3b	*def.*	2276	1A1a	3B1b
2181	d2b	2A1a	2229	*def.*	*def.*	2277	1D5	3B*1c
2182	3E1	2C1b	2230	*def.*	2B1d	2278	d3b	2A3a
2183	1D5	1A1a	2231	*def.*	3B1b	2279	1A1a	3E2
2184	3B1c	1A*1a	2232	d2b	1*A*1	2280	2*A*1	2B1d

2281	1A1a	3E2	2329	1A*1a	d1b
2282	2A1a	3E2	2330	3B1b	2A1a
2283	2A1a	2C1b	2331	1A*1a	3E2
2284	1D5	1A*1a	2332	1A*1a	3B*1c
2285	3E1	1D1	2333	d3b	2A1a
2286	1D*4	2A1a	2334	2A3a	2A3b
2287	2B1b	1A1b	2335	1A*1a	d3b
2288	a1d	2E2a	2336	2A1a	1D1
2289	2A2	2B1b	2337	a1d	3E1
2290	2A1a	3E2	2338	1*D*1	2A1a
2291	d1b	1A*1a	2339	2A3a	2A1a
2292	1A2a	d1b	2340	d3b	1A*1a
2293	1A*1a	2A3a	2341	1A1a	d3b
2294	1A*1b	2C1b	2342	2A1a	1A*1a
2295	a1e	1A*1a	2343	2A1a	2C2b
2296	1A2a	2E2b	2344	d3b	2A1a
2297	*hyp.*	3B1b	2345	3B1b	2A1a
2298	d1c	3B*1b	2346	d3d	1A*1a
2299	2A1a	2B1c	2347	2A1a	3B*1d
2300	2A3a	3B*1b	2348	3B1c	2C2a
2301	3B1c	1A*1a	2349	1A1a	2C2c
2302	1*A*1	2E2a	2350	1D1	1A*1a
2303	2*A*1	3B1b	2351	2*A*1	d1c
2304	a1c	2A1a	2352	3E2	1D1
2305	a1c	1A*1a	2353	3B*1b	2A1a
2306	2A3a	2C2b	2354	2A1a	3B1b
2307	1A*1a	3B1b	2355	1*A*1	3B1b
2308	2A1a	3B1b	2356	3B1b	2A1a
2309	1A*1a	2C1b	2357	2A3a	3E1
2310	1A*1a	3B1b	2358	2A1a	3E2
2311	d3b	1A*1a	2359	1A*1a	3B1b
2312	2B1b	2A1a	2360	2A1a	3E2
2313	2A3a	3E2	2361	a1d	2A1a
2314	1A*1a	2C2b	2362	2*A*1	3B1c
2315	1D3	2A1a	2363	d1b	2A1a
2316	3B1b	1A*1a	2364	2*A*1	2B1b
2317	3E2	1A1a	2365	2A1a	2E2a
2318	d3b	2A1a	2366	d3b	2A1a
2319	1A*1a	2E2a	2367	3B*1d	1D1
2320	2A3a	2C1a	2368	1D3	1A1a
2321	d3b	1A*1a	2369	2B1b	1A1a
2322	1A*1a	1A*1a	2370	1A*2	1A*1a
2323	1A*1a	2B1b	2371	d2c	2*A*1
2324	d1b	1A*1a	2372	2A1a	3B1b
2325	1A*1a	3B1b	2373	d1c	2A1a
2326	2A1a	3E2	2374	d1b	2A1a
2327	2A3a	3B1b	2375	d1b	2A1a
2328	1A1a	3E2	2376	a1d	2A1a

2377	a1f	3E2
2378	1A*1a	3B1c
2379	3E1	d2b
2380	2C1b	1D1
2381	a1d	1D1
2382	d1b	1*D*1
2383	d2d	1D1
2384	2A1a	3B1c
2385	a1c	3E2
2386	2A1a	1D1
2387	2B1b	3E1
2388	2A1a	3B1b
2389	a2c	2A1a
2390	2A1a	2C2b
2391	d3b	1A1a
2392	2A1a	3E1
2393	3E1	1A*1a
2394	2C1b	1D1
2395	1A1a	2C1b
2396	1D*2	3E*2
2397	3B*1b	2C1a
2398	1A*1a	1D1
2399	2*A*1	3B1c
2400	a1d	2C1a
2401	3B1c	1A*1a
2402	2A1a	1D1
2403	a1d	2B1c
2404	2A3a	3B1b
2405	2A3a	3B1b
2406	a1d	3E1
2407	d1b	1A1a
2408	1D2	2C2b
2409	1D1	3B1c
2410	d3d	2A1a
2411	1A1b	3E2
2412	1*A*1	3B1b
2413	1A*1a	1D1
2414	1D3	3E2
2415	1A1b	3B1b
2416	d1b	2A1a
2417	a1d	2A3b
2418	3B*1b	1*A*1
2419	2A3a	2C2b
2420	1A*2	*rem.*
2421	a1c	2A1a
2422	1D*5	1A*1a
2423	1A1a	3E1b
2424	1D1	1A*1a

2425	2A1a	1D1	2473	2C2b	1A1a	2521	1A*1a	3B1d
2426	a1d	3E*2	2474	2A3a	3B1b	2522	d2c	2A1a
2427	2A1	2B1b	2475	d1c	2A1a	2523	1A*1a	2C2d
2428	d2b	3B1b	2476	1D3	1A*1a	2524	1A1a	3B1c
2429	2A3a	2B1c	2477	2C1b	d5b	2525	1D*5	3B1b
2430	a1c	2C2–	2478	1D*5	1A1a	2526	1A*1a	2B1b
2431	2B1b	1A*1a	2479	d3a	1A*1a	2527	1D6	3B1c
2432	a1d	2A1a	2480	1A*1a	3B1c	2528	d3e	1A1b
2433	1A1a	3B1c	2481	3B1b	1A*1a	2529	a1e	2A1a
2434	1A*1a	3B1b	2482	2A1a	3E1	2530	1A*1a	2C2b
2435	d1b	rem.	2483	2A1a	1D1	2531	d2b	1A*1a
2436	2A1a	2A3a	2484	3B*1c	1D1	2532	2A1a	3B1b
2437	a1d	d3a	2485	2A1a	2C1a	2533	2C1b	2C1b
2438	d3a	1A*1a	2486	d1a	2A1a	2534	d1c	2A1a
2439	1D*1	2B1b	2487	2E2a	2A1a	2535	2A1a	3B1b
2440	1D1	2A1a	2488	rem.	1A1a	2536	1A1a	2C2b
2441	3B*1b	1A*1a	2489	1A*1a	2E2b	2537	2A3a	1D1
2442	1D*2	3B*1b	2490	a1c	2C1b	2538	a1d	1D1
2443	1D*1	2A1a	2491	1A1a	3B1b	2539	1A1b	3E2
2444	d1b	2A1a	2492	2A1a	2B1b	2540	d3b	1A*1a
2445	d1b	2C1b	2493	1D5	3B1b	2541	2A1a	3B1c
2446	1A1a	2C2c	2494	a1c	d3c	2542	a1d	3B1b
2447	3E1	2C1c	2495	d2c	2A1a	2543	3E2	1A*1a
2448	1A*1a	3B*1c	2496	1D*3	1A*1a	2544	2A1	2C1b
2449	1A1a	1A*1a	2497	a1e	2C1a	2545	1D*3	2A3b
2450	a1d	1A*1a	2498	1A*1a	3B1c	2546	1A1a	3B1c
2451	1D*5	1A*1a	2499	2A1a	2C2c	2547	3E2	3B1c
2452	d1b	1A*1a	2500	2B1b	1A1a	2548	1D1	2A1a
2453	2A1	2C2c	2501	a1d	3E1	2549	1A1a	2C1a
2454	3B1a	1A*1a	2502	d3a	2A1a	2550	a1c	3B1c
2455	1D3	2C1b	2503	a1d	1D1	2551	3E1	2A3b
2456	2A3a	2A1a	2504	1D1	2A1a	2552	2A3a	2E2a
2457	1A*1a	2A1b	2505	3B*1b	2A1a	2553	2A3a	3B1b
2458	1A1a	3B1b	2506	1A*1a	2C2b	2554	1A1b	2E2a
2459	1A1a	2C1c	2507	d5b	2A1a	2555	2A1a	3B1b
2460	a1f	2A3b	2508	2E2a	3B1b	2556	1A*1a	3E2
2461	1A1b	2B1c	2509	1A1a	2C1a	2557	1D1	1A1a
2462	1A*2	3B1a	2510	2A1a	3E2	2558	1D5	2A1a
2463	d1b	2A1a	2511	2A1a	3B1b	2559	1A1b	2E2a
2464	3E1	1A*1a	2512	1A*1a	1A1a	2560	d2b	2A1a
2465	d3b	1A*1a	2513	1D5	2A1a	2561	d3b	1A*1a
2466	a2f	1A*1a	2514	2A1a	d3c	2562	1A*1a	2E2a
2467	2A1a	2B1b	2515	d3a	1A1a	2563	1D3	2A1a
2468	a1e	2B1c	2516	3B1a	1A*1a	2564	2A1a	3E1
2469	2E2a	2E2a	2517	1D3	2A1a	2565	1D1	1A*1a
2470	2A1a	3B1b	2518	1A*1a	2C2c	2566	2E2a	3B1a
2471	1A2a	3B*1c	2519	1A*1a	3B1b	2567	2A1a	2B1b
2472	2B1b	1A*1a	2520	d1b	2A1a	2568	1A*1a	3B1b

2569	d1c	2C1a	2617	d1a	1A1	2665	a1d	d1b
2570	2C1b	2E2a	2618	2A3a	3B1d	2666	1A1a	3B1b
2571	1A*1a	2A1a	2619	3B1d	d1a	2667	1D*1	2A1a
2572	2A1a	2C1c	2620	3B*1d	1D1	2668	1D1	d1b
2573	a1c	2A1a	2621	1A1a	2C1c	2669	a1c	3E2
2574	2A1a	2B2b	2622	2A1a	d3b	2670	1D5	2A1a
2575	1A1a	2E2a	2623	a1d	1A1	2671	3E2	2A1a
2576	2A1a	3E2	2624	2A1a	3B*1c	2672	2A1a	3E*2
2577	2A1	2B1b	2625	1A2a	3B1b	2673	2B1–	1A*1a
2578	1A1a	1D1	2626	2A1a	3B1b	2674	1D*3	1A*1a
2579	d3c	2A1a	2627	d2b	2A1a	2675	2C1b	3B1c
2580	1A*1a	3B1b	2628	d3e	3B1b	2676	1A*1a	3B1b
2581	d2b	2C1a	2629	1A1a	2B1b	2677	1A*1a	d3b
2582	1D2	2A1a	2630	a1d	2C1a	2678	1A*1a	3E2
2583	2A1	3E*2	2631	2A1a	3E2	2679	2A1	3B1c
2584	2A3a	2E2a	2632	1A*1a	2C1b	2680	1A*1a	2E1a
2585	1A1a	2C1b	2633	2B1b	2C1b	2681	1A1a	1D1
2586	2A2	3B1c	2634	a1d	d1b	2682	1A2a	3B*1b
2587	a1b	1D1	2635	d3a	3B1c	2683	d1b	2A1a
2588	2A3b	2C1a	2636	d4d	2A1a	2684	1A*1a	2B1b
2589	a1d	1D1	2637	d1b	1A1a	2685	3B*1b	1A*1a
2590	2A1a	3B1b	2638	1A*2	3B*1e	2686	1A*1b	3B1d
2591	1D*3	2B1b	2639	d1c	2A1a	2687	1D*5	3B*1b
2592	d1b	1A1a	2640	a1e	3B1c	2688	d3b	2A1a
2593	a2d	3E2	2641	d2d	2A1a	2689	1D*3	1A*1a
2594	2A1a	1D1	2642	1D3	3B1b	2690	1A*1c	2B1b
2595	1A*1a	3B1c	2643	d5a	1A*1a	2691	1A2a	3E*2
2596	a1d	1A1	2644	d1b	2A1a	2692	2A1a	3B1b
2597	3E1	1A*1a	2645	3B1c	1A*1a	2693	2A1a	3E2
2598	2A1	2C2c	2646	1D*1	2C2c	2694	3B*1c	1D1
2599	2A1a	3B1c	2647	d2c	1A*1a	2695	3E1	2A1a
2600	1A1a	3E*2	2648	1D*2	3B1b	2696	1A1a	3B1c
2601	1A1a	2C1b	2649	1D*3	2C1b	2697	a1e	2B1b
2602	1A*1a	3E1	2650	3E2	2E2a	2698	2A1a	3B1c
2603	1D*3	1D1	2651	a1e	d3c	2699	a2d	3E2
2604	1D1	d2c	2652	d3c	1D1	2700	1A1a	2B1b
2605	d2b	1D1	2653	a1e	3B1b	2701	1A1a	2B1b
2606	a1e	2B1c	2654	1A1a	3B1c	2702	2A1a	2C2b
2607	2A3a	1D1	2655	1A*1a	1D1	2703	1A1b	3E*2
2608	3E*2	2C1b	2656	2A1a	2C2a	2704	1A2a	3B1c
2609	a1e	2E2a	2657	d4c	3B1b	2705	1D5	1A1a
2610	2A1a	2E2a	2658	2A1a	1D1	2706	1A1a	3E2
2611	a1c	3E1	2659	1A*1a	2B1c	2707	a1e	2C1a
2612	1D1	3B1b	2660	1A*2	1A1a	2708	1D1	2C2c
2613	1D*1	2A1b	2661	a2e	3E2	2709	1A1a	3B1b
2614	2A1a	3B*1b	2662	1A1a	3E2	2710	1D*2	2A1a
2615	3E2	2A1a	2663	2A1a	2A3b	2711	1A*1a	2B1b
2616	2A3a	3B*1b	2664	d3c	1A*1a	2712	d3c	1A1a

2713	1A1a	3B*1b	2761	3E2	2A1	2809	a1d	1D1
2714	a1c	3E2	2762	1A*1a	2C2b	2810	1D*2	1A*1a
2715	1A*1a	3B1b	2763	1A1a	3E2	2811	1D*3	3E2
2716	a1c	1D1	2764	1A*1a	3E2	2812	1A1a	3B1c
2717	1A1a	rem.	2765	1A1a	3E*2	2813	d5b	2A1a
2718	d3b	2A1a	2766	d1b	1A*1b	2814	1D1	2B1b
2719	1D*3	2A1a	2767	3B*1c	2A3a	2815	2A1a	d2a
2720	a1d	1D1	2768	1A1b	3E2	2816	1A*1a	3B1b
2721	2A1a	rem.	2769	1D2	3B1b	2817	a1c	3E1
2722	3E2	1A*1a	2770	a2d	2C1a	2818	1A1	2C2b
2723	2A1a	2B1b	2771	1A*1a	3B1b	2819	1D*2	3B*1b
2724	2A1a	3B1c	2772	2A1a	2B1c	2820	2A1a	3E2
2725	1D*2	2A1a	2773	3B*1c	1D1	2821	a1c	1D1
2726	d2b	2C1a	2774	1D6	2A1a	2822	2A1	3B*1c
2727	2A1a	2C2b	2775	2C2b	1A1a	2823	d1b	1A*1a
2728	1A1	rem.	2776	2A1a	2E2a	2824	1A*1a	3E2
2729	2C1b	2A1a	2777	2A1a	2E2a	2825	1D*3	1A*1a
2730	1A1	3B1b	2778	1A1a	1D1	2826	1A*1a	3E2
2731	1D*5	2A1a	2779	a1c	3E3	2827	1D3	1A*1a
2732	1A*1a	3B1b	2780	2A1a	3E2	2828	d1b	1A*1a
2733	2A1a	d3b	2781	1A*1a	1D1	2829	1D*2	2A1a
2734	1D1	2A1a	2782	2A1	3B1c	2830	d3b	2A1a
2735	d3b	2A1a	2783	1A1b	3E2	2831	1A1a	3E2
2736	2A1a	3B1b	2784	1A*1a	3B1b	2832	a1d	3E1
2737	1A1	2C2a	2785	d5b	1A*1a	2833	2A1	3E2
2738	1D*2	2C2b	2786	d3b	2A1a	2834	2A1a	3B*1b
2739	1A*1a	3B1b	2787	2A1	2B1d	2835	d3b	1A1
2740	3E2	2C1a	2788	a1d	2A1a	2836	a1d	3E2
2741	3B*1c	2A1a	2789	2A1a	3E1	2837	1D1	1A*1a
2742	2A3a	2C2b	2790	1A*1a	2B1c	2838	3B*1c	2A1a
2743	1A1a	3B1b	2791	2A1a	3B1b	2839	d3c	1A*1a
2744	1D1	3B1b	2792	2E2a	3E3	2840	d3b	2A1a
2745	2A1a	2C2b	2793	1A1a	1D1	2841	d1b	1A1a
2746	1D5	1A*1a	2794	a1c	3E2	2842	1A*1a	3E1
2747	a1c	d3b	2795	2A1	2A1a	2843	3E2	1A*1a
2748	2E2a	1D1	2796	2A1a	2C1c	2844	d1b	1A*1a
2749	1D*2	2C2c	2797	a1c	2A1a	2845	2A1a	2B1b
2750	d3b	1A1a	2798	d3a	1A1a	2846	d3b	1A1a
2751	1A1a	3B1c	2799	3B1c	1A*1a	2847	1D*3	1A*1a
2752	3B*1b	1D1	2800	1D*3	2A1a	2848	3B1b	2A1a
2753	d3b	2A1a	2801	2A1a	2C2d	2849	d2c	2A1a
2754	1D*2	2A3b	2802	d2b	1A1a	2850	d1b	2A1a
2755	1D*2	3B1b	2803	1A*1b	2C1a	2851	1A1	3B1b
2756	d2c	3B1c	2804	a1d	2A1a	2852	1A1a	3B1b
2757	2A3a	3E2	2805	1D1	d2a	2853	2A1	3E2
2758	1D1	1A*1a	2806	d2b	2A1a	2854	a1d	2B1a
2759	1A*1a	3B1b	2807	3E1	d1b	2855	a1e	3B1b
2760	1D*3	2A1a	2808	3B*1b	2A1a	2856	d2b	1A1a

2857	dıb 1Aıa	2905	dıb 2Aıa	2953	2A2 1A*ıa
2858	2C2b 2Aıa	2906	1A*ıa 2Aıb	2954	d2b 2Cıa
2859	1A*ıa 2Cıc	2907	dıb 1Dı	2955	1Dı 1Aıa
2860	aıd 1Dı	2908	1Aıb 1Dı	2956	1Aıa 2A3b
2861	1A1 3B*ıd	2909	1D*2 2A1	2957	1A2b 2C2b
2862	2Aıa 3Eı	2910	1A*ıa 3Bıb	2958	2Aıa 1Dı
2863	1D5 1Aıb	2911	2A1 dıb	2959	2A3b 1Aıb
2864	aıc 2C2d	2912	1A*ıa 1Dı	2960	dıb 2Cıa
2865	d2b 3Bıc	2913	2Aıa 2C2b	2961	dıb 2Aıa
2866	2A1 2Cıc	2914	1Aıa 3Bıb	2962	2A1 2C2a
2867	d2d 1Aıa	2915	1D2 3Bıa	2963	d3b 2Aıa
2868	1Dı 1Aıa	2916	dıc 1A*ıa	2964	1D*5 dıb
2869	1A*ıa dıc	2917	1A*ıa dıb	2965	1Dı 1A*ıa
2870	2B2b 2Aıa	2918	d3b 2Aıa	2966	aıc 3E2
2871	dıb 1A1	2919	1Aıa 3Bıb	2967	1Aıb 2Bıb
2872	1A*ıa 2Bıc	2920	2Aıa 2Cıb	2968	2Aıa 2C2b
2873	d3b 1A1	2921	1Dı 1Aıa	2969	2Aıa 2A3b
2874	2Aıa 2Cıc	2922	d2c 1A*ıb	2970	d3b 1Aıa
2875	2Aıa 3B*ıd	2923	1A*ıa 3Bıb	2971	aıd 1Dı
2876	1A*ıa 3Bıc	2924	dıb 1A*ıa	2972	2Aıa 2Aıb
2877	d3b 2Aıa	2925	2Aıa d5a	2973	aıd 2E2a
2878	1Aıa 2Bıb	2926	dıb 1A*ıa	2974	3Bıb 2Aıa
2879	3Bıb 2Aıa	2927	2Aıa 1Dı	2975	1Aıa 3B*ıb
2880	1A*ıb 3Bıc	2928	aıd 1Dı	2976	aıe 2C2c
2881	1A1 1Dı	2929	1Aıa 2Eıa	2977	aıb 3Eı
2882	1Aıb 3E*ı	2930	1D2 1Aıa	2978	2Aıa 3Bıb
2883	1Aıb 2Bıd	2931	1D*2 1A*ıa	2979	2A3b 3Eı
2884	d3b d3a	2932	2Aıa dıa	2980	1A2b 2C2b
2885	1D5 2Aıa	2933	dıb 1A1	2981	2Aıa 2C2b
2886	1Aıa 3E2	2934	aıd 2A1	2982	aıc 2C2b
2887	d2b 2Aıa	2935	d5a 2A1	2983	1A*ıa 3Bıc
2888	2Aıa dıb	2936	d2c 2Aıa	2984	d2b 2Aıa
2889	1A*ıa 1Dı	2937	2Aıa 2E2a	2985	dıb 1Dı
2890	3Eı 1Aıa	2938	2Aıa 3Eı	2986	dıb 2A1
2891	1A*ıa d5b	2939	dıc 2Aıa	2987	2A3a 2C2b
2892	a2c 2Cıa	2940	2Aıa d2c	2988	2Aıa 3Eı
2893	1A2b d3b	2941	1A*ıa 2E2a	2989	3Bıb 3B*ıb
2894	3E2 3E2	2942	2A1 1Dı	2990	1A*ıa 3Bıb
2895	1Dı 1A*ıa	2943	dıc 1Aıa	2991	1A2b 2Aıa
2896	2A1 d3a	2944	1A*ıa 3Bıb	2992	2Aıa 2Bıc
2897	2Aıa 1Dı	2945	2Aıa 2C2a	2993	1A*ıa d2a
2898	2Aıa 2Bıb	2946	d3b 1A*ıa	2994	aıe 1Dı
2899	dıb 1A*ıb	2947	2A3b 1A*ıa	2995	hyp. hyp.
2900	d3b 2Aıa	2948	2Bıb 1A*ıa	2996	hyp. hyp.
2901	2Aıa 3E2	2949	aıe dıb	2997	3B*ıb 2Aıa
2902	1D2 2Aıa	2950	1D2 2Aıa	2998	1Dı 1A*ıa
2903	2C2b 1A1	2951	1Dı 1Aıa	2999	aıc dıb
2904	3E2 1A*ıa	2952	dıb 1A*ıa	3000	2A3b 2C2c

3001	3B1b	2A1a	3049	1A*1a	3B1c
3002	a1d	1D1	3050	2A1a	1D1
3003	2*A*1	2B1c	3051	a1d	2*A*1
3004	d1a	1A1a	3052	3E2	1A*1a
3005	3B1b	1D1	3053	d3b	1A*1a
3006	2A3a	3B1b	3054	2A1a	2C1b
3007	2A1a	2C2b	3055	1D*3	1A*1c
3008	d3b	1D1	3056	*rem.*	1D1
3009	a1d	3B1b	3057	a1e	2C1c
3010	d3a	3B1b	3058	a1c	2B1b
3011	1A*1b	3B1c	3059	d1b	1A*1a
3012	1D1	1A*1a	3060	1A*1b	2E2a
3013	d1c	2A1a	3061	2A1a	2B1b
3014	1A*1a	2C2b	3062	1D1	2A3a
3015	2A1a	2C2b	3063	1D5	1A*1a
3016	1A*1b	2C1a	3064	1*A*1	2B1b
3017	1A*1a	1D1	3065	1A1b	2A3a
3018	d5b	1A*1a	3066	d1b	3B1b
3019	1A1b	2A3b	3067	1D*2	1A*1a
3020	d2b	1A*1a	3068	3B*1c	2A1a
3021	1A2a	2C2c	3069	3B1c	1A*1a
3022	1D5	1A*1a	3070	2A1a	2C2b
3023	1A1a	3B1b	3071	2C1b	2A1a
3024	2A1a	3B1b	3072	1A*1a	3E2
3025	1A1b	1D1	3073	1A*1a	2C1c
3026	2A1a	3B1c	3074	d3b	2A1a
3027	e1d	1D1	3075	3E1	1A1a
3028	2C2b	3E1	3076	2A1a	3E1
3029	2A1a	2C2b	3077	2C2b	2A1a
3030	1A*1a	2E2a	3078	1A1a	3B1c
3031	1D*2	d5b	3079	a1e	2A1a
3032	2*A*1	1D1	3080	2A1a	1D1
3033	a1d	2*A*1	3081	a1c	2A3b
3034	2A3a	3B1d	3082	a1d	3B1b
3035	2A1a	d5b	3083	2A1a	d2a
3036	1A*1a	d3b	3084	1D*4	1A1b
3037	2A1a	3E2	3085	1A*1a	3B*1b
3038	a1d	3E1	3086	d3c	1A1a
3039	1A1a	3E2	3087	a1c	2B1b
3040	2A1a	d3b	3088	2A1a	3B1c
3041	2A2	1A*1a	3089	d1b	1A1a
3042	d1b	1*A*1	3090	1A2b	3B*1b
3043	1A1a	3E2	3091	1A*1a	1D1
3044	2A1a	2E2a	3092	1*A*1	2E2a
3045	2A1a	3B1b	3093	2A1a	1A1b
3046	d3b	1A*1a	3094	1A1b	2E2a
3047	2C1a	1A1a	3095	1A1a	3B1c
3048	2A1a	3B1a	3096	a1d	2C1b

3097	d3a	1A1b
3098	1A*1a	3B1b
3099	1D*1	1A*1a
3100	d3c	2A1a
3101	a1c	2A1a
3102	1A1a	3E*2
3103	1A*1b	d1b
3104	a1c	1D1
3105	1A*2	2C2b
3106	1A*1a	2C2c
3107	a1d	1D1
3108	2A1a	3B1b
3109	d1b	1A*1a
3110	a1c	1D1
3111	1D5	2A1a
3112	1D1	d3b
3113	2A1a	1D1
3114	1A*1a	2C2b
3115	1D*5	2A1a
3116	2B1c	2*A*1
3117	3B1b	1A*1a
3118	1A2b	3E2
3119	3E2	1A*1a
3120	a1c	1D1
3121	1A*1a	2A1a
3122	1A*1a	d1a
3123	1D*5	d5b
3124	2*A*1	3B1b
3125	2*A*1	3B1c
3126	a1c	2C1b
3127	d1b	3E1
3128	1A*1a	2C1a
3129	2A1a	3E2
3130	d1b	1A1a
3131	2A1a	2A3b
3132	1A2b	2C2b
3133	1D1	2A1a
3134	3B1b	2C2a
3135	2A1a	2A1b
3136	1D5	d2a
3137	a1c	2A1a
3138	1A1a	1D1
3139	1A*1a	2*A*1
3140	2A1a	3B1b
3141	a1e	2A1a
3142	1D1	2A1a
3143	a1e	3E2
3144	2A1a	2E2a

3145	1A1b	3E1	3158	1D1	1A*1a	3171	2C1b	2C1a
3146	1A*1a	2E2a	3159	d1b	2C2a	3172	2A3b	2C2b
3147	a2d	2C1a	3160	3E2	2A1a	3173	1D*1	d5b
3148	1A1a	1D1	3161	1A*1a	d1b	3174	2A1a	3B1c
3149	2A3a	3E2	3162	3E2	2A1a	3175	d2c	2A1a
3150	d5b	d2a	3163	2C2b	1A1a	3176	2A1a	2C2c
3151	d1b	2A1	3164	a1c	3B1c	3177	d3a	2A1a
3152	1D3	1A*1a	3165	3E2	2C1a	3178	d1b	2A1a
3153	d3d	1A*1a	3166	3B*1c	2A1a	3179	3E1	1A1
3154	3E2	2A1a	3167	1A1a	2C2c	3180	a1d	1D1
3155	1A*2	3E2	3168	1A*1a	3B1b	3181	2A1a	d2a
3156	3B1a	2A1a	3169	2C2c	2A1	3182	2A1a	d2a
3157	1A1a	2B1b	3170	3E1	2A1a			

INDEX TO THE SCANSION OF THE HYPERMETRIC VERSES IN OLD ENGLISH

The following is the order in which the various pieces are listed:

Beowulf	The Order of the World
Judith	The Riming Poem
Andreas	Riddle 16
The Fates of the Apostles	Resignation
The Dream of the Rood	The Lord's Prayer I
Elene	Genesis A
Christ	Exodus
Guthlac	Daniel
The Phoenix	Christ and Satan
The Wanderer	The Metres of Boethius
Precepts	The Rune Poem
The Seafarer	Solomon and Saturn
The Fortunes of Men	Maxims II
Maxims I	Psalm 50

BEOWULF

1163	1A1b(2A1a)	a1b(2A1a)
1164	2A1(1A*1a)	a1e(1A1a)
1165	2A1(2A1a)	a1c(2A1b)
1166	2C1a(3B1,1D1)	a1e(2A1a)
1167	—	a1d(2A1a)
1168	1A*1a(1A*1a)	a1b(1D1)
1705	1A1b(1A*1a)	a1d(2A1a)
1706	1A1a(2A1a)	a1c(1A*1a)
1707	1A*1b(2A1a)	a1c(2A1a)
2173	3E1(2C1)	—
2297	2A1(2A1a)	—
2995	1A*1a(2A1a)	a1e(1A1a)
2996	1A1a(2A1a)	a1d(1A*1a)

JUDITH

2	1A*1b(2A1a)	a1c(2A1a)
3	1A*3b(2A1a)	a1d(2A1a)
4	1A*1a(2A1a)	a1e(2A1a)
5	2A1(2A1a)	a1c(1A1a)
6	2A3(1A*1a)	a1d(1A*1a)

JUDITH (cont.)

7	1A1b(1D1)	a1e(2A1a)
8	3A3(2A1a)	a1c(2A1a)
9	2A1(1D1)	a1d(2A1a)
10	1A*1a(3A1)	a1b(2A1a)
11	2A1(1D1)	a1d(2A1a)
12	2A1(2A1a)	a1c(2A1a)
16	1A*1a(1A1a)	a1c(1A1a)
17	2A1(1D1)	a1c(2A1a)
18	1A1b(1A*1a)	a1c(1A*1a)
19	2A1(1D1)	a1b(2A1a)
20	2A1(1D1)	a1c(1A*1a)
21	2A1(2A1a)	a1b(2A1a)
30	2A3(2A1a)	a1d(2A1a)
31	1A*1a(2A1a)	a1e(1A*1a)
32	2A1(1A*1a)	a1c(2A1a)
33	2A1(1D1)	a1b(2A1a)
34	3A1(1A1a)	a1b(1A*1a)
54	1A*1a(1A*1a)	a1c(1A*1a)
55	1A*1a(2A1a)	a1c(2A1a)
56	1A1a(2A1a)	a1c(2A1a)
57	1A1b(1A1a)	a1c(1A*1a)

JUDITH (cont.)

58	2A1(2A1a)	a1c(2A1a)
59	1A*1b(1A*1a)	a1d(2A1a)
60	2A1(2A1a)	a1d(1A*1a)
61	2A1(2A1a)	a1d(2A1a)
62	2A3(2A1a)	—
63	1A*1a(2A1a)	a1e(1A1a)
64	1A*1b(2A1a)	a1d(1A*1a)
65	2A1(1D1)	a1d(2A1a)
66	2A3(2A1a)	a1d(2A1a)
67	1A*1b(2A1a)	a1c(1A*1a)
68	1A*1b(2A1a)	a1d(2A1a)
88	1A*1a(1A*1a)	a1c(2A1a)
89	1A1a(1A*1a)	a1d(2A1a)
90	a1e(2A1a)	a1d(1A*1a)
91	2A3(2A1a)	a1c(2A1a)
92	1A*1a(2A1a)	a1c(2A1a)
93	2A3(2A1a)	a1d(1A*1a)
94	1A*1a(2A1a)	a1c(2A1a)
95	1A*1a(1A*1a)	a1c(1A*1a)
96	—	a1e(2A1a)
97	1A*1b(1A*1a)	a1d(1A*1a)
98	3A1(1A1a)	a1e(2A1a)
99	1A*1a(2A1a)	a1c(1A1a)
132	2A1(2A1a)	a1c(2A1a)
272	2A1(1D1)	a1d(1A*1a)
273	1A*1a(2A1a)	a1d(1A*1a)
287	2A1(1A1a)	a1d(1D1)
289	1A1a(1A*1a)	a1b(1A*1a)
290	2A1(2A1a)	a1b(2A1a)
291	1A*1b(1A*1a)	a1d(2A1a)
338	1A1a(3E1)	a1c(2A1a)
339	2A1(2A1a)	a1d(2A1a)
340	2A3(2A1a)	a1b(2A1a)
341	1A*1a(2A1a)	a1d(2A1a)
342	2A1(1D1)	a1c(2A1a)
343	2A1(2A1a)	a1c(3E1)
344	1A*1a(2A1a)	a1c(1A*1a)
345	1A*3a(2A1a)	a1e(1A*1a)
346	1A1b(1D1)	a1d(1A*1a)
347	1A*1b(2A1a)	a1c(2A1a)
348	1A*1a(2A1a)	a1c(1A1a)
349	1A*1a(2A1a)	a1c(2A1a)
350	1A1a(2A1a)	a1b(2A1a)

ANDREAS

51	1A*1a(2A1a)	a1d(2E1a)
303	1A*1a(2A1a)	a1e(1A1a)

ANDREAS (cont.)

795	1A*1a(1A*1a)	a1d(2A1a)
796	1A1a(2A1a)	a1d(1A*1a)
799	a1b(2A1a)	a1b(1D1)
801	—	a1e(3E1)
802	2A1(2A3b)	a1c(2A3a)
803	—	a1c(1A*1a)
1022	—	a1c(1A1a)
1023	2A1(2A1a)	a1c(1A1a)
1114	1A1a(1A1a)	—

THE FATES OF THE APOSTLES

98	a1b(2A1a)	1A1b(2A1a)
99	1A*1b(2A1a)	a1d(1A*1a)
102	2A1(2A1a)	a1c(1A1a)

THE DREAM OF THE ROOD

8	1A*1a(2A1a)	a1c(2A1a)
9	1A*1b(1A*1a)	a1d(3E2)
10	2E1a(2B1)	a1e(2A1a)
20	1A*1b(2A1a)	a1d(1A*1a)
21	1A1e(1A*1a)	a1d(2A1a)
22	2A1(1A*1a)	a1e(1A*1a)
23	1A1a(2A1a)	a1c(1A*1a)
30	1A1a(2A1a)	a1e(2A1a)
31	a1f(2A1a)	a1e(2A1a)
32	a1d(1A*1a)	a1e(1A1a)
33	a1f(1A*1a)	a1d(1D2)
34	2A1(2A1a)	a1e(1A1a)
39	—	a1b(1D1)
40	—	1A*1a(2A1a)
41	1A*1a(1A*1a)	a1d(2A1a)
42	a1g(1A1a)	a1f(1A*1a)
43	1A*1a(2A1a)	a1d(2A1a)
46	a1f(2A1a)	a1e(1A1a)
47	2A1(2A1a)	a1f(2A1a)
48	a1f(1A*1a)	a1d(1A*1a)
49	2B2a(2C1)	a1f(1A1a)
59	1A*1c(1A*1a)	a1e(1A*1a)
60	2A3(2A1a)	a1e(3E1)
61	a1g(2A1a)	a1e(2A1a)
62	2A1(1A*1a)	a1d(1A*1a)
63	a1e(1D1)	a1f(2A1a)
64	a1e(2A1a)	a1c(2A1a)
65	1A*1c(1A*1a)	a1e(2A3a)
66	1A*1a(1A1a)	a1e(2A1a)

THE DREAM OF THE ROOD (cont.)

67	a1f(2A1a)	a1e(2A3b)
68	1A*1b(2A1a)	a1d(1D1)
69	1A*1b(2A1a)	a1d(2A1a)
75	a1e(2A1a)	a1d(2A1a)

ELENE

163	a1c(1A1a)	a1c(1A*1a)
580	—	a1d(1A1a)
581	1A*1a(1A1a)	a1e(1A1a)
582	—	a1d(1A1a)
583	1A1b(2A1a)	a1e(1A1a)
584	1A*1a(2A1a)	a1d(1A*1a)
585	1A*1a(2A1a)	a1c(1A*1a)
586	2A1(1D1)	a1b(2A1b)
587	2E1a(2C1)	a1e(1A*1a)
588	a1d(2A1a)	a1c(1A1a)
589	2C1a(2E1a)	a1d(2A1a)
609	1A*1c(1D1)	a1e(1A*1a)
610	2A1(1A1a)	a1e(1A*1a)
667	1A*1c(1D1)	a1c(1A*1a)
668	a1b(2A1a)	a1c(2A1a)
701	1A*1a(1A*1a)	—
1102	—	a1d(2A1a)
1157	—	a1d(2A1a)
1159	—	a1d(2A1a)

CHRIST

621	a1d(1A*1a)	a1e(2A1a)
888	1A*1c(2A1a)	a1c(1A1a)
889	1A*1a(1A*1a)	a1c(3E1)
921	3B*1b(2C1)	—
981	—	a1b(1A*1a)
1049	a1d(2A1a)	—
1107	a1c(2A1a)	
1162	1A*1b(2A1a)	1A1a(2A1a)
1163	2A1(1A*1a)	—
1208	2C1a(2A1a)	—

CHRIST (cont.)

1304	—	a1c(2A1a)
1359	a1e(2A1a)	—
1377	—	a1c(2A1a)
1380	—	a1b(2A1a)
1381	1A*1b(1A1a)	a1c(2A1a)
1382	a1f(1A*1a)	a1f(2A1a)
1383	2A3(1A1a)	—
1384	1A1b(3E*2)	2C1c(3E1)
1385	1A*1b(2A1a)	a1b(1A1a)
1409	—	a1b(2A1a)
1422	1A*1a(2A1a)	a1d(1A*1a)
1423	3A*1a(2A1a)	a1d(1A*1a)
1424	1A*1c(2A1a)	1A*1a(2A1a)
1425	—	a1f(1A1a)
1426	—	a1d(2A1a)
1427	1A*1b(2A1a)	a1d(3E1)
1460	—	a1b(1A*1a)
1463	—	a1c(2A1a)
1467	—	a1d(2A1a)
1487	—	a1c(2A1a)
1488	—	a1c(2A1a)
1495	a1c(2A1a)	a1d(1A1a)
1496	1A1c(2A1a)	a1d(1A*1a)
1513	3B1a(2C1)	a1d(1A*1a)
1514	1A*1a(2A1a)	1A1a(1A*1a)
1546	a1e(2A1a)	a1c(2A1a)
1560	1A1b(2A1a)	—

GUTHLAC

1	a1c(2A1a)	a1d(1A*1a)
2	2E1b(3B1)	a1e(2A1a)
3	1A*1a(2A1a)	a1d(1A*1a)
5	2A1(1D1)	a1d(1D1)
25	1A*1b(2A1a)	a1d(2A1a)
80	2A1(2A1a)	a1c(2A1a)

GUTHLAC (cont.)

88	2A1(1D1)	a1c(2A1a)
89	1A*1a(2A1a)	a1c(1A*1a)
90	2A1(3E1)	a1d(1A1a)
91	a1d(2A1a)	a1b(2A1a)
92	a1d(1A1a)	a1c(1A1a)
190	1A*1b(2A1a)	a1d(2A1a)
191	2A1(2A1a)	a1d(2A1a)
239	1A*1b(1D1)	a1c(1A*1a)
240	1A*1a(2A1a)	a1d(1A1a)
241	a1e(1A*1a)	a1d(2A1a)
242	1A1a(3E1)	a1c(1A*1a)
289	2A1(2A1a)	a1d(2A1a)
290	a1b(1A*1a)	a1d(1D1)
291	1A1b(2A1a)	a1d(2A1a)
363	a1d(2A1a)	a1d(2A1a)
376	a1g(1A*1a)	a1e(1A1a)
377	a1e(1A*1a)	a1f(2A1a)
378	a1c(1A*1a)	a1d(2A1a)
379	a1d(2A1a)	—
465	a1e(2A1a)	a1d(1A*1a)
466	a1d(2A1a)	a1e(1A*1a)
467	a1c(1A1c)	a1d(2A1a)
468	a1d(1A*1a)	a1c(1A1a)
469	a1d(1A*1a)	a1e(1A*1a)
510	a1d(2A1a)	a1c(1A1a)
636	1A1a(2A1a)	a1d(1A*1a)
701	a1d(1A*1a)	a1d(1A*1a)
702	a1c(2A1a)	a1f(1A1a)
741	a1d(3A2)	a1d(1A1a)
1110	1A*1b(2A1a)	a1d(1D1)
1158	—	a1d(2A1a)
1160	—	a1c(1A*1a)
1161	2C1a(2A1a)	a1c(2A1a)
1162	1A*1c(2A1a)	a1d(1A1a)
1294	2A1(1A*1a)	a1c(2A1a)
1295	1A1b(1A*1a)	—
1301	1A*3a(2A1a)	a1d(1A*1a)
1302	2A1(2A1a)	a1d(2A1a)
1303	1A*3a(2A1a)	a1c(1A1a)

THE PHOENIX

10	2A1(2A1a)	a1b(1A*1a)
630	a1e(2A1a)	a1b(1D1)

THE WANDERER

65	2B1–(3B1,2C1)	—
111	a1b(1A1a)	a1c(1A*1a)
112	1A1d(1A*1a)	a1e(1A1a)
113	1A1b(1A*1a)	a1e(2A1a)
114	1A1a(1A*1a)	a1e(2A1a)
115	1A*1a(1A1a)	a1d(2A1a)

PRECEPTS

17	—	a1c(2A1a)
18	—	a1c(1A1a)
19	—	a1c(2A1a)

THE SEAFARER

23	1A*1a(2A3a)	—
103	1A1b(2A1a)	a1d(1A*1a)
106	1A1e(1A*1a)	a1d(1A1a)
107	1A*1a(2A3b)	a1d(1A1a)
108	1A1b(1A1a)	a1e(1A*1a)
109	1A*1b(2A1a)	a1c(2A1a)

THE FORTUNES OF MEN

15	a1c(1A*1a)	a1c(1A1a)
16	a1c(1A1a)	a1b(1A1a)

MAXIMS I

1	a1c(2A1a)	a1d(1A1a)
2	1A*1b(2A1a)	a1e(1A*1a)
3	a1e(2A3b)	a1c(1A*1a)
4	1A1b(3B1,2A1a)	1A1b(2A1a)
5	2A1(1D1)	a1e(1A*1a)
6	1A1a(2A1a)	a1g(1A*1a)
30	—	a1d(1A*1a)
35	remainder	a1e(1A1a)
36	2C1–(3B1,2A1a)	a1d(1A1a)
37	1A*1e(1A*1a)	1A1c(1A1a)
38	1A*1d(1A1a)	1A*1a(1A*1a)
39	1A*1a(2A1a)	1A1b(2A1a)
40	1A1b(1A*1a)	a1d(1A*1a)
41	2A3(1A*1a)	a1c(1A1b)
42	2E1d(3B1)	a1f(2A1b)

MAXIMS I (cont.)

43	1A*1b(2A1a)	a1c(2A1a)
44	1A*1a(2A1a)	a1c(2A1a)
45	2A3(1A*1a)	1A*1b(2A1a)
46	2E1b(1A*1a,2C1)	a1f(2A1a)
47	a1c(1A1a)	a1g(1A*1a)
48	a1e(3E*2)	a1e(2A1a)
49	a1c(1A*1a)	a1d(1D1)
50	1A*1b(2A1a)	2A3(1A1a)
51	1A1a(2A1a)	2A1(1D1)
52	1A*1a(1A*1a)	a1c(2A1a)
53	1A*1a(2A1a)	a1b(1A1a)
56	a1b(1A*1a)	a1d(2A1a)
57	a1f(2A1a)	a1e(2A1a1)
58	1A1a(3B1,2A1a)	1A1a(3E1)
59	2B2–(3B1)	1A1b(2A1a)
62	1A1b(2A1a)	2B2–(2C1)
63	2A1a(2A1a)	1A*1c(1A*1a)
64	2A1(3E2,1A1a)	a1c(1A*1a)
65	1A1a(2A1a)	a1c(1A1a)
66	2E1b(3E1,2C1)	1A1a(1A*1a)
67	1A1a(1A*1a)	1A1a(2A1a)
68	1A*3a(2A1a)	a1d(1A1a)
69	1A*1c(1A*1a)	1A1b(3E*2)
70	1A1c(2A1a)	a1d(1A*1a)
98	2E1a(3B1)	a1d(2A1a)
100	2C1–(2B2,1A*1a)	a1c(1A*1a)
101	1A1a(1D1)	1A1a(2A1a)
102	a1b(2A1a)	a1e(1A1a)
103	1A1a(1A*1a)	a1e(2A1a)
104	1A*1c(2E1a)	—
105	2E2b(2C2)	—
109	1A1a(2A1a)	a1d(1A1a)
110	2E2b(3B1)	a1d(2A1a)
111	remainder	a1e(2A1a)
112	—	a1c(1A1a)
113	remainder	a1f(2A1a)
114	1A1c(2A1a)	1A*1b(1A*1a)
116	—	a1d(2A1a)
124	remainder	1A1b(2A1a)
144	2B2–(2C1)	—
145	2C1b(1A1a)	a1c(1A1a)
146	2A1(3E2)	a1d(1A*1b)
147	—	a1f(2A1a)
149	—	a1c(1A*1a)

MAXIMS I (cont.)

151	—	a1c(2A1a)
164	2B2–(2B1,2B1)	—
167	1A*1a(1A1b)	a1b(1A1a)
174	1A*1e(2A1a)	1A*1a(2A1a)
175	2A1(2A1a)	a1d(1A1a)
181	1A*1b(2A1a)	a1e(1A1a)
182	1A1b(1A*1a)	a1c(1A1a)
183	—	a1b(2A1a)
184	1A*1a(2A1a)	a1e(2A1a)
185	1A1a(3B1,2A1a)	a1c(2A1a)
186	1A*1b(1A*1a)	a1c(1A1a)
192	2A1(2A1a)	—
193	2A1(2A1a)	a1b(3E1)
196	—	a1b(2A1a)
197	2E1b(2C1)	1A1a(2A1a)
198	remainder	—

THE ORDER OF THE WORLD

98	a1d(1A1a)	a1b(2A1a)
99	2A1(2A1a)	a1c(2A1a)
100	2A1(2A1a)	a1e(2A1a)
102	a1a(2A1a)	a1e(2A1a)

THE RIMING POEM

80	a1b(1A*1a)	a1c(2A1a)
81	a1d(2A1a)	a1e(2A1a)
82	2C1a(2A1a)	a1c(2A1a)
83	1A*1a(2A1a)	a1c(1A*1a)

RIDDLE 16

1	a1d(2A1a)	a1b(2A1a)
2	—	a1c(1A*1a)
3	—	a1c(2A1a)
4	a1b(1A1b)	a1b(2A1a)

RESIGNATION

1	a1d(3E1)	—
2	a1d(2A1a)	a1d(1A1a)
79	2A1(1D1)	—
80	1A*1a(2A1a)	a1c(2A1a)

THE LORD'S PRAYER I

1	—	a1c(2A1a)
2	2A1(2A1a)	a1c(2A1a)
3	2C1–(2A1a)	a1b(2A1b)
4	a1c(2A1a)	a1b(2A1a)
5	1A*1b(2A1a)	a1c(2A1a)

GENESIS A

44	1A*1a(2A1a)	a1d(3E1)
45	2A1(2A1a)	a1c(1A1a)
46	1A*1a(1A1a)	a1b(2E2a)
155	2A1(2A1a)	a1b(1A*1a)
156	2E2a(2C1)	—
913	1A1a(2A1a)	a1b(2A1a)
1015	1A*1a(2A1a)	a1d(2A1a)
1016	2E1a(2C1)	a1b(3E2)
1017	1A*1a(2A1a)	a1d(1A*1a)
1018	2A1(2A1a)	a1b(2A1a)
1019	1A*1a(2A1a)	a1b(2A1a)
1522	—	a1d(2A1a)
1523	2A1(1A*1a)	a1d(3E*1)
2167	2A1(1D1)	a1b(1D1)
2168	1A*1b(2A1a)	a1e(1A1a)
2169	2A1(2A1a)	a1d(1A1a)
2170	a1e(2A1a)	a1c(3E1)
2174	2A3(2A1a)	a1c(3E2)
2328	1A1a(2A1a)	a1d(1D1)
2329	2A1(2A1a)	a1d(2A1a)
2406	1A1b(2A1a)	a1c(2A1a)
2407	2E1a(3B2)	a1c(3E1)
2411	1A1b(2A1a)	a1b(3E1)
2412	2A1(2A1a)	a1c(3E1)
2855	1A1a(2A1a)	a1c(1A1a)
2856	a1c(2A1a)	a1c(1A1a)
2857	2A3(2A1a)	—
2858	1A1a(2A1a)	a1c(2A1a)
2859	2A1(1A1a)	a1b(1A1a)
2866	2A1(2A1a)	a1d(2A1a)
2867	1A*1a(2A1a)	a1d(2A1a)
2868	2A3(2A1a)	a1c(2A1a)
2869	2A1(1D1)	1A1b(2A1a)

EXODUS

570	—	a1c(2A1a)
571	1A1a(2A1a)	a1d(1A*1a)
572	1A1b(2A1a)	a1e(2A1a)
573	2C1c(2A1a)	a1d(2A3a)
574	2A1(2A1a)	a1d(1A*1a)

DANIEL

59	a1e(2A1a)	—
106	2A1(2A1a)	a1b(2A1a)
203	2A1(2A1a)	a1d(2A1a)
204	1A1b(2A1a)	a1d(1A1a)
205	2A1(2A1a)	a1e(2A1a)
207	a1b(1A*1a)	a1c(1D1)
224	2A1(2A1b)	a1b(1A1a)
225	2C1a(2A1a)	a1e(1A*1a)
226	—	a1b(2A1a)
227	2A1(2A1a)	a1d(1D1)
232	1A1c(1A*1a)	—
233	2C1a(2A1a)	a1e(1A1a)
234	—	a1b(1A*1a)
235	1A*1b(1A1a)	a1d(2A1a)
237	2A1(2E1c,2E1a)	a1c(2A1b)
238	2A3(1A*1a)	a1c(2A1a)
240	1A1a(2A1a)	a1c(2A1a)
241	1A*3b(2A1a)	—
242	2E1a(3B2)	a1c(1A1a)
243	2A1(1A1a)	a1c(2A1a)
244	2A1(1A1a)	a1d(1A*1a)
261	2A1(2A1a)	—
262	2A1(2A1a)	—
263	a1c(1A1a)	a1c(2A1a)
264	a1b(1D2)	a1c(2A1a)
265	—	a1d(2A1d)
266	1A1b(2A1a)	a1b(2A1a)
267	2A1(1D1)	a1c(1A*1a)
268	a1c(2A3b)	a1c(1A1a)
269	1A*1a(1A*1a)	a1b(2A1a)
270	2A1(2A1a)	a1b(2A1a)
271	2A1(3E1)	a1d(1A1b)
273	2A1(1D1)	a1b(1A*1a)
434	a1c(1A*1a)	a1c(2A1a)
435	2A3(2A1a)	a1c(1A*1a)
436	a1c(1A1a)	a1c(1A1a)
437	2C1a(1A*1a)	—
440	—	a1c(2A1a)
446	—	a1c(1A*1a)
447	a1d(2A1a)	a1e(1A*1a)

DANIEL (cont.)

449	2A3(2A1a)	a1e(2A1a)
451	2A1(2A1a)	a1d(1A*1a)
452	a1d(2A1a)	a1c(2A1a)
453	—	a1b(2A1a)
454	a1c(1A1a)	a1e(1D1)
455	1A1c(1A*1a)	a1c(1A*1a)
456	a1d(2A1a)	a1c(2A1a)
457	2A1(3E2)	a1c(1A1a)

CHRIST AND SATAN

201	2E1b(2C1)	a1f(2A1a)
202	2A1(1A*1a)	a1c(1A1a)
203	a1c(2A1a)	a1b(1A1a)
230	2A1a(3E*1)	—
604	1A*1a(1A*1a)	—

THE METRES OF BOETHIUS

5.45	1A*1b(2A1a)	a1d(2A1a)
7.23	2A1(1A1b)	1A1c(2E1a)
10.67	1A1b(2A1a)	a1d(2A1a)
16.1	a1d(2A1a)	a1d(2A1a)
17.11	1A*1b(2A1a)	a1c(1A1a)
25.45	a1d(2A1a)	a1c(2A1a)
26.79	a1d(2A1a)	a1e(1A1a)
29.31	a1d(2A1a)	a1d(1A1a)
32	1A*1b(2A1a)	a1d(2A1a)
31.8	a1d(2A1a)	a1e(2A1a)

THE RUNE POEM

25	1A1a(2A1a)	a1c(2A1a)
26	a1c(2A1a)	a1d(2A1a)
27	1A1a(1A1a)	a1e(2A1a)
28	1A*1b(1A*1a)	a1c(2A1a)

SOLOMON AND SATURN

312	1A1a(2A1a)	1A1a(2A1a)
313	1A1a(2A1a)	1A1a(1A*1a)
327	a1f(2A1a)	a1e(2A1a)
328	1A*1c(1A*1a)	a1d(1A*1a)
329	*remainder*	a1d(1A1b)
330	a1f(1A*1a)	a1d(2A1a)
331	2A1(2A1a)	a1f(1A*1a)
338	a1d(2A1a)	a1c(1A*1a)
339	1A*1a(2A1a)	—
367	a1c(1A*1a)	a1c(2A1a)
368	1A*3a(2A1a)	2C1b(2A1a)
370	1A*1c(1A*1a)	a1e(1A*1a)
371	a1d(2A1a)	1A*1c(2A1a)
437	1A1a(2A1a)	2A1(1A*1a)
453	a1c(2A1a)	a1h(2A1a)
454	1A1a(2A1a)	a1f(2A1a)
455	1A*1a(2A1a)	a1e(2A1a)
456	1A*1c(2A1a)	a1d(1A*1a)
457	2E1a(2C1)	a1c(2A1a)
458	1A*1b(1A*1a)	a1f(1A*1a)
459	—	a1b(2A1a)
460	a1d(1A*1a)	—
488	a1c(2A1a)	a1c(2A1a)
490	—	a1c(2A1a)

MAXIMS II

1	1A1a(2A1a)	1A*1a(1A*1a)
2	2A1(2E1a)	a1e(2A1a)
3	2A1(3E*2)	1A1b(2A1a)
4	1A1a(2A1a)	1A*1b(2A1a)
42	2A1(1A1a,2A1a)	1A1b(1A*1a)
43	2A1(2A1a)	1A1a(2A1a)
44	1A*1b(1A1a)	a1e(1A*1a)
45	a1c(1A*1a)	1A1a(2A1a)
47	2A1(2A1a)	—

PSALM 50

31	a1d(2A1a)	a1c(1A*1a)

INDEX OF VERSES SPECIALLY DISCUSSED

[This index includes all the verses in *Beowulf* for which an emendation is suggested, together with a number of others which offer some special difficulty. References are to paragraphs.]

25a	47		1111b	61, 78	2093a	44, 47, 87
53b	64		1125b	65	2152b	63
107a	46, 47		1177b	52	2241b	62, 77
141a	49		1224b	52	2252a	48
208b	49		1230b	62, 77	2339b	51
274b	79		1236a	50	2432b	64
368a	72		1329b	50, 59	2435b	87
395b	72		1424b	81	2441a	50
402b	49		1441b	79	2488a	87
414a	46, 47		1454a	44	2562a	44
469b	59		1525b	77	2636a	72
473a	44, 52		1537a	20	2671b	65
501b	50, 59		1573b	54	2691b	82
502a	54		1663b	65	2725b	51
517b	57, 59		1697a	66	2734a	75
525a	20		1724b	44	2767b	61, 78
534a	56		1830b	50, 59	2803b	60
662a	50		1859a	52	2863b	44
673a	66		1863a	44	2921b	61
758a	20		1869b	77	3005b	62
768a	75		1880b	48	3032b	65
840b	65		1892b	60	3045a	65
932b	50, 59		1941a	44	3062a	49
949b	50, 59		1941b	50, 59	3062b	78
960b	51		1997b	78	3084a	45
988a	81		2008a	48	3154b	4
1068a	46, 47		2032b	64		

ADDENDUM

In the classification here adopted the position of the cæsura in the verse has been indicated by 'prefixing to Sievers' letters the numbers 1, 2 or 3, indicating that the first breath-group is shorter than, equal to, or longer than the second breath-group' (§ 91). For this purpose the length of a breath-group is to be measured not in syllables but in metrical units, i.e. thesis and arsis. The breath-groups of a verse of Type 2 may differ considerably in number of syllables: e.g. in Types 2B and 2C there may be as many as six syllables in the first breath-group against only two in the second. In Type 2A the number of syllables in the two breath-groups can differ only when one of the metrical units is resolved. It has been suggested to me by Professor Kemp Malone that in Type 2A the greater number of syllables in the second breath-group resulting from the resolution of one of the metrical units might be sufficient to justify anacrusis—cf. § 49(1): if so, there could be no further objection to *gesawon seledream* 2252a (§ 48). However, the weight of probability seems to be against this suggestion: in all other respects the resolution of a metrical unit makes no significant difference; moreover, the solitary example in *Beowulf* has been held by many editors to be objectionable on other grounds.[1] No final conclusion could be reached without searching the whole corpus of Old English poetry for further examples, an undertaking which is outside the scope of this study.

[1] For a defence of the reading *secga seledream* accepted in § 48 see Klaeber, *op. cit.* 209-10. On the superficially similar verse *Ne sorga, snotor guma* 1384a see § 81.